W9-BSZ-877

THE RISE AND FALL OF AL-QAEDA

THE RISE AND FALL
OF AL-QAEDA

Fawaz A. Gerges

OXFORD
UNIVERSITY PRESS

OXFORD
UNIVERSITY PRESS

Oxford University Press, Inc., publishes works that further
Oxford University's objective of excellence
in research, scholarship, and education.

Oxford   New York
Auckland   Cape Town   Dar es Salaam   Hong Kong   Karachi
Kuala Lumpur   Madrid   Melbourne   Mexico City   Nairobi
New Delhi   Shanghai   Taipei   Toronto

With offices in
Argentina   Austria   Brazil   Chile   Czech Republic   France   Greece
Guatemala   Hungary   Italy   Japan   Poland   Portugal   Singapore
South Korea   Switzerland   Thailand   Turkey   Ukraine   Vietnam

Published by Oxford University Press, Inc.
198 Madison Avenue, New York, New York 10016

www.oup.com

Oxford is a registered trademark of Oxford University Press

Library of Congress Cataloging-in-Publication Data
Gerges, Fawaz A., 1958–
The rise and fall of Al-Qaeda / Fawaz A. Gerges.
p.   c.m
Includes bibliographical references.
ISBN 978-0-19-979065-4 (alk. paper)
1. Qaida (Organization) 2. Terrorism.
3. Terrorism—Religious aspects—Islam. I. Title.
HV6432.5.Q2G47   2011
363.325—dc22   2011013771

1 3 5 7 9 8 6 4 2

Printed in the United States of America
on acid-free paper

To Avi Shlaim

CONTENTS

ACKNOWLEDGMENTS

There is no space to list all of the numerous colleagues, activists, and strangers in the Middle East who over the years spent countless hours with me, patiently answering my questions and deepening my knowledge of the Islamist and jihadist phenomena. I owe them gratitude for their time and insights, and for sharing their experience with me. I could not have written this book without their personal stories, feedback, and competing narratives.

I want to thank my research assistant Andrew Bowen, a Ph.D. candidate at LSE, who went beyond the call of duty in editing, summarizing, and synthesizing several sections of *The Rise and Fall*. His work ethic and generosity of spirit are exceptional. I also want to thank Hadi Makarem, a Ph.D. candidate at LSE, who has just joined me as a research assistant. Special thanks are due to colleagues who read and critiqued separate chapters of the book, including Farid Senzai, Mohammed Ayoob, Nader Hashemi, Hassan Abbas, Kamran Bokhari, Antonio Giustozzi, Karim Mezran, Avi Shlaim, Charles Tripp, Claudio Franco, Tarak Barkawi, Omar Ashour, and Marvin Weinbaum.

I appreciate the meticulous and rigorous editing and feedback of my OUP editor, Tim Bent, who invested considerable time and energy in the book. Tim edited my previous book, *Journey of the Jihadist*, and showed a deep commitment and dedication to its quality.

ACKNOWLEDGMENTS

While at Sarah Lawrence College, New York, I began writing *The Rise and Fall* and completed it at my present home—London School of Economics. Sarah Lawrence, a unique, civilized community, nourishes a fierce sense of academic freedom and critical inquiry and reflection. For all that and more, I am grateful to Sarah Lawrence and Julie Kidd, a visionary and enlightened educator who established my Christian A. Johnson Endeavor Foundation Chair at SLC and provided me with the time to travel and undertake field research. I want to thank the Carnegie Foundation for awarding me a grant that allowed me to spend more than a year in the Middle East. I owe special gratitude to Mike Mahoney who has always been there for me.

The Rise and Fall of Al-Qaeda is dedicated to Oxford Professor Avi Shlaim, not only because he is a dear friend but also because he has debunked a more entrenched and challenging narrative on the Arab-Israeli conflict.

Last but not least, I could not have written this book without my family's love and support. Nora generously offered her insights on Yemen and sharpened the narrative. My son Bassam Gergi, a student of history, put up with my ceaseless inquiries about comparative historical developments in early modern Europe and editorial and technological questions as well. My daughter Annie-Marie was mainly concerned about the rigor of my central argument and often pressed me, are you confident that al-Qaeda no longer poses a real threat? Hannah and Laith only wanted to know when I would complete the book and take them on their favorite outings. Tearing myself away from the family took a lot of willpower and selfishness. In many ways, this book belongs to them.

Fawaz A. Gerges
London
June 1, 2011

THE RISE AND FALL OF AL-QAEDA

Introduction: Life After Death

It committed one of the most chilling and brutal attacks in the memory of a generation, transforming the landscape of international affairs, and inexorably changing the course of its greatest superpower—launching not one but two wars, which have lasted longer than the two great world wars of the twentieth century combined. The radical politics of a small band of Muslim extremists became everyone's business, and their actions, particularly those of a single day now ten years ago, set into motion reactions and counter-reactions that continue to dominate headlines, guide foreign policy, and define domestic agendas.

And yet, like Osama bin Laden himself, the world's most feared and hated terrorist organization, indeed the very embodiment of what "terrorist organization" has come to mean in the minds of Americans and Westerners alike and the symbol of everything that is antithetical to Western values, no longer exists. It has all but vanished, or at least dwindled to the palest shadow of its former self.

News of bin Laden's killing by US Special Forces at a compound near the capital city of Islamabad, deep in the heart of Pakistan, has sunk in. News of al-Qaeda's demise, on the other hand, has not. A gulf has emerged between the perception of the threat posed by al-Qaeda and its actual capabilities, and this gulf continues to widen.

Six weeks after bin Laden's death, Ayman al-Zawahiri, bin Laden's second-in-command, and now officially his successor, said that his former leader and comrade-in-arms had "terrified America in his life" and would "continue to terrify it after his death." Al-Qaeda continues to have a hold over the Western imagination, in part because the West will not let it go.

Al-Qaeda remains shrouded in myth, lurking everywhere, ceaselessly plotting to kill innocent people en masse. While there is currently extensive and ongoing analysis of bin Laden's compound in Abbottabad and what it contained, and whether or not the evidence suggests his active participation in al-Qaeda's operations up to the moment of his death, there remains little debate in the media about his organization and its viability. Commentators and analysts readily accept the narrative advanced by officials and so-called terrorism experts, who argue that al-Qaeda remains the West's greatest threat.

Yet even more than the killing of bin Laden, the Arab awakening of the spring of 2011—in Tunisia, Egypt, Libya, Yemen, Bahrain, Oman, and Syria—has not only shaken the very foundation of the regional authoritarian order but threatened to unravel the standard terrorism narrative. As the Arab revolutions gathered steam, al-Qaeda Central was notably absent. Neither jihadist slogans and rituals nor its violent tactics found a receptive audience among the millions of Arab protesters.

Al-Qaeda offers no economic blueprint, no political horizon, and no vision for the future. While millions of Arabs demand genuine elections and the separation of powers, al-Qaeda considers elections and democracy "heresy" and an "evil principle." Its leaders have shunned political participation and activism, preaching that only violence and terrorism will bring about political change. Yet the millions of Arabs who took to the streets openly have shown that politics matters and that peaceful protests are

more effective at delivering change. Constitutionalism, not militant Islamism, is their rallying cry, an utter rejection of al-Qaeda's
ideology. The Arab revolutions are post-Islamists in that while
religion-based activists, such as the Muslim Brotherhood and
independent Islamists, represent an important segment of the protesters, they are dwarfed by centrists, nationalists, liberals, and
non-affiliated activists. Although Islamic-oriented groups like the
Muslim Brotherhood and the Salafis will be a force to reckon with in
the post-autocratic order, they have little in common with al-Qaeda
and will become one among many competing forces.

Thus, the revolutions have reinforced what many of us have
already known: al-Qaeda's core ideology is incompatible with the
universal aspirations of the Arabs. Arabs and Muslims do not hate
America and the West but rather admire their democratic institutions, including free elections, peaceful transition of leadership, and
separation of powers. The millions of Arabs involved have neither
burned American and Western flags nor blamed the West for their
predicament. Neither bin Laden nor now his successor Zawahiri
speak for the umma (the global Muslim community) or exercise any
influence over Arab public opinion.

So what remains of al-Qaeda? Very little. Today it is composed
of roving bands limited to the mountains and valleys of Pakistan
tribal areas along the Afghan border (where bin Laden was assumed
to be hiding), remote areas in Yemen along the Saudi border, and
the wastes of the African Sahara and the Maghreb. Its actions show
a consistent pattern of ineptitude. Its leadership relies, increasingly,
on inexperienced freelancers or unskilled recruits.

Few in the West—Americans specifically—realize that their fear
of terrorism is misplaced. Yet the threat they feel from al-Qaeda has
acquired a life of its own. The mainstream media restricts the param-
eters of the debate and does not give alternative voices time and

space. Every incident—no matter how amateurish—is blown out of proportion, reinforcing anxiety and paranoia about terrorism generally and al-Qaeda specifically. Moreover, Western politicians—again, particularly American—embrace this distorted view of al-Qaeda's threat capability; it justifies their careers and affords political opportunities, enhancing their ability to shape foreign policy and national security strategy.

While the Bush administration catered to this monolithic and mostly ideological perception of al-Qaeda's omnipotence and invincibility—and indeed promoted it—President Obama has walked a fine line between changing his predecessor's language and terms on the "War on Terror" and adopting "a new strategic approach" that exemplifies the structural continuities in US foreign policy. It is an approach designed to reassure Americans that, "faced with that persistent and evolving terrorist threat," the president and his administration would be "unrelenting, unwavering, and unyielding in its efforts to defeat, disrupt, and dismantle al-Qaeda and its allies."[1] For example, Secretary of State Hillary Clinton has said that "for most of us" al-Qaeda and its affiliates—"trans-national non-state networks"—represented a more potent threat to US security than a nuclear-armed Iran or North Korea.[2] Although by "most of us" Clinton meant the US foreign policy and security establishment, she implied that the entire West faced a strategic threat from al-Qaeda.

Similarly, President Obama has emphasized the danger posed by rogue terror groups over that posed by North Korea and Iran. Efforts by al-Qaeda to acquire atomic weapons represented "the single biggest threat to US security—both short-term, medium-term and long term."[3] "We know that organizations like al Qaeda are in the process of trying to secure a nuclear weapon—a weapon of mass destruction that they have no compunction at using." Obama added, "If there was ever a detonation in New York City or London or Johannesburg, the ramifications economically, politically and from a security perspective would be devastating."[4]

Preparing Americans for potentially bad news, Obama's attorney general, Eric Holder, admitted that the danger of homegrown terrorists "keeps [him] up at night." In an interview with ABC's *Good Morning America*, Holder warned Americans that the terror threat is grave and immediate. "What I am trying to do in this interview is to make people aware of the fact that the threat is real, the threat is different, the threat is constant," he said. "The threat has changed from simply worrying about foreigners coming here, to worrying about people in the United States, American citizens—raised here, born here, and who for whatever reason, have decided that they are going to become radicalized and take up arms against the nation in which they were born," Holder added.[5]

These pronouncements by Obama, Clinton, and Holder show that the "terrorism narrative," as I would call it—the notion that the West remains under constant and imminent threat of attack—has become institutionalized among policymakers, government officials, and now the general public. American neoconservatives can largely be credited with this shift in attitude. Indeed the neoconservatives' most enduring legacy on US foreign policy may not be the Iraq war—American involvement in which President Obama pledged to end by the close of 2011—but rather the transformation of the American psyche after September 11.

In truth the only conceivable scenario by which al-Qaeda could obtain a nuclear device is if it built one for itself. For a group that has never displayed any technical sophistication in its attacks, this would involve a monumentally steep learning curve. Even were al-Qaeda to acquire the technical sophistication to build a nuclear bomb—and here we enter the sphere of science fiction—it lacks the structural capacity to develop such a weapon, let alone the necessary ingredients.[6]

Last year, a group of nuclear non-proliferation experts issued a statement in which they declared that there were no known instances of terrorist groups obtaining materials—enriched uranium or plutonium—that could be used to make even a crude nuclear device. They noted that there had been eighteen instances of nuclear materials being stolen or going missing since the early 1990s, but that this was before al-Qaeda was fully developed, and that therefore it was extremely unlikely that it had the materials.[7]

Moreover, financing a nuclear bomb is beyond al-Qaeda's reach. Peter Zimmerman, a nuclear physicist, and Jeffrey Lewis, a nuclear specialist at the Kennedy School, conservatively estimate the cost of building a bomb at $10 million.[8] At the height of its prowess in the 1990s, al-Qaeda's entire WMD budget was estimated at a mere fraction of that: $3,000.[9]

In the (unlikely) event that al-Qaeda were to obtain the right materials and finances, the odds are stacked heavily against success. John Mueller, an expert on al-Qaeda's atomic potential, notes that the organization would have to address no fewer than twenty different technical scenarios to complete and deploy one bomb, a challenge for a country like Iran. Even were one to allow al-Qaeda the benefit of a 30 percent chance of overcoming each one of these twenty scenarios to deploy a bomb, the odds are one in over three billion for a single successful deployment.[10]

It therefore remains a mystery how a roving band of extremists—most of them on the run and under constant fire in Pakistan's lawless tribal areas along the Afghan border—might be "in the process of trying to secure a nuclear weapon," which they would then be able to detonate in a major Western city. The evidence of al-Qaeda's strategic reach and capability seems to foreclose any need for hard evidence and discussion. Nonetheless the media faithfully reports the alarming refrain and avoids subjecting these stories to critical scrutiny and analysis, thus indirectly reinforcing widely held perceptions of al-Qaeda's prowess.

When the Soviet Union was in its final stage of decline, the majority of the US foreign policy establishment—the Republican camp in particular, though also mainstream intellectual and media commentators—firmly believed that the Soviets were expanding their influence and posed new threats to the West. US intelligence assessments were often doctored to confirm this alarmist view. Even when the evidence of Soviet weakness was presented, it was dismissed as a ploy by Moscow to dupe the West into lowering its guard.

The parallels between the dominant view of the Soviet Union during the Cold War and the present-day view of al-Qaeda are apparent. Many current US officials are former Soviet specialists, and they now view the War on Terror through the prism of the Cold War. There is no better way to illustrate the continuity between the Cold War and the War on Terror than to examine the priority that Obama's national security team assigns to terrorism. During the Cold War, when the president—the commander-in-chief—traveled away from the White House, his Soviet and nuclear aides were his shadow, accompanying him everywhere. Now his counterterrorism advisers do the same. In the official US worldview, the terrorism menace has replaced the nuclear threat.

In short, for many Western government officials and policymakers, terrorism has become a "Level A."[11] The notion of "Islamic terrorism" has merely replaced the specter of the "evil empire," or Soviet communism. And, so far, the cost of waging the War on Terror has been exorbitant; it soon will top 5 trillion dollars in direct and indirect costs. The longest conflict since World War II is not between the United States and the former Soviet Union, but rather the one currently being waged in Afghanistan. And even with bin Laden out of the picture, there is no clear end in sight.[12]

Not unlike the "military-industrial complex," against which President Dwight Eisenhower warned during the Cold War and which centered on building nuclear weapons to deter the Soviet Union, a new "national security complex" has been constructed since September 11.[13] A two-year investigation by the *Washington Post* discovered a "Top Secret America" that has mushroomed in ten years to include some 1,271 government organizations and nearly 2,000 private companies, working on counterterrorism in 10,000 locations across the United States, with at least 854,000 people—or nearly one and one half times the population of Washington, DC—holding top-secret security clearance (even janitors have top-secret clearances because of where they work). The annual US intelligence budget has risen from $40 billion a year in 2001 to more than $80 billion in 2011, a figure that does not include a number of military activities or domestic counterterrorism programs. That $80 billion far exceeds the $51 billion spent on the State Department and foreign aid programs in 2010.[14]

According to the *Washington Post* series, published in the summer of 2010, "[t]he top-secret world the government created in response to the terrorist attacks of September 11, 2001, has become so large, so unwieldy, and so secretive that no one knows how much money it costs, how many people it employs, how many programs exist within it or exactly how many agencies do the same work."[15] The study captured the massive expansion of the national security complex. It noted that by the end of 2001 no fewer than twenty-four organizations were created, including the Office of Homeland Security and the Foreign Terrorist Asset Tracking Task Force. The following year, 37 more were created—"to track weapons of mass destruction, collect threat tips and coordinate the new focus on counterterrorism." Their number was increased in 2003 by 36 new organizations, in 2004 by another 26, and in 2005 by 31 more. In

2007, 2008, and 2009, respectively, 31, 32, and 20 new organizations were launched.[16]

Massive as it is, the post–September 11 security bureaucracy remains mostly invisible to the people it is meant to protect. It is also extremely inefficient. No fewer than 51 federal agencies and military commands, operating in 15 US cities, track the flow of money to and from terrorist networks. Their reports recycle the same facts and overwhelm anyone's ability to analyze them. Every day, collection systems at the National Security Agency intercept and store 1.7 billion e-mails, phone calls, and other types of communications, a fraction of which is sorted. The complex publishes 50,000 reports each year—a volume so great that many are routinely ignored. The government has recently begun to integrate the latest technology, in an effort at "data mining" this huge amount of information. In an interview with the *Washington Post*, outgoing Defense Secretary Robert Gates acknowledged the "challenge" and "difficulty" of obtaining precise data.[17]

Despite the phenomenal expansion of the intelligence machine, the *Washington Post* pointed out that this machine has failed to detect the few serious attacks and plots against the US homeland, such as the Fort Hood, Texas, shooting that left thirteen dead, the so-called underwear bomber plot, or the 2009 Christmas Day bomb attempt, which was thwarted not by one of the almost one million individuals with top-secret clearances employed to find lone terrorists but by an alert airline passenger who saw smoke coming from a seatmate. In the Times Square bombing, an alert vendor called the police after he saw smoke coming out of a parked SUV.

Particularly alarming was the failure to prevent the Christmas Day bomber, Umar Farouk Abdulmutallab, from boarding a US airline in Amsterdam, despite having been warned beforehand of a potential attack originating from Yemen by an Algerian national. "A systemic failure has occurred, and I consider that totally unacceptable," Obama said, referring to what authorities allege was Abdumutallab's failed attempt to blow up a Northwest Airlines plane preparing to land in Detroit, Michigan.[18] The US government had sufficient information to uncover and disrupt this plot, but the intelligence community failed to connect the dots. "We need to learn from this episode and act quickly to fix the flaws in our system because our security is at stake and lives are at stake," President Obama concluded.[19]

According to the *Washington Post*, while intelligence officials have told Congress that the system has become so big that the lines of responsibility have become hopelessly blurred, the response has been to throw more money at it and create another organization. Before he resigned, Director of National Intelligence Admiral Dennis Blair told Congress that he needed more money and more analysts to prevent another mistake. Similarly, the Department of Homeland Security has asked for air marshals, more body scanners, and more analysts, though it cannot find enough qualified people to fill the current positions for which it has funding.[20] President Obama has said that he will not freeze spending on national security, making it likely that requests for more money and personnel will be honored. After bin Laden was killed, American officials and terrorism experts were quick to warn that the fight against al-Qaeda had not yet been won. Secretary of State Clinton said that although bin Laden is dead, al-Qaeda still poses a serious threat. The United States will continue aggressive operations against militants, added Clinton, which means that the terror narrative continues to dominate discussion and al-Qaeda will remain big business.[21]

It has also become big business in education. New programs and courses for the study of terrorism have sprung up in Western universities and colleges. There is great demand for the study of terrorism and plenty of people all too eager to meet it. Both demand and supply follow the money, and the federal government keeps supplying it. And yet, ironically, established scholars of the Middle East have shied away from engaging the subject, believing such discussion to be politically suspicious, and thus leaving the field to terrorism "experts" in think tanks and related policy institutions.

Nonetheless, there is no better yardstick to measure the demand for the study of terrorism than the number of post-graduate students and doctoral candidates who specialize in the topic. In 2009, when I arrived at the London School of Economics and Political Science, the majority of doctoral applications from Western countries were in subjects related to counterterrorism and militant Islamism. LSE represents the norm, not the exception, among top Western universities. Prospective graduate candidates are merely following research funding and future post-doctoral fellowships and academic posts, abundant in terrorism-related topics. There is a causal link between the multi-billion-dollar national security complex and the training of a new generation of experts. The latter, whose umbilical cord is tied to the national security apparatus and who perform complementary functions, are naturally averse to offering an alternate narrative.

More than the experts, many of whom maintain a semblance of institutional and financial independence, private contractors play a direct and active role in maintaining the national security machine. The aforementioned *Washington Post* investigative series uncovered an explosion in the number of private contractors who perform many functions, including killing enemy fighters, spying on foreign nationals, eavesdropping on terrorists, and crafting war plans. It is estimated that, of the 854,000 personnel with top-secret clearances, 265,000 are private contractors, or close to 30 percent.

The privatization of national security raises serious questions about inherent conflicts of interest between loyalty to the country and to the shareholders. Contractor misdeeds in Iraq and Afghanistan have damaged US credibility worldwide.[22] The abuse of prisoners at Abu Ghraib, some of it done by contractors, ignited a call for vengeance against the United States that continues to this day, as does the killing of Iraqi civilians by private contractors working for Blackwater. Both of them became, and remain, symbols of an America run amok.[23]

A longtime conservative staffer on the Senate Services Committee described the privatization of national security as the creation of "a living, breathing organism." "We've built such a vast instrument. What are you going to do with this thing?"[24] Nothing like the Western national security complex existed even at the height of the Cold War when the United States and the Soviet Union fought wars-by-proxy worldwide, from Vietnam to Afghanistan. History may provide some perspective. At the height of its power, the USSR possessed almost 10,000 nuclear bombs, an army of millions of men and thousands of fighter jets, submarines, armored vehicles, and tanks that could have destroyed the US homeland and its Western allies several times over. In contrast, even at its peak in the late 1990s, al-Qaeda's membership ranged between 3,000 and 4,000 fighters.[25] There are no brigades, fighter jets, and heavy tanks in al-Qaeda's armory, much less weapons of mass destruction (WMD).

American and Western intelligence agencies now believe that there are somewhere around 300 surviving members of al-Qaeda, based mainly in Pakistan and Afghanistan, into which the United States has poured nearly 100,000 troops.[26] Most of al-Qaeda's skilled operatives and mid-level field lieutenants have been either killed or captured, depleting the ranks of seasoned fighters and effective managers, and depriving it of significant operational capability. Cooks, drivers, bodyguards, and foot soldiers now make up the bulk of al-Qaeda's membership.

Al-Qaeda's centralized command and control has been disman-tled and its top leaders have gone deeper and deeper underground, choosing personal safety over operational efficacy—even according to US intelligence. While hiding in Abbottabad, Pakistan, for five years, bin Laden reportedly relied almost exclusively—and rather pathetically—on only one courier, Sheikh Abu Ahmed, a Pakistani born in Kuwait (his nom de guerre was Abu Ahmed al-Kuwaiti), to communicate with the outside world.[27]

Suicide bombers remain al-Qaeda's weapon of choice, but its ability to carry out complex suicide attacks along the lines of Sep-tember 11 has degraded considerably. After reviewing computer files and documents seized at the compound where bin Laden was killed, American officials say that the evidence suggests that until his death bin Laden encouraged his followers to strike inside the United States. US officials acknowledge that bin Laden's directions were, however, "aspirational" rather than granular in their details.[28] Although the remnants of al-Qaeda are fixated on attacking Western targets, they not only face more vigilant security, but they lack oper-ational capabilities—a functioning command and control, military and intelligence infrastructure, financial means, and rudimentary training—to carry out their ambitious schemes.

Moreover, al-Qaeda faces a leadership crisis that could further di-minish its capabilities. By selecting Ayman al-Zawahiri as its new emir, it has opted for continuity over change. According to a statement, Zawahiri's appointment shows respect for the "righteous martyrs" and honors the legacy of bin Laden. For his part, Zawahiri has vowed to continue the struggle against the Western powers and to avenge bin Laden. Perhaps even more alarmingly, he has pledged allegiance to Mullah Omar, leader of the Taliban, clearly an attempt to steady a rocky relationship between their two respective organizations. The appointment is nonetheless a risky one. As we will see, Zawahiri is a divisive figure and lacks the appeal of a bin Laden. However, his likely rivals for the position, including Sayf al-Adl, lacked his intellect, his theological credentials, and his operational experience.

Nevertheless, al-Qaeda and other similar factions might succeed in carrying out an attack in the short- to mid-term because of the escalation of the conflict in Afghanistan-Pakistan and the consequent radicalization wave affecting tiny elements of these two communities in the West. (There is, moreover, the motive to avenge bin Laden's killing, which they view as an assassination, effectively cold-blooded murder.) Most of the recent arrests have involved young Pakistani and Afghan men. But that likelihood, troubling as it is, must not blind us to the limited nature of the challenge posed by al-Qaeda and the gradual and steady dismantling of its military apparatus.

Similarly, local al-Qaeda branches in Iraq, Saudi Arabia, Yemen, the Maghreb, and elsewhere have exposed al-Qaeda Central's loss of operational control and damaged its outreach efforts to Muslims. Indiscriminate targeting of civilians has turned Muslim opinion against al-Qaeda, its tactics, and its ideology. For most Muslims, al-Qaeda stands accused of having brought ruin to the umma.[29] Some insist that al-Qaeda is an American invention, a pretext to intervene in Muslim lands.

In other words, the bin Laden group—as we might term its remnants—has lost the struggle for Muslim hearts and minds. In many countries, information about al-Qaeda suspects now comes from citizens, including family members, friends, and neighbors, not from surveillance and intelligence sources. This shift demonstrates a hardening of Muslim public sentiment against bin Laden's men, preaching of a transnational jihad centered on violence no longer resonates with ordinary Muslims, and their organization suffers from a grave crisis of legitimacy and authority.

Contrary to received wisdom in the West, there never was any swell of Muslim public support for bin Laden and his transnational jihadi contingent. More of a fringe phenomenon than a popular social movement, transnational jihad has never enjoyed a big constituency in Muslim societies.[30] The majority of Arabs and Muslims were (and are) highly critical of US and Western foreign policies, particularly involving the wars in Afghanistan and Pakistan. Nonetheless, only a small segment condones and sanctions a direct war with the West, or the killing of noncombatants. No prominent Muslim theorists or ideologues called for attacking the West. The struggle within—an intra-civilizational rift between secular nationalists on the one hand, and religious nationalists on the other—overshadowed and eclipsed the struggle without a so-called clash of cultures and civilizations.

After September 11, bin Laden, Zawahiri and their cohorts discovered that neither domestic jihadis nor the umma had any desire to join their caravan. Indeed influential opinion makers, clerics, and chiefs of domestic jihadis warned that al-Qaeda's reckless conduct risked embroiling Muslims in unnecessary, costly wars and endangered the very survival of the Islamist movement. With the exception of one or two pockets of refugee camps, the Muslim world did not see September 11 as a triumph but as a catastrophe.

And nearly ten years later, the broadly based peaceful revolutions of this past spring have demolished al-Qaeda's claim that the Islamist vanguard will spearhead revolutionary change in Muslim societies. On the whole, the revolts are peaceful, non-ideological, post-Islamist, and led by the embattled middle class, including a coalition of men and women of all ages and political colors: liberal-leaning centrists, democrats, leftists, nationalists, and Islamists. Clerics and mullahs are not key drivers; there is no Ayatollah Khomeini waiting in the wings to hijack the revolution and to seize power. Even mainstream

Islamists like the Muslim Brotherhood are only one tile in a social mosaic. The Arab revolutions have left bin Laden's vanguard behind.

The terrorism narrative has suffered an equally hard blow. The question is not why the Arabs and Muslims hate America so much, as the conventional wisdom would have it after September 11, but why Western pundits and policy makers underestimated the millions of Arabs and Muslims yearning for universal values such as human rights, the rule of law, open and pluralistic societies, and individual freedom and liberty. Although Middle Easterners are critical of US foreign policy, the Arab revolts show that they admire democratic ideals.[31]

Nonetheless, the dominant opinion in Western circles was, and remains, that al-Qaeda reflects a significant segment of Muslims and for Islamists of all stripes. No distinction is made between domestic jihadis and transnational al-Qaeda types, or between al-Qaeda and politically based Islamists, such as the Muslim Brotherhood, Palestinian Hamas, or Hizbullah. The conclusion reached after September 11 still holds: that the West faces an immediate and present danger that must be met with full force in one stroke.[32]

The War on Terror was a boon to bin Laden and Zawahiri's organization, elevating a dangerous but inconsequential insurgency into a geo-strategic threat and elevating them to the ranks of global actors. From 2003 until 2006, their defiant message fell on receptive ears, particularly among politically radicalized religious activists outraged by what they saw as the occupation of Muslim territories. From London to Algiers and Islamabad to Sana'a, young Muslim men tried to journey to Iraq and fight alongside members of Tanzim al-Qaeda fi Bilad al-Rafidayn (al-Qaeda in the Land of the Two Rivers), a group that embraces bin Laden's ideology but maintains its independence.

I have met many young men—Libyans, Tunisians, Syrians, Palestinians, Jordanians, Lebanese, Saudis, Yemenis, Algerians, Moroccans, Pakistanis, and others—who relayed stories of their failed efforts to travel to Iraq and join the "martyrs" brigade. America was waging a "crusade" against Islam and Muslims and al-Qaeda was a vanguard of Islamic resistance. None of them accepted the premise that the invasion and occupation of Iraq had anything to do with September 11. The consensus was that it was a pretext to occupy Arab territories, siphon their oil resources, and humiliate their people.

Nonetheless, as we'll see, al-Qaeda lost Iraq and Abu Musab al-Zarqawi, chief of al-Qaeda in Iraq, was the reason. Zarqawi terrorized Iraqis and fueled all-out sectarian war.[33] To cut his losses, and to distance himself from his reckless lieutenant, bin Laden publicly apologized to Muslims for the mistakes and misdeeds perpetrated by his men and reminded them that even the prophet had made mistakes. But bin Laden's apology was too little, too late. Sunni Iraqis had turned against bin Laden's men with a vengeance, and the reverberations of that civil war are still felt in Iraq and beyond.

All of this information is more or less public record now. Yet the politics of terrorism in the West sustains al-Qaeda, or at least the idea of al-Qaeda. America's political culture in particular remains obsessed with al-Qaeda and the terrorism narrative continues to resonate both with ordinary Americans and with top military commanders in charge of national security. "You can't find a four-star general without a security detail," said one three-star general posted in Washington after years of service abroad. "Fear has caused everyone to have [platoons of personal bodyguards and staff]."[34] Defense Secretary Robert Gates acknowledged the problem in an interview in August 2010. Since September 11, "what little discipline existed in the Defense Department when it came to spending has gone completely out of the window," he says. Gates argues that the bureaucracy had "swelled to cumbersome and top-heavy proportions, grown over-reliant on contractors, and grown accustomed to operating with little consideration to cost."[35]

The politics of terrorism have driven military adventurism, provided the environment for a mushrooming national debt, and militarized domestic affairs (torture, military tribunals, and the massive expansion of the national security machine).[36] They have also exposed deep cultural, legal, and philosophical fault lines within Western societies, giving rise to attempts to demonize Muslims and portray them as aliens, as fifth columns. Though driven by powerful far-right grassroots groups, Islamophobia, sometimes called the "new anti-Semitism," has gone mainstream. In Europe, the alarm over the Islamicization of the continent, masquerading as the demographic crisis in which Muslims outbreed their Christian counterparts, has become commonplace, reflected in the literature, ranging from more sophisticated treatments like Christopher Caldwell's *Reflections on the Revolution in Europe* to cruder polemics like Mark Steyn's *America Alone* and Bat Ye'or's *Eurabia*.[37]

Many surveys and public opinion polls suggested that an increasing number of Western citizens accept the fringe's depiction of Muslims. According to a poll conducted by Cornell University, nearly half of all Americans (44 percent) say that the government should restrict the civil liberties of American Muslims.[38] There is a growing cottage industry of Western commentators and politicians who thrive on bashing Islam. The War on Terror has provided a substantial level of cover for their views.[39] While initially terror experts such as Daniel Pipes, Steven Emerson, and Robert Spencer led the anti-Islam charge, it has spread widely. For a glimpse of this venomous rhetoric, read a now-notorious blog post by Martin Peretz, the *New Republic*'s editor in chief, which stated, "Frankly, Muslim life is cheap, most notably to Muslims." Peretz added: "I wonder whether I need honor these people and pretend that they are worthy of the privileges of the First Amendment which I have in my gut the sense they will abuse."[40] Although Peretz apologized twice, he nevertheless defended his assertion that Muslim life is cheap. "This is a statement of fact, not value," he said.[41]

Similarly, the cultural reverberations of the War on Terror have put America's values of religious tolerance and individual freedom under stress. As of early 2011, there are between 2.5 and 7 million Muslims in the United States (out of a total population of 300 million), a third of whom are African American. Confrontations have broken out over proposed mosques in Tennessee, California, Georgia, Kentucky, Wisconsin, and Illinois, as well as Brooklyn, Staten Island, Midland Beach, and Sheepshead Bay in New York.[42] Islamophobes seized on the proposed mosque and Islamic center in Lower Manhattan to stir up anti-Muslim sentiment. Newt Gingrich spearheaded opposition to building such a mosque so long as Saudi Arabia bars construction of churches and synagogues. To do so "a few blocks from the site where Islamist extremists killed more than 3,000 Americans," Gingrich opined, is a "political act" of "triumphalism," he said.[43] He justified his opposition by drawing an analogy with the Holocaust: "Nazis don't have the right to put up a sign next to the Holocaust museum in Washington," he said.[44] A number of politicians and citizens backed the mosque project based on the principle of freedom of religion, including New York's Mayor Michael Bloomberg and, eventually, President Obama, who came out in support after the New York City Landmarks Commission approved construction.

This virulent debate, however, illustrates how the politics of terrorism and the War on Terror threaten American values, the same values embraced by those taking to the streets through the Middle East.[45] Even President Obama raised the issue of the "wisdom" of building the Islamic center at the location in question.[46] The corrupting effects of war on state and society have been debated since America's beginnings. "Of all the enemies of public liberty, war is perhaps the most to be dreaded, because it comprises and develops the germ of every other," famously observed James Madison, essentially the author of the United States Constitution, in 1795. "No nation could preserve its freedom in the midst of continual warfare."[47]

A decade of anti-Muslim sentiment has taken its toll. In 2010, Gallup's Muslim West Facts Project published the results of a major poll about American prejudices toward Islam. They showed a causal link between rising anti-Islam and the politics of terrorism. The most significant finding is also the least surprising: A slight majority of Americans—53 percent—stated that their opinion of the faith is either "not too favorable"—22 percent—or "not favorable at all"— 31 percent. Americans were more than twice as likely to express negative feelings toward Muslims than they are toward Buddhists, Christians, or Jews. A majority of Americans disagreed with the statement that most Muslims are accepting of other religions—66 percent—and also admitted that they know either very little—40 percent—about Islam, or nothing at all—23 percent.[48] Putting the best face on the Gallup's finding, *Boston Globe* columnist James Carroll said that Muslims are wildly misperceived and wrongly judged, but that Americans are "at war, and afraid," and therefore that "exaggerated fears fuel themselves, and the dynamic of prejudice can be a riptide."[49] He compared the blanket stereotyping of Muslims to an unseen current that has run below the surface of Western culture for a millennium.[50]

Where is the debate today? As I mentioned earlier, most scholars of the Middle East have avoided discussion of the War on Terrorism, either fearful or suspicious of the politics involved. Despite a number of books encouraging greater and more sophisticated treatment—John Mueller's *Overblown*, Peter Beinert's *The Icarus Syndrome*, and Sandra Silbertstein's *War or Words*—neat concepts and convenient theoretical premises continue to dominate and the terrorism narrative has become deeply entrenched, both within American political culture and in the national psyche. Now active policies from Washington or self-interested advocacy parties no longer appear to provide the main momentum for this worldview. The response to the challenge and threat of terrorism has become an ideology of its own. Consequently, there is very little chance of reevaluating the country's overall strategy, particularly the expansion of the national security complex—even for a progressive president such as Obama—except, perhaps, on the rhetorical level. Obama's discourse does represent a break with the inflammatory rhetoric advocated by his predecessor. Time and again, the president and his senior advisers have stressed that the United States is not engaged in a "global war" against either "jihadists" or "militant Islamic radicalism," Bush's preferred ideological label for al-Qaeda and its allies. Instead, the Obama National Security Strategy (NSS) released in May 2010 defines "a far-reaching network of hatred and violence," a less hyperbolic and more ideologically neutral phrase.[51] According to Obama's top counterterrorism aide John Brennan, the new terminology aims at counteracting the notion that the United States is in conflict with the rest of the world—and that al-Qaeda is a global entity capable of replacing sovereign nation-states.[52]

Obama has offered a more nuanced and realistic interpretation of the fight against al-Qaeda, as was the case during a commencement speech to the 2010 graduating class at the United

States Military Academy at West Point in which he previewed key elements of his NSS: "Al Qaeda and its affiliates are small men on the wrong side of history. They lead no nation. They lead no religion. We need not give in to fear every time a terrorist tries to scare us. We should not discard our freedoms because extremists try to exploit them."[53] Although Obama explicitly reserves the right to act unilaterally and to use preemptive military force, he pledged to shape a new "international order" based on engagement, diplomacy, and collaboration with traditional allies and rising new influential actors.[54]

Brennan has reiterated the message: "Why should a great and powerful nation like the United States allow its relationship with more than a billion Muslims around the world [to] be defined by the narrow hatred and nihilistic actions of an exceptionally small minority of Muslims?"[55]

An important rhetorical shift in emphasis has taken place between the Obama administration and that of its predecessor. Yet, the Obama administration's rhetoric is at odds with institutional reality. Although the phrase "War on Terror" is no longer used, it still reflects its state of mind.[56] Obama's national security advisers have been unable to break free from this mindset in part because of Republican criticism that the president is weak on national security.[57] Any attempt on Obama's part to reassess the war effort is instantly met with a barrage of attacks by hawks and neoconservatives alike.

The American political landscape has become so toxic and polarized that the mere mention of reassessing the strategy against al-Qaeda is treated as a sign of weakness. The administration is perfectly aware of this. Yet al-Qaeda still looms large over American foreign policy. The Obama administration has not deviated significantly from its overall strategy: it has intensified the war in Afghanistan and Pakistan and has preserved many controversial Bush programs, such as the so-called secret surveillance and the Guantanamo military commissions. Although it ordered so-called black sites closed, it is impossible to know how much has changed in the methods intelligence services employ to capture and detain terrorist suspects, at least without access to highly classified information.[58]

Stressing the president's commitment to wage war against al-Qaeda and its allies, such as the Taliban in Afghanistan, Pakistan, and Yemen, Obama's advisers reminded Americans that he is fighting the "right war." They also emphasize that Obama has escalated covert operations in Pakistan against al-Qaeda and the Taliban, though without explicitly mentioning that the administration's weapon of choice is the CIA's Predator drones. Obama ordered more drone attacks in his first year in office than President Bush did in two full presidential terms.[59] He also expanded the use of drones to include low-level targets, such as foot soldiers, and even, reportedly, drug lords who give money to the Taliban—a remarkably aggressive definition of "material support" to terrorism. Although drone strikes have killed scores of al-Qaeda and Taliban leaders, they have also incinerated more than 1,000 civilians since 2004, including women and children. According to an analysis of US government sources, since the drone attacks intensified in the summer of 2008 the CIA has killed many more low-level fighters than mid- to high-level al-Qaeda and Taliban.[60]

In 2010, Predator drones fired more than 100 missiles in Pakistan alone, more than twice the number of strikes in Afghanistan, the recognized war theater. In Pakistan, the pace of drone strikes became almost a daily affair, a more than fourfold increase from the Bush years. The Obama administration even diverted additional aerial drones and weaponry from the Afghan battlefront to significantly expand the CIA's campaign against militants in their Pakistani havens, reported the *New York Times* and the *Wall Street Journal*. This put more strain on US-Pakistani relations and intensified tensions between the two allies, tensions which since bin Laden's killing have risen almost to the breaking point.

Despite its rhetoric, the Obama administration has therefore effectively escalated the War on Terror in the Afghanistan-Pakistan theater and targeted the remnants of al-Qaeda, as well as what it calls its "extremist allies" in both countries, a highly ambitious plan. Obama's national security team seems to group al-Qaeda with the Taliban, particularly the Pakistani Taliban. In contrast to its predecessor, the Obama administration has focused more on killing individual terrorists than on capturing them. The administration has its rationale for drone attacks; for example, stressing that they have degraded the capabilities of the Pakistani Taliban and al-Qaeda, and without needing to put US troops in harm's way on Pakistani soil. After bin Laden's death, American officials continued to defended them as instrumental in the destruction of al-Qaeda's central network in Pakistan and Afghanistan.[61]

But this calculus ignores the damage drone attacks have inflicted on America's reputation in the Muslim world and the "possibilities of blowback," about which the CIA, which is waging the Predator strikes, has warned. These attacks have inflamed anti-American rage among Afghanis and Pakistanis, including elite members of the security services and the urban middle class who feel their country is impotent to stand up to its powerful patron. There is a widespread perception among Pakistani elites, including the military, that the drone attacks violate Pakistan's sovereignty and dignity. Moreover, the ability of the United States to invade Pakistani airspace, kill bin Laden, and leave without detection was a humiliation to the Pakistani military. There is seething anger among the ranks of the Pakistan army—the world's seventh-largest in terms of active personnel—in barracks across the country.⁶² Both Secretary of Defense Gates and Chairman of the Joint Chiefs of Staff Admiral Mike Mullen argue the operation to kill bin Laden was a "humbling experience" for the Pakistanis and one that has tarnished their self-image.⁶³

This might come back to haunt the United States in ways more far-reaching than those of al-Qaeda in its heyday. Many Pakistanis, including some who live in the West, view the escalating war as an attack on their Muslim identity, and it is no coincidence that large numbers of Pakistanis and Afghans are behind some of the recent terror plots. The Pakistani Taliban and other militants are moving to exploit this anger, vowing to carry out suicide bombings in major American cities. Drone attacks have become a rallying cry, feeding the flow of volunteers into a small, loose network that is harder to trace even than shadowy al-Qaeda. Jeffrey Addicott, former legal adviser to Army Special Operations, said the strategy is "creating more enemies than we're killing or capturing."⁶⁴

In the US view, the attacks of September 11 constitute a turning point in contemporary American history and have been internalized by official Washington and ordinary citizens alike. Al-Qaeda shattered the collective peace of mind of Americans, who helplessly watched the collapse of the Twin Towers live on their television screens. In contrast to the Cold War, this was real and verifiable. Al-Qaeda and bin Laden had accomplished something that the powerful Soviet Union never achieved: they attacked the homeland and caused Americans to question their personal safety while going about everyday tasks, such as working in an office. We should not diminish the emotional toll it has had on the psyche of a nation. Many who were mere children when the September 11 attacks took place took to the streets to celebrate the announcement of bin Laden's death. For them and for Americans of all ages, bin Laden's elimination was a "significant and cathartic moment" for the nation, as Obama's press secretary, Jay Carney, put it.[65] More than a decade later, few Americans and Westerners realize the degree to which their fear of terrorism and terrorists is misplaced. But there can be no closure so long as ideology and reality remain confused.

Al-Qaeda's leaders and their local allies are perfectly aware of this. Indeed what stature they still have depends upon it. Spreading fear is the most effective means of staying in business. In an editorial in its English-language online magazine, *Inspire,* al-Qaeda in the Arabian Peninsula (AQAP) claimed responsibility for its attempts to bomb two US-bound cargo planes, boasting that what they call Operation Hemorrhage in October 2010 was cheap and easy, costing only $4,200 to carry out. "On the other hand this . . . will without a doubt cost America and other Western countries billions of dollars in new security measures. This is what we call leverage," the AQAP editors boasted.[66]

> AQAP unveiled what it called its "strategy of a thousand cuts," which will "bleed the enemy to death"; the goal, said the group's head of foreign operations, was to foment fear among Westerners, forcing them to invest huge amounts in new security procedures. Spending a few thousand to make the West spend billions was "such a good bargain."[67]

That is al-Qaeda's current war game, one that despite all odds it believes will give it the upper hand in its struggle against the most powerful country in the world. If al-Qaeda succeeds it will be because of its hold over the American imagination. To understand how it achieved this hold, we need to look at the full story of its rise and fall.

1

The Rise of Al-Qaeda

As an operationally organized, independent, and centralized transnational group, al-Qaeda did not exist until the second half of the 1990s—not the late 1980s, as received wisdom in the United States and the West would have it. By the time American forces had expelled bin Laden and his associates from their home base in Afghanistan at the end of 2001, al-Qaeda was but five years old.

Far from being a social movement with deep historical roots in Muslim societies, al-Qaeda, and transnational jihad in general, is an orphan within the militant Islamist family, an ambitious venture founded and led by a small vanguard. "Small" is the key word. Al-Qaeda has only ever attracted a limited number of ardent adherents and has never developed a mass following. Its brief history has been characterized by the absence of a thick and durable social base, and by its essentially nomadic quality. Any overview of the rise of al-Qaeda must acknowledge these humble and limited social origins, for they reveal the context and conditions that have given rise to the bin Laden generation.

And they are very limited. From the very beginning, al-Qaeda has been structurally constrained by weak societal ties and links. There is, in fact, less to it than meets the eye. Nonetheless, the conventional terrorism narrative continues to portray al-Qaeda as a potent global power. Rohan Gunaratna, whose book on al-Qaeda was a bestseller in the United States, claims that since September 11 al-Qaeda has become stronger:

> Despite the losses Al Qaeda has suffered in Afghanistan as a result of the destruction of its operational and training infrastructure, its cells overseas have moved from strength to strength. While Al Qaeda has been hunted down by the US, its allies and its friends, Al Qaeda has been able to replenish its human losses and material wastage.[1]

Gunaratna and others contend that radical Islam is "slowly growing."[2] In fact, once al-Qaeda's core elite—the Afghan Arabs— disappear, it will be incapable of replenishing its skilled, depleted ranks whose *asabiya*, tribal loyalty, has powered the transnational organization.

The organization's beginnings are key to unlocking the riddle of this transnational group, revealing its relative weight and inevitable decline and fall. Al-Qaeda has always contained the seeds of its own destruction.

From its origins in the late 1950s until the mid-1990s, a period of almost forty years, the militant Islamist movement known as "jihadism" was inward-looking, obsessed with replacing "renegade" secular Muslim rulers with Qur'anic-based states or states governed by the sharia (Islamic law). Sayyid Qutb, while in prison from 1954 until 1965, spearheaded a paramilitary group called al-Tanzim al-Sirri or "the Secret Apparatus." Qutb instructed his followers to prioritize the fight against the enemy within and oust Muslim "tyrants" who did not apply the sharia. According to my interviews with several of his contemporary disciples over the years, Qutb cautioned them against any activity or engagement that detracted them from this existential domestic struggle between God's sovereignty (faith) and apostasy, or between *hakimiya* and *jahiliya*. For Qutb, the clash within was the defining moment of the day because local secular rulers allowed the West to culturally dominate the abode of Islam.

For almost four decades, politically radicalized religious activists, the disciples of Qutb, fought a prolonged war against the near enemy—pro-Western Muslim leaders. They refrained from attacking the far enemy—Western powers. They kept their focus on the home front. There existed no constituency within the militant Islamist movement calling for an armed confrontation with the West, nor any manifestos that demanded such a clash. Jihadism was a solely domestic affair. After September 11, Western commentators and analysts suddenly discovered Qutb, and portrayed him as the "philosopher of terror," the spiritual and operational godfather to bin Laden and Zawahiri; they have drawn a direct, unbroken line between Qutb and al-Qaeda.

This connection fits perfectly with al-Qaeda's own designs. The organization has engaged in a systematic effort to claim the Qutbian legacy.[3] Bin Laden and Zawahiri repeatedly pronounced themselves ardent disciples of Qutb, warriors in his Islamic pioneering vanguard. Zawahiri's relationship with Qutb goes back to the latter's execution in 1966. Zawahiri, then in high school in a middle-class neighborhood in Cairo, was so moved by Qutb's martyrdom that he established a small underground cell, together with a few of his schoolmates. Ever since, Zawahiri has looked to *al-shahid* ("the martyr") as his model and inspiration, and frequently cites him in his pronouncements and manifestos. Zawahiri's senior associate, Sayyid Imam al-Sharif (alias "Abd al-Qadir Ibn Abd al-Aziz" and also known as "Dr. Fadl"), who as we shall see is a key figure in the story of the rise and fall of al-Qaeda, notes that Zawahiri's theological growth stopped with Qutb's writing more than thirty years ago, and that he never really evolved beyond that point. Other close associates of Zawahiri testify that Qutb has shaped Zawahiri's worldview.[4]

Despite their claim of kinship, bin Laden and Zawahiri twisted Qutb's ideas to suit their purposes. According to Qutb's contemporary followers, some of whom spent years with him in prison and underground, Qutb never called for a confrontation with the West and instead exhorted them to strike at Arab rulers who conspired with Islam's external enemies and allowed them to infiltrate Muslim lands.[5] Contemporary followers maintain that he showed no interest in either the internationalization of jihad or the targeting of Western powers. Nonetheless Qutb essentially called on Muslims to defend *dar al-Islam* (the abode of Islam) against crusading intrusion and cultural invasion. Yet both bin Laden and his detractors have claimed that Qutb supplied the fuel that powered al-Qaeda's transnational jihad.

This could not be further from the truth. Qutb was the master theorist of the concept of the "enemy within" and his organization, the Secret Apparatus, targeted the secular-leaning nationalist regime of Egyptian President Gamal Abdel Nasser. None of the surviving chiefs of the Secret Apparatus whom I interviewed ever mentioned that Qutb had instructed them to attack the United States and its Western allies or had theorized about the need to confront the enemy without. "Qutb's raison d'être was the replacement of *jahiliya* with *hakimiya* at home and the establishment of a Qur'anic state," pointed out Sayyid Eid, now 80, who spent years with Qutb in prison and who was one of his closest confidants inside and outside jail. "I do not ever recall *al-shahid* saying that we should wage war against America or Britain; rather he wanted us to be vigilant against the West's cultural penetration of our societies."

After Qutb's execution by Nasser in 1966, the overwhelming majority of politically radicalized religious activists, or domestic jihadis, who heeded his call have focused on the enemy within. What Zawahiri and bin Laden did was to substitute the enemy without for the enemy within, and subsequently collapse all distinctions between the two, a testament to Qutb's absolutist and opaque ideological categories. Qutb's anti-American narrative coupled with his revolutionary idea of *al-Islam al-haraki* (dynamic and operational Islam), facilitated al-Qaeda's efforts and allowed it to reclaim him as the spiritual force behind its "blessed" transnational jihad.

Qutb did not advocate an armed confrontation with the United States, even though he lashed out angrily against its crusading spirit. Nonetheless many dismiss such distinctions as hair splitting, insisting that his hostility to America—where he spent a formative period in the 1950s—created a fertile environment for extremist transnational organizations like al-Qaeda; rooted in absolutist cultural and civilization polarities, the Qutbian legacy has been theologically and ideologically deformed. By portraying the United States as Islam's Public Enemy No. 1 and cautioning Muslims that Islam is under threat, Qutb, it is argued, institutionalized anti-US sentiment among Arabs and Muslims and paved the road to September 11.

While Qutb's diatribe against America has widely resonated among Islamists, al-Qaeda's actions cannot be traced to his rhetoric. Indeed, transnational jihad took Qutb's strategic priorities and turned them on their head. While Qutb's Secret Apparatus and al-Qaeda strive to establish a Qur'anic state, they disagreed on how to bring it about. Qutb spent his life in prison and the underground nourishing and training a pioneering vanguard to confront local tyrants and Islamize society from the bottom up.

In contrast, al-Qaeda was a top-down, militarized organization designed to wage a transnational war against the West, trying to bog it down in a total war against the greater Islamic world. Al-Qaeda aimed at winning the hearts and minds of Muslims and spearheading popular resistance against the Western crusade against the umma.[6] Once bin Laden and Zawahiri gained credibility in the eyes of the Muslim masses, they would level the playing field with local rulers and then seize power in their native lands.

Thus the transition from Qutb's Secret Apparatus to bin Laden's al-Qaeda has been marked by continuities and discontinuities. Bin Laden and Zawahiri adopted some of Qutb's key concepts and terms, and then adapted them to their transnational jihad cause. For example, they borrowed the concept of al-Islam al-haraki ("a pioneering vanguard")—which Qutb coined and popularized—and deployed it against the religious and political establishment at home and against foreign powers. Qutb was a theorist of domestic jihadism, not al-Qaeda's transnational jihadism. Since his execution, domestic jihadis have struggled to enact his vision and exact vengeance on secular-leaning Arab rulers, such as Nasser and his successors.

Al-Qaeda and transnational jihad in general are primarily creatures of the Afghan war against the Soviets, a conflict that lasted almost a decade and brought together between 10,000 and 50,000 volunteers from every region of the Muslim world. Afghanistan was the cradle of a new generation of mujahideen, baptized by blood and fire, who tasted the sweetness of victory over one of the most powerful fighting machines the world has known. The Afghan jihad molded the character and worldview of many members of this generation and bred among then a sense of invincibility. This helps explain the resilience and perseverance of this generation whose asabiya has withstood considerable adversity.

The Afghan jihad was pivotal to the rise of al-Qaeda and to transnational jihad, fertilizing two powerful ideological currents—Egyptian radical Islamism and Saudi ultra-conservatism. Al-Qaeda was born out of a marriage of convenience between Zawahiri and a powerful Egyptian contingent on the one hand, and bin Laden, including Saudi and Yemeni volunteers, on the other: an alliance of two Islamist tribes. Although this unholy union will survive despite bin Laden's death, it faces a bleak future and its descendants are few and isolated from the mainstream Islamist family.

Zawahiri and the Egyptian contingent have spent a lifetime battling the secular-nationalist Egyptian regime. As late as 1995, he authored an essay entitled "The Road to Jerusalem Goes through Cairo," which appeared in his group's newsletter, *al-Mujahidun* (April 26) published by Tanzim al-Jihad. He wrote, "Jerusalem will not be liberated unless the battle for Egypt and Algeria is won and unless Egypt is liberated," thus reaffirming his commitment to battle Muslim rulers. According to Fadl, Zawahiri's senior associate, from the 1960s through the mid-1990s Zawahiri never showed any operational interest in attacking the far enemy.[7] That would have squandered his precious, limited resources and contradicted deeply held theoretical and theological percepts.

For the Zawahiri generation, the struggle against the near enemy was a strategic necessity as well as a religious duty; only Qur'anic-based states would protect and promote Islam against the West's corrupting cultural influences and imperial crusades. His associates were even more steadfast in their belief that the domestic jihad must take priority over everything else. For example, in the late 1990s Zawahiri appealed to his key lieutenants and associates in Afghanistan, Yemen, Egypt, and elsewhere to join the recently formed World Islamic Front for Jihad against the Jews and Crusaders (referred to hereafter as the "World Islamic Front") with bin Laden; he faced an internal revolt within his own organization, a group known as "al-Jihad," later renamed "Tanzim al-Jihad," and fierce opposition against the new transnational venture with bin Laden.

A good number of Zawahiri's associates pointedly accused him of recklessness, of endangering the survival of the Islamist movement as a whole. Several of his top cohorts also cautioned him against falling under the spell of bin Laden, whom they perceived as an untrustworthy amateur, a self-promoter more interested in cultivating his media image than in struggling to make God's words supreme. At a key meeting in Afghanistan in the late 1990s, Zawahiri tendered his resignation as emir of Tanzim al-Jihad because of the intensity of opposition to his joint venture with bin Laden. According to accounts by some participants, senior members expressed shock that their leader would join bin Laden's World Islamic Front without consulting them first and examining the repercussions of such a dangerous venture.[8]

In addition to the opposition within Zawahiri's inner circle to attacking the United States, there were few buyers of transnational jihad within the jihadist movement generally. In particular, incarcerated leaders of al-Gamaa al-Islamiya, the largest jihadist organization in the Muslim world, called on their members to refrain from joining the World Islamic Front and to abide by the unilateral cease-fire that they declared in 1997. A war of words developed between al-Gamaa's senior chiefs and Zawahiri, who labored to drive a wedge between these imprisoned leaders and their counterparts in exile.[9]

The World Islamic Front was a foolish idea that was bound to exact a heavy toll on the sons of Islam, according to some of Zawahiri's former cohorts, whom I interviewed in Egypt, Yemen, and elsewhere in the late 1990s. None of them bought into Zawahiri's sudden switch to transnational jihad. The consensus was that pressing financial and operational circumstances forced his hand and caused him to join bin Laden's front, a tactical move to rescue his sinking ship. Bankrupt and without independent financial resources in the second half of the 1990s, Zawahiri could not pay the meager salaries of his fighters' widows, a painful blow, nor the living expenses of his dispersed lieutenants and foot soldiers. Moreover, Zawahiri's Tanzim al-Jihad had suffered a catastrophic military setback (in 1993 almost a thousand members, including senior lieutenants, were captured by the Egyptian authorities because of tactical blunders by low- and mid-ranks). In 1995 Zawahiri sent a memo to his subordinates and suspended attacks against the Egyptian regime at home because of operational difficulties, thus implicitly conceding defeat.

Others asserted that Zawahiri had no genuine interest in transnational jihad but believed that he had thought he would ultimately outsmart and outmaneuver bin Laden and recalibrate the World Islamic Front to serve his lifelong struggle against the near enemy. Zawahiri himself argues that his decision to go on the offensive against the far enemy stems from US involvement in the late 1990s in the capture and rendition to Egypt of al-Jihad senior chiefs from Albania and other countries, a number of whom received death sentences. Zawahiri vowed to retaliate against America. Whatever the case, his call for transnational jihad did not resonate with his inner circle or with the jihadist movement at large. But, once committed, he could not back down. Abandoning a thirty-year struggle against the near enemy, Zawahiri converted wholeheartedly to battling the far enemy; in 2000 he authored an autobiographical manifesto—*Fursan tahta rayat al-nabi* [Knights under the prophet's banner]—in which he justified his new conversion and called for prioritizing the fight against the head of *kufr* or infidelity: the United States.[10]

The story of al-Qaeda is that of a union between two driven and charismatic men with differing sensibilities, backgrounds, and lifestyles. From a very young age, growing up during a period of profound socioeconomic and political change in Egypt in the 1950s and 1960s, the young Zawahiri sought to bring Qutb's unfinished struggle to fruition and establish a Qur'anic-based state. One of his prison mates told me, "Zawahiri is a Qutbian from head to toe." While at high school in Maadi, Cairo, he established an underground cell and invited a few of his classmates and close friends to join it. Though he belongs to a professional family with roots in pan-Arab politics, Zawahiri completely rejected the political process and embraced the underground and paramilitary tactics. Several of his contemporary associates have told me that Zawahiri never believed in religious or political activism as a means to overthrow the secular Egyptian regime and did not even use the mosque for recruitment or mobilization, though he participated in a few protests.

Ironically, Zawahiri emulated his sworn enemy, Nasser, in enacting a military coup to bring about radical change. He tried to infiltrate the Egyptian officer corps by recruiting and co-opting junior officers into his cell, avoiding a direct armed confrontation with the Egyptian authorities, and instead plotting in the shadows until the time was right. While Zawahiri was not directly involved in the assassination of Sadat in 1981, he was imprisoned for three years because of his close connection with the perpetrators. Through intensive interrogation and torture, Zawahiri's shadowy life was brought to light, and his jihadist cell was crushed by President Hosni Mubarak's security forces. Similar to Qutb's experience in prison, Zawahiri's years in jail did not turn him away from the underground; they hardened his resolve. His experience of hard labor, psychological and physical abuse, humiliation, and torture left a permanent scar. In 1984, he left prison with abiding grievances against the state and a deep thirst for revenge. Despite the twists and turns of his violent journey—from local jihad to transnational jihad, Zawahiri has been consumed by the fight against "renegade" Egyptian secular rulers—Nasser, Anwar Sadat, and Hosni Mubarak. For almost fifty years he waged a crusade against them, a crusade that took him from a high school in an upper middle-class neighborhood in Egypt to the killing fields of Afghanistan and Pakistan.

In contrast, until the 1980s, bin Laden lived a simpler life than that of his Egyptian co-conspirator. One of the fifty-four children of Mohammed bin Laden, Saudi Arabia's construction czar, bin Laden enjoyed wealth, privilege, and opportunity from a young age. Bin

Laden spent his formative years in the Red Sea city of Jeddah, and many hours at his family's ranch in the hills and valleys between Jeddah and Mecca. He also frequently visited his mother's family in Latakia, Syria, and received some of his early schooling there and in Beirut.[11]

His father, who arrived in Saudi Arabia from the rugged terrain of northern Yemen with only what he had in his pockets, built a multibillion-dollar construction empire from the ground up, and established strong ties with the royal family. He rebuilt the great mosque complexes at Mecca and Medina, Islam's two holiest shrines. Even after his untimely death—Osama was just ten years old—Mohammed bin Laden continued to serve as a role model for his son, who embraced his father's work ethic, humility, piety, and independence. Mohammed instilled in the young Osama stamina, endurance, and a dogged faith that hardship could be overcome. His hands-on approach to business deeply influenced bin Laden's leadership style. He preferred to be directly involved in a project rather than remain behind a desk in an office.

From a young age, bin Laden was more religious than his half-brothers, and he felt deeply the upheaval in the Arab world after the 1967 Arab-Israeli war, in which Israel crushed the Arab armies, and the tumultuous events of the 1970s, culminating in the Islamic revolution in Iran, the Soviet invasion of Afghanistan, the siege of the mosque at Mecca, and the signing of the peace treaty between Egypt and Israel. His joining an after-school Islamic study group at al-Thaghr, an elite private school in Jeddah, in 1973, marked a transformational moment for bin Laden. He considered himself reborn. This religious awakening helped fill the void left by the loss of his father.

While bin Laden was perhaps more pious than his brothers, he was not all that different from other young Saudis whose sensibilities and worldview were shaped by pivotal developments in the late 1960s and 1970s. He never exhibited a propensity for breaking away from his family, let alone leaving home to wage a borderless, transnational war. Until the late 1970s bin Laden remained largely apolitical and did not engage in political causes.

Like many young Saudis of his generation, bin Laden studied economics at King Abdul Aziz University in Jeddah and came in contact with two lecturers there—Abdullah Azzam, a charismatic Islamic scholar who would become his mentor during the Afghan jihad in the 1980s, and Muhammad Qutb, the brother of Sayyid—both of whom played a key role in his subsequent transformation. In addition to studying macroeconomics, Osama read Sayyid Qutb's revolutionary manifestos and internalized some of his ideas and concepts. Although his piety deepened at the university, it did not preclude him from expanding his role in his family's construction company. He spent countless hours at various construction sites, overseeing building projects, and traveled in Europe on company business on private jets. At home in Jeddah, however, bin Laden led a more humble and simple life than his brothers, and started a family of his own. Afghanistan transformed him, and his deepening and expanding role in the conflict helped strengthen his family's position within Saudi Arabia, a leading driver behind the Afghan jihad.

Bin Laden and Zawahiri led two different lives: one above ground and the other deep underground. Bin Laden was a builder, Zawahiri a demolisher. They met in Afghanistan in the 1980s and their divergent lives converged. The Afghan jihad transformed bin Laden, took hold of his imagination, and left a deep imprint on his psyche. He found his calling among young and old mujahideen battling a godless enemy, seeking martyrdom, and dreaming of heavenly, not earthly, fruits and rewards. The wealthy man from Islam's holy land,

Saudi Arabia, felt at home with humble Muslims—many of whom came from afar and sold precious belongings, including their wives' jewelry and life savings—who were willing to sacrifice themselves to defend the umma. Bin Laden realized that that lesson, mobilizing the collective will of Muslims and undertaking jihad, a personal duty in the Afghan case or *fard kifaya* (a collective obligation), represented a powerful weapon, one that could be profitably leveraged and deployed to great effect.

Psychologically and spiritually, the Afghan jihad shaped bin Laden more than any school had. His mentor, Shaykh Abdullah Azzam, a charismatic Jordanian of Palestinian descent, provided ideological and theological guidance and became a driving force behind bin Laden's entry into the jihad environment. Bin Laden looked on Azzam as a spiritual father and mentor, and fell under his spell. Azzam was to bin Laden what Qutb was to Zawahiri. Both Azzam and Qutb belonged to a radical Islamist school of thought, though with similarities and differences, and both were martyred.

Like Qutb, Azzam favored the formation of a "pioneering vanguard" that would build an ideal Qur'anic society and bring about an Islamic revival worldwide. In his widely read manifesto, *Join the Caravan*, Azzam states that establishing a solid foundation, a homeland, as a base for Islam was crucial:

> The establishment of the Muslim community on an area of land is a necessity, as vital as water and air. This homeland will not come about without an organized Islamic movement which perseveres consciously and realistically upon jihad, and which regards fighting as a decisive factor and as a protective cover.[12]

But unlike Qutb, Azzam opposed taking arms against fellow Muslims, including nationalist rulers like Nasser and Mubarak.

From 1987 until his assassination in 1989, Azzam doggedly opposed initiatives by the Egyptian and Algerian contingents led by Zawahiri to deploy the Afghan Arabs (those mujahideen from the Arab region who fought against the Soviets in Afghanistan) against pro-Western secular Muslim regimes and to spread the Islamic revolution throughout Muslim lands, starting with Egypt and Algeria. Azzam felt that "violence should not be used against Muslim regimes no matter how far they had deviated from *shariah* principles."[13]

Zawahiri railed against Azzam for poisoning bin Laden's mind, several former associates of Zawahiri told me in the 1990s; he resented Azzam's dominant influence over the Saudi and labored hard to drive a wedge between disciple and mentor. In a meeting of Afghan Arabs, according to a participant, Zawahiri publicly criticized Azzam, saying that he was "not the Abdullah Azzam we know."[14] The Egyptian contingent, led by Fadl and Zawahiri, hoped to convert bin Laden to their fight against "apostate" Arab rulers—the near enemy—and to tap into his resources. However, bin Laden would have none of that. Throughout the 1980s and 1990s he opposed a war of Muslim against Muslim, counseling the Afghan Arabs against shedding Muslim blood. Contrary to widespread accounts of bin Laden's financing attacks against Egyptian and Algerian targets by domestic jihadis in the 1990s, he withheld his support.

Zawahiri and his allies were furious with bin Laden, and accused him of being greedy and selfish, of not being one of them. For example, when in 1995 bin Laden reduced his financial assistance to Zawahiri's Tanzim al-Jihad, Zawahiri wrote an article in al-Jihad's magazine *Kalimat Haq* ("Word of Truth"), in which he criticized bin Laden: "While *al-shabab* [the youth] sacrifice their souls, the wealthy withhold their money."[15] Bin Laden's withholding of financing partly explains the fierce opposition among Zawahiri's inner circle and cohorts alike to merging with bin Laden's transnational jihad in the late 1990s.

Like Qutb, Azzam did not call for the internationalization of jihad and never envisioned a transnational organization along al-Qaeda ideology, structure, and tactics. He might have conceived of an idea called *al-qaeda al-sulba*, or "the solid base," in 1987, but, contrary to simplistic and misleading claims by so-called terrorism experts like Gunaratna, the "solid base" had a dramatically different character than the entity born in the second half of the 1990s.[16]

Azzam's *al-qaeda al-sulba* had nothing in common with bin Laden's military organization, formally launched as the World Islamic Front in 1998, except in name.[17] In fact, according to the aforementioned Fadl, the emir of Tanzim al-Jihad and senior associate of Zawahiri, as well as the lead man behind the theological wooing of bin Laden away from Azzam in the late 1980s, "people ought to know that the rise of al-Qaeda was a splinter away from Sheikh Abdullah Azzam, a rejection of his ideas."[18] Azzam certainly saw al-Qaeda as a base, one that was to be composed of individuals committed to the cause who would, through the cumulative weight of their actions, instigate great change. Azzam was referring to a tactic, however, not an organization.[19]

Many take terms, such as Azzam's *al-qaeda al-sulba*, out of their historical and sociological contexts and apply them to dramatically different settings. In their minds, Azzam's *al-qaeda al-sulba* becomes synonymous with bin Laden's transnational organization founded almost a decade later, effectively comparing apples and oranges. To equate Azzam's theory with bin Laden's organization is to distort history, and to ignore important differences and disagreements among leaders of the Afghan Arabs. For example, Azzam attempted to restrain what he saw as reckless adventurers, such as Fadl and Zawahiri and their cohorts, and to prevent them from hijacking the

Afghan jihad. Before his assassination in 1989, and to the chagrin of Zawahiri, Azzam also tried to extract bin Laden from the clutches of the Egyptian contingent.

In his memoir, *The Exposure*, as well as in various media interviews in Arabic, Fadl throws light on the fierce struggle that took place between the Egyptian contingent and Azzam for the future of the Afghan Arabs in the late 1980s. Zawahiri spearheaded the effort to discredit Azzam in the eyes of the Afghan Arabs, particularly bin Laden. Fadl's efforts suggest that had Azzam not been killed, bin Laden's organization would not have taken the murderous transnational path that it has since the mid-1990s. Azzam was the unchallenged leader of the Afghan Arabs and possessed considerable prestige and charisma. At the height of the Afghan war, Azzam opposed attacking civilians, including Russians, though between 1979 and 1989 Soviet troops nearly destroyed Afghanistan and killed and injured millions of its inhabitants. He opposed terrorism as a tool of war as well as aggression against noncombatants.

In interviews, Azzam's disciples confided to me that he vetoed proposals by extremists like Zawahiri and others to attack Russian civilians, arguing that it would tarnish the reputation of the mujahideen and jihad. Unlike Zawahiri, Azzam possessed an ethical view that distinguished right from wrong and proscribed belligerence. Azzam, they said, rejected the premise that the end justified the means—that is, he did not believe the imperative to liberate Afghanistan from Soviet occupation justified the use of terrorism against Russian noncombatants.

Of course, Azzam was not an angel, and some of his inflammatory pronouncements at the height of the Afghan jihad suggest a militaristic sensibility. The Afghan war left deep scars on all combatants, particularly the winners, such as those of the Azzam generation. Victory made them arrogant and they lost perspective. I would contend that Azzam's statements must be contextualized, and compared and contrasted with his actions during the Afghan war. There is a critical debate over the nature of the divisions between and contradictions among leading members of this generation.

The debate goes to the very heart of why and when bin Laden broke from Azzam and set up his military network. A comparative historical approach shows that the Afghan Arabs were not a monolith, as the post–September 11 terrorism narrative would have it, and that serious disagreements existed among their top chiefs. The standard narrative overlooks the ideological diversity of the Afghan Arabs and the presence of more powerful figures than bin Laden and Zawahiri—such as Azzam; Shaykh Omar Abdel Rahman, the blind cleric and leader of Egyptian al-Gamaa al-Islamiya; and, of course, Fadl.

For example, in *Inside Al Qaeda*, Rohan Gunaratna groups all Islamists with al-Qaeda and argues that the nature of the threat they pose is existential. Gunaratna further claims that al-Qaeda has penetrated existing Islamist networks around the world—the Middle East, East Asia, Southeast Asia, including southern Thailand, Malaysia, Singapore, Brunei, Indonesia, Cambodia, and Mindanao. "Al Qaeda is a worldwide movement capable of mobilizing a new and hitherto unimagined global conflict," he warns Western audiences. "It is a pioneering operational vanguard of a global Islamist threat posing the likelihood of long term, more or less continuous conflict with the West."[20] He envisions and calls for an ongoing, open-ended global War on Terror.

In fact, as I have suggested, not all Islamists are synonymous with bin Laden's al-Qaeda. Azzam was by far the most influential of the founding fathers of the Afghan Arabs, and his words and actions continue to matter considerably, particularly to bin Laden, who he groomed as a future leader of his "pioneering vanguard." As the

Afghan war was winding down, Azzam turned his sights to Palestine, his native home—about which he felt passionately all of his life—as a potential base for the new jihad. The need to liberate occupied Palestine, he argued, was a sacred duty, and he called on Muslims to join the jihad caravan there.

Although the plight of Palestine resonated with most mujahideen, Qutb's disciples—particularly the Egyptian contingent, such as Fadl, Zawahiri, Subhy Abu Sitta (also known as Abu Hafs al-Masri), and Ali Amin al-Rashidi (alias Abu Ubayda al-Banshiri), Sayf al-Adl (also known as Mohammed Ibrahim Makkawi)—argued that it must wait until the replacement of secular Muslim regimes with Qur'anic-based states. Instead of confronting the Zionist enemy, Zawahiri and Fadl called for taking war to "renegade" Muslim rulers and seizing power; once the Islamist movement is empowered, the liberation of Palestine would commence. "Palestine is not the central and fundamental question for Arabs and Muslims, as some cynics propagate," stated Fadl. "The first priority is the restoration of the Islamic caliphate rule that unites Muslims."[21] Hence, Zawahiri's much-cited dictum that the road to Jerusalem goes through Cairo, Algiers, and Amman.

Both camps attempted to bring bin Laden to their cause. But at this stage, in the late 1980s, captivated by the struggle against Soviet communism, he hoped to shift the jihad caravan to the Central Asian republics and continue the struggle against Russia.[22]

It is worth stressing that at the end of the Afghan war in 1989, none of the leading figures—neither Azzam, Fadl, Zawahiri, nor bin Laden—called for targeting the United States. At this stage, none of the important voices advocated an armed confrontation with the West. The United States, along with its allies, was in the same trenches as the mujahideen battling the "evil empire." Indeed,

America and the holy warriors in Afghanistan were so close that few differences could be found between them.

After September 11, commentators went to great lengths to ferret out clues about bin Laden's intrinsic hostility and hatred toward the United States and the West in general. Several points are in order. To begin with, most of the accounts of bin Laden's al-Qaeda tend to impose the present on the past, or to read the past through the distorted lens of September 11 and its bloody aftermath—the War on Terror. For example, *Wall Street Journal* reporter Yaroslav Trofimov authored a book widely cited in the US press, *The Siege of Mecca*, in which he traces the rise of al-Qaeda to an uprising in 1979 by a small group of extremists who took over the holy shrine in Mecca and precipitated a troublesome battle with the Saudi authorities. "But with the benefit of hindsight, it's painfully clear: the count-down to September 11, to the terrorist bombings in London and Madrid, and to the grisly Islamist violence ravaging Afghanistan and Iraq all began on that warm November morning in the shade of the Kaba."[23] Trofimov does not provide any credible evidence to show how the battle in Mecca—"in the shade of the Kaba"—shaped the mindset and sensibility of bin Laden; it is, rather, a farfetched conclusion.

Contrary to what Trofimov and others say, there exists no hard evidence for bin Laden entertaining or expressing anti-American sentiments before 1990–91. During the Afghan war, bin Laden was the main point man between the Saudi security services and their Pakistani counterparts, an integral part of the American chain of support for the Afghan mujahideen. According to his close confidants, bin Laden often met with Pakistani military intelligence officers, particularly General Mahmoud Ahmad, in order to coordinate tactics and strategy with them. He was in direct contact with the office of Prince Turki al-Faisal, head of Saudi intelligence, and frequently requested and received instructions from him.[24] In fact, in the 1980s the CIA nicknamed bin Laden a "good-gooder" because initially he spent his own money as well as raising for the Afghan jihad from wealthy men from the Gulf. He then utilized his skills in construction and his family's wealth to build clinics, roads, and barracks for the Afghan mujahideen.

Bin Laden's worldview was shaped by the jihad against the Soviet Union, not the United States, an ally in the fight against "godless communism." Members of the Saudi royal family recall that during the Afghan jihad bin Laden approached them and expressed his gratitude for America's active support for the mujahideen.[25] This is not surprising given the unholy alliance between US foreign policy and political Islamists, united by a mutual perception of a rising Soviet threat. Although there was little love lost between the two camps, the Soviet invasion of Afghanistan, which coincided with the Islamic revolution in Shiite Iran, brought Sunni-based mujahideen and America closer. Fadl, who worked closely with bin Laden in Afghanistan, acknowledges that the interests of the jihadist movement and America coincided and converged in Afghanistan for the benefit of both camps. Both suspended their misgivings against one another and focused on the common goal, battling the greater communist menace. But when the Soviet army retreated in defeat from Afghanistan and the Soviet empire collapsed soon after, inherent tensions between an emboldened mujahideen movement and the lone surviving superpower quickly reasserted themselves.

Bin Laden did not express strong anti-US views until after the 1990–91 Gulf War. When he returned to Saudi Arabia in 1989, he was welcomed like a hero and was on good terms with the royal family. He continued to wage an anti-Marxist crusade, targeting the socialist-based government of South Yemen for ouster. Between 1989 and 1990, there was no marked change in his conduct or worldview. Some analysts note that bin Laden encouraged a boycott of US products because of America's support for Israel.[26] But this example hardly characterizes bin Laden as a belligerent anti-American voice or disproves the hypothesis that before 1991 he was at war with communist Russia, not capitalist America.

The catalyst for change was American military intervention in the Gulf and its permanently stationing troops in Saudi Arabia, Islam's birthplace and bin Laden's home. He viewed actions in the Gulf War and afterward as part of an American conspiracy to establish military bases and dominate Muslim lands and siphon their oil resources. Bin Laden also resented Saudi rulers for disregarding his proposal to mobilize a mujahideen force to confront the army of Saddam Hussein, and, instead, for relying on the Americans to defend their regime.

Although there is no single explanation for bin Laden's antipathy to America, the Gulf War and its aftermath, particularly the stationing of troops in Saudi Arabia, were primary. But bin Laden still did not yet translate this hostility into concrete action by establishing a paramilitary organization along al-Qaeda lines. After the Saudi authorities seized his passport in 1991 in an effort to keep him under control, he used his family contacts to retrieve it. He left the country, never to return.

There was nothing inevitable about bin Laden's journey, which first took him briefly to the western Pakistani frontier city of Peshawar in March 1992, and then to Sudan, where he stayed for four years until his departure to Afghanistan in May 1996. According to the dominant terrorism narrative, as soon as bin Laden left Saudi Arabia in exile in 1992, he activated al-Qaeda al-Askariya, which he had set up in 1988 before he left Afghanistan. This relates to the assertion—a false one, as I have argued—that al-Qaeda al-Askariya was merely an extension of Azzam's *al-qaeda al-sulba*.[27]

As noted previously, Azzam's "solid base" was more theoretical than actual; it was not a true organization with operational capacity. There is debate as to whether bin Laden founded a group called "al-Qaeda" in either late 1987 or early 1988. Although the evidence is sketchy and inconclusive, in 1988 in Peshawar, bin Laden and a dozen or so close associates appeared to have set up al-Qaeda al-Askariya, or "a training base"—as bin Laden subsequently recalled—"and that is where the name came from."[28]

One rationale for the training base stems from a late 1987 complaint from some young Afghan Arabs to bin Laden about Azzam's services bureau. Bin Laden had been raising funds from Saudi Arabia for Azzam and the Afghan leaders, but decided to set up a separate facility near the Afghan-Pakistan border and called on the Egyptian Tanzim al-Jihad to run it. Bin Laden's camp was a limited venture and primarily focused on training recruits for the front against the Soviets, notes Fadl, who provided bin Laden with skilled cadres to train Afghan Arab fighters. In a series of interviews with the Arabic newspaper *al-Hayat* from the Egyptian prison, Tura, Fadl conceded that his Tanzim al-Jihad had established bin Laden's original training base and, moreover, that he had "tried to direct him to the right path," by which he meant battling the near enemy. Bin Laden proved to be a huge disappointment to Fadl, who maintained that by the end of the Afghan war bin Laden was more interested in waging jihad against the socialist-based government in South Yemen than anything else.[29]

It should be no surprise that few of bin Laden's associates remembered calling themselves "al-Qaeda" and that there is no mention of the group in the comprehensive *Encyclopedia of Jihad* published by Azzam's Maktab al-Khidmat (services bureau) between 1991 and 1993. Nevertheless, at this stage, the term "al-Qaeda" referred more to "fundamentals," as they called them—maxims, or rules—rather than to an organization.[30]

Peshawar, the alleged home of bin Laden's 1988 al-Qaeda, was not as welcoming the next time around, when he arrived as an exile in 1992. He had no organizational infrastructure and few ardent supporters left over from the Afghan jihad. In addition, Pakistan, a close ally of the Saudi royal family, had come under intense pressure from Arab countries as well as the United States to repatriate the Afghan Arabs, many of whom had been battling their own regimes. Although he had planned to provoke the Saudi authorities and incite trouble, bin Laden soon discovered that Pakistan was hostile and thus immediately left for Sudan, a state ruled by a friendly Islamic-based coalition.

Sudan was an important way station on bin Laden's journey to al-Qaeda and transnational jihad. He spent almost four years in this poor African-Arab country and utilized his skills in construction to build roads and experiment with arboriculture and a soap-making factory and tannery in Khartoum. Welcomed as "the great Islamic investor" by Hassan al-Turabi, the country's most important Islamic scholar, bin Laden duly invested tens of millions of dollars in road construction and other projects.[31]

During the next four years bin Laden built a complex network, one that combined business practices with ideological indoctrination and recruitment. Management and militancy were intertwined. Most of the managers employed by bin Laden were either hardcore Islamist ideologues, associates of the Afghan jihad, or exiled militants who sought refuge in the friendly Sudan. Although at this stage al-Qaeda was not yet an operational organization, the plans to make it into one were put in place.

In the first half of the 1990s Sudan was a focal point for radical Islamists and Afghan Arabs on the run. With the Afghan mujahideen embroiled in a vicious civil war and Pakistan repatriating the Afghan Arabs to their respective countries, Islamic Sudan emerged as the new jihad headquarters, offering shelter and ideological and theological substance to a new breed of Salafi-Jihadi traveling fighters. Turabi was the man behind the transformation of Sudan from a military junta to a pan-Islamic hub. In particular, he welcomed Algerian and Egyptian jihadis, such as Zawahiri, who were then battling regimes in their respective countries, and precipitated a serious crisis with the two neighboring Arab states, particularly Egypt.

For example, when bin Laden refused to finance Zawahiri's Tanzim al-Jihad to carry out attacks inside Egypt, the Sudanese intelligence service reportedly provided the financing. In late 1993 Zawahiri told Fadl that the Sudanese authorities gave him 100,000 dollars on the condition that he execute ten operations against the Egyptian regime.[32] According to Fadl, when, in the mid-1990s, bin Laden began to excommunicate Saudi rulers, Fadl warned him that this may incur the wrath of the Sudanese government. Bin Laden retorted by saying that the Sudanese authorities had encouraged him to undertake these operations.[33]

At critical junctures in the 1980s, 1990s, and after September 11, state actors have used non-state actors, such as the Afghan mujahideen, the Afghan Arabs, Tanzim al-Jihad, al-Gamaa al-Islamiya, al-Qaeda, and others, to serve their interests. Transnational actors allowed themselves to be used to wage wars by proxy; their own survival was at stake, as was their ability to go on the offensive against secular Muslim rulers and ultimately to replace them.[34] Far from being passive victims of the games nations play, Zawahiri, bin Laden, and their cohorts were active participants. They desperately struggled to shed their non-state status and to join the privileged and exclusive nation club.

Despite tensions over money in Sudan, bin Laden, who had drawn closer to the Egyptian contingent at the end of the Afghan war, was now surrounded by lieutenants of Tanzim al-Jihad and al-Gamaa al-Islamiya who offered their services. In Afghanistan, bin Laden had had Azzam to counterbalance the weight of Zawahiri and other militant Egyptians; in Sudan he had no such countervailing authority. His inner circle consisted almost entirely of Egyptian travelers from the Afghan jihad, who fed him an extreme theological and ideological diet tailored to his rigid, authoritarian sensibility and worldview. Herein lie the origins of the marriage of ideas between Egyptian radicalism of the Qutbian variety and the ultra-conservative Saudi variety, a marriage that gave birth to al-Qaeda. Sudan was an incubator of this union, subsequently consummated in Afghanistan.

Moreover, while in Sudan, bin Laden was torn between confrontation and accommodation, pursuing both approaches simultaneously and sending out feelers to the Saudi authorities about a potential rapprochement and a return home. Until mid-1995, bin Laden was on record as saying that he opposed the killing of innocent noncombatants, including Americans, and it is not clear whether he was involved in some of the attacks carried out in the early 1990s. After September 11 there was a tendency among observers to blame bin Laden while he was in Sudan for all the bombings that occurred in that period; many accept al-Qaeda's exaggerated claims about its early military exploits as fact. Elevated to new heights of prowess and invincibility, bin Laden's reach was portrayed as extensive, even limitless. The reality is more complicated than that.

In the first half of the 1990s a number of domestic jihadis exiled in Sudan fought their own governments and carried out attacks in their various home countries. Bin Laden had never been in favor of waging war against the near enemy, though he provided limited financial assistance to militants battling certain Muslim rulers. This partly explains why bin Laden was not on the radar screen of Western intelligence services, which monitored transnational jihadis operating in the world during the 1990s; he was seen more as a "financier of terrorists" than as an operational leader plotting and ordering attacks.[35]

Jason Burke, who has written a thoroughly researched book on al-Qaeda, notes that bin Laden had little or nothing to do with most of the attacks in the first half of the 1990s: while bin Laden is often linked to the bombings in Aden in December of 1992, in fact it is far more likely that Tariq al-Fadhli organized the attacks. Burke also asserts that bin Laden was falsely linked to the attempted assassination of Egyptian President Hosni Mubarak and the 1995 and 1996 attacks in Saudi Arabia. Prince Turki blamed him for the 1995 bombing of the National Guard Training Center in Riyadh, which was considered the first "terrorist blow" against the Arabian kingdom.[36]

In any case, by late 1994 the pendulum tilted against reconciliation between bin Laden and the rulers of his native land. He mistrusted King Fahd and his senior advisers who, in return, demanded that he give up jihad and disband his militant network in Sudan. King Fahd's alleged support of secular laws and the stationing of American troops in the kingdom definitively turned bin Laden against the ruling royal family. Bin Laden listened more and more to his inner circle, which fed him reports about American plots to expand its military presence to Sudan and other Arab countries after Somalia.

Bin Laden's views of America hardened into overt hostility. In a message addressed to the "honorable scholars of the Arabian peninsula and Saudi Arabia in particular," he called on Muslims to rise up and resist the enemy that had invaded the land of the umma, violated her honor, shed her blood, and occupied its sanctuaries. It is "a calamity unprecedented in the history of our ummah, namely the invasion by the American and Western Crusader forces of the Arabian peninsula and Saudi Arabia, the home of the Noble Ka'ba, the sacred House of God . . . where the Prophetic revelation was received."[37] All this happened, added bin Laden, on the watch of the region's "apostate" rulers, and with their active participation and sponsorship. Bin Laden vowed to expel US troops from the lands of the two holy places—Mecca and Medina—regardless of how long it would take and how costly it would be. The lone surviving superpower was on the offensive, unstoppable, and no Muslim state seemed willing to or capable of resisting it. Only a pioneering vanguard could step forward and raise the banner of resistance, embroiling America in an endless and unwinnable war with the umma.

Bin Laden and his inner circle developed a strategic vision that involved forcing the United States to fight the war on bin Laden's terms and lash out angrily against the Muslim world at large. As a small elitist vanguard, they could neither challenge American power nor survive a direct confrontation with it. The only way to level the playing field lay in asymmetric warfare, one that ignited a greater clash between America and the world of Islam. It is on this level that the success or failure of bin Laden's enterprise must be assessed.

By the end of 1995, bin Laden appears to have reached a decision from which there was no turning back: transnational jihad would be the only effective means to stem the tide of the American offensive and force it either to retreat from Arab and Muslim territories or fight on multiple fronts. This marked a radical transformation in bin Laden's stance. He would henceforth sanction the killing of civilians, including Muslims. He and his circle issued two fatwas, authorizing attacks on American troops, as well as the murder of innocents.[38] The fatwas signaled the beginning of a new phase in bin

Laden's journey, one that culminated in the establishment of the 1998 World Islamic Front—the formal launch of al-Qaeda.

In March 1995 bin Laden made another decision to issue a public indictment of the House of Saud, which signaled a final break with the Kingdom. Deploying the Qur'an and commentaries by Islamic scholars, he accused the king of being an "apostate," and demanded his abdication. "You have brought to our people the two worst calamities, blasphemy and poverty. Our best advice to you now is to submit your resignation."[39]

Bin Laden's rupture with the House of Saud was in essence a declaration of war. The Saudi authorities, who blamed bin Laden for the 1995 attacks on the national guard, fought hard to have him expelled from Sudan and shut down his propaganda shop. There were also, allegedly, Saudi attempts to assassinate him. The United States and its allies in turn exerted intense pressure on Khartoum to expel bin Laden and the small army of seasoned militants and new volunteers who journeyed to Sudan either to train or to escape persecution at home. By 1996 Sudan could no longer withstand the concerted international campaign, particularly after the 1995 assassination attempt on Mubarak (Egypt accused Sudan of sheltering the perpetrators), and after Zawahiri rather disastrously ordered the execution of an associate's child for being an alleged spy for Egyptian intelligence. The Sudanese government warned Zawahiri and his associates and let bin Laden know that he was no longer welcome in the country.

As bin Laden boarded a small Russian-made airplane to transport him and his family back to Afghanistan in 1996, the future must have looked bleak indeed. Stripped of his Saudi citizenship in the spring of 1994, he was nearly penniless, having lost his financial empire, amounting to millions of dollars, in Sudan, and found himself on the run. His investment in various domestic jihadist groups, such as Zawahiri's Tanzim al-Jihad, al-Gamaa al-Islamiya, and Algeria's Groupes Islamiques Armés (GIA; Armed Islamic Groups), had gone sour—their extreme violence turned Muslim public opinion against them and they were more of a liability than an asset. Bin Laden had nothing concrete to show after spending four years in Sudan and squandering his fortune. Al-Qaeda was not yet operational. Armed with an opaque, untested ideology and surrounded by a small core of loyalists, bin Laden's prospects were at a low point. His survival and that of his family hung in the balance.

All was not lost, however. While in Sudan, bin Laden's fierce opposition to the Saudi royal family had earned him precious political capital among disaffected members of his generation and the youth in Saudi Arabia. He became a magnet for the opposition both inside and outside the Kingdom, having grown in both stature and popularity. The years in Sudan had enriched bin Laden's religious education and sharpened his rhetorical skills. Once he arrived in Afghanistan in 1996 and established his headquarters there, he swiftly built on these new strengths. He leveraged his status as the spearhead of resistance to the American-Saudi alliance in the Middle East to raise money in the Gulf and elsewhere, and to recruit volunteers. Young Saudis and Yemenis flocked first to Sudan and then to Afghanistan to swear *baya*, or fealty, to bin Laden and to join his new jihad caravan.

Beginning in Afghanistan in May 1996, bin Laden embarked on a systematic campaign to operationalize al-Qaeda and turn it into a coherent transnational organization—an umbrella organization that could encompass a broad spectrum of jihadist factions. Soon after being forced out of Sudan, Zawahiri and other domestic jihadis joined bin Laden in Afghanistan and became increasingly dependent on his financial assistance. Patronage and organizational skills allowed bin Laden to co-opt key figures and lieutenants, even those who did not share his methods and strategy regarding the far enemy. Zawahiri is a case in point. Before he fully aligned himself with bin Laden, Zawahiri had dedicated his life to overthrowing the secular-nationalist leaning Egyptian state. Yet, starved financially and weakened militarily, Zawahiri joined the transnational jihad caravan.

Most of Zawahiri's contemporary cohorts whom I interviewed said that his desperate finances forced him to embrace bin Laden's agenda and to fuse Tanzim al-Jihad to al-Qaeda. "Zawahiri may rationalize and justify his merger with al-Qaeda any way he wants," a founder of Tanzim al-Jihad told me, "[b]ut he has always believed in the primacy and urgency of battling the near enemy. He joined bin Laden out of necessity and desperation not choice or belief." Nevertheless, the migration of Zawahiri and others to transnational jihad in the second half of the 1990s testifies to bin Laden's managerial and leadership skills, as well as his canny use of patronage and money to restructure the jihadist landscape. Little wonder then that many of Zawahiri's associates resented bin Laden and accused him of opportunism.

Ambitious and driven, bin Laden constructed an efficient structure with decision-making capabilities. Designed like a corporation, al-Qaeda was distinctive for its collective corporate ethos, a feature that dates back to the days of the Afghan jihad. Bin Laden's inner circle—or shura council—consisted mainly of the same Afghan Arabs who fought side by side in Afghanistan. They possessed a similar worldview and a similar *asabiya,* or tribal loyalty, as well. Al-Qaeda's survival has depended on the unity and cohesion of this elite vanguard, a fact that has not received enough critical scrutiny in the West. The dissolution of this inner circle would likely cripple al-Qaeda operationally and sever its umbilical cord: its *asabiya.*

Between 1996 and 1998, bin Laden invested considerable time and energy recruiting bands of young fighters—veterans of combat in Bosnia, Chechnya, Algeria, Egypt, Iraq, and elsewhere—who journeyed to Afghanistan either to join one of the warring factions or to find out about bin Laden's new jihadist project. Afghanistan, a broken, war-torn country essentially under full Taliban control by the end of 1996, opened its gates to these recruits. From the late 1990s until September 11, Afghanistan was the Mecca of the jihad world and bin Laden was its chief draw. Training camps were set up all over the country to meet the needs of young volunteers flocking to Afghanistan. Bin Laden and his inner circle targeted the most promising of these recruits for their organization.

Some of the fighters who joined the bin Laden group recall that he took an active role in their recruitment and was relentless in pursuing them; in particular, bin Laden zeroed in on young men from Saudi Arabia and Yemen, a clear indication that despite all his preaching about transnational jihad, his central goal was to seize power in Saudi Arabia. According to these recruits, bin Laden spent countless hours with them and endlessly preached the gospel that America possessed evil designs on the world of Islam, and that America maintained the oppressive status quo in the Middle East. America was now the only force blocking the restoration of sharia-based states and the caliphate, a pan-Islamist rule. Setting an example for his volunteers, he lived among them, leading a humble existence and eschewing leisure and privilege. To these young fighters, bin Laden was more tribal chief than corporate CEO. Abu Abdullah, as his fighters affectionately called bin Laden, won their hearts. They revered him. Most would end up dying for him.

By 2001 bin Laden had built a cadre of around 3,000 operators, though he sent few recruits to fight in foreign combat zones, such as Chechnya. While al-Qaeda fielded specialized, well-trained units, it did not maintain a standing army in the traditional sense; after training, recruits either remained temporarily in Afghanistan or left for their home countries, if that was feasible. Al-Qaeda resembled a small and transient private army. It vetted requests for financial assistance by various militant groups with local jihadist agendas in Pakistan, Chechnya, Bosnia, Algeria, and Egypt. This allowed bin Laden to broaden his reach and establish connections that proved vital, particularly in Pakistan, after al-Qaeda's expulsion from Afghanistan in 2001. He also leveraged his private army to gain favor with his hosts, the Taliban, providing them with logistical and operational services at critical junctures in their prolonged struggle against the Northern Alliance adversary.

The relationship between bin Laden's al-Qaeda and the Taliban is far more complex and fractious than the dominant terrorism narrative would have it. The conventional view is that the two camps have always been bosom buddies. This could not be further from the truth. Beginning in 1996 until the ouster of the Taliban in 2001, relations between the two camps were marked by considerable tensions. In contrast to bin Laden, the Taliban had no interest in transnational jihad and had frequently cautioned their Arabian guest against using Afghanistan as a staging ground for attacks against the United States and its allies. The Taliban were inward-looking, preoccupied by a prolonged struggle to pacify the country and consolidate their regressive rule. According to several jihadis privy to the internal debate between the Taliban and al-Qaeda, Mullah Omar, supreme leader, repeatedly "ordered" bin Laden to refrain from militarily confronting America because it would endanger the survival of the nascent Islamic emirate. Omar reportedly told bin Laden that the Taliban could not afford to antagonize the United States because that was beyond its capability.[40]

A memoir, *The Story of the Afghan Arabs: From the Entry to Afghanistan to the Final Exodus with the Taliban*, by Abu al-Walid al-Masri, a close confidant of Mullah Omar and bin Laden, who apparently denies ever being part of the organization formally, sheds light on the tangled relationship between the Taliban and al-Qaeda, and particularly on bin Laden's disdain for Omar and his sacred code of honor and hospitality. For example, at the height of al-Qaeda's prowess in Afghanistan in the late 1990s, several senior Taliban leaders, including the then foreign minister Mullah Wakil Ahmad Mutawakkil, resented al-Qaeda's presence in the country and lobbied to get rid of bin Laden and Zawahiri and expel foreign fighters.[41]

In particular, Abu al-Walid recalls that a group of Taliban hardliners criticized bin Laden's reckless conduct. He was, they believed, deciding Afghan foreign policy, and his controversial media statements were politically and financially costly to the Taliban. They advocated the mass expulsion of the Afghan Arabs, who had become a local and international liability to the Taliban. Another anti–bin Laden faction opposed to his presence in Afghanistan advanced a conspiracy theory—that bin Laden had been sent by the Americans as a ploy to destroy the Taliban Islamic emirate. Both factions, Abu al-Walid recounts, wanted to rid Afghanistan of bin Laden and the crises associated with the Afghan Arabs.[42]

Against the wishes of the majority of his aides, Omar protected bin Laden but, once again, ordered him to refrain from granting inflammatory media interviews, as well as from plotting and carrying out attacks from Afghan territories. According to Abu al-Walid, who witnessed the most important moments of the drama in Afghanistan, Omar's decision not to expel bin Laden was driven more by emotional and utilitarian considerations than by agreement with his transnational worldview. He also apparently believed that bin Laden would obey a superior's orders. The Taliban ruler was swayed by gratitude for the sacrifice of the Arab mujahideen contingent during the Afghan war, and hoped that bin Laden would invest in development and reconstruction in the war-torn Islamic emirate, just as he had in Sudan in the first half of the 1990s. Omar used to order his subordinates to meet with bin Laden and seek out technical advice and financial support.[43]

Abu al-Walid and Fadl accused bin Laden of embroiling the Taliban in regional and international conflicts against their will and thereby bringing about the final destruction of the Islamic emirate. They argued that the Taliban were defeated and Afghanistan lost because of bin Laden's reckless conduct, which culminated in the September 11 attacks. Yet despite great odds and fierce opposition by senior Taliban leaders, bin Laden successfully navigated the Afghan minefields and executed his design. While dependent on the Taliban's goodwill, particularly that of Mullah Omar, bin Laden played his cards well, dragging them with him into all-out war against the only remaining superpower.

In his memoir, Abu al-Walid describes a key "historical" meeting in 1997 between bin Laden and Omar to which he was a witness, one that shows bin Laden's leadership skills and absolute determination to wage transnational jihad. For two hours Mullah Omar "pleaded" with his Saudi guest to desist from contacting the international media and inciting others against Saudi Arabia and America. Bin Laden insisted that he should be permitted to call for the liberation of the holy places—a code word for waging transnational jihad against the West. He also made the case that Muslims worldwide must support the Taliban financially and invest in the Islamic emirate. Despite this offer from bin Laden, Mullah Omar disagreed.

Nonetheless bin Laden persisted with his argument. At the end of the meeting Mullah Omar stood up and told his guest, "You are a Mujahid [Islamic warrior]. This is your country and you are welcome to do whatever you like."[44]

It is important to stress that bin Laden arrived in Afghanistan in May 1996—before the Taliban seized power in the autumn of that year. He had had no meaningful relationship with the Taliban and was merely anxious to find a safe shelter. Less than a year later the Taliban supreme leader protected bin Laden against the express wishes of his own senior aides and sent him an equivocal, conflicted message about what he could and could not do in Afghanistan. This achievement is magnified by the fact that the Taliban did not share bin Laden's interest in launching attacks against either the far enemy or the near enemy—specifically, Saudi Arabia, a country that had been friendly to the Taliban rule and had for a time assisted them. The Taliban and al-Qaeda had very different priorities. Yet bin Laden relentlessly pushed his agenda, eventually to the ruin of the Taliban regime.

Bin Laden not only outmaneuvered the Taliban and Mullah Omar but also outfoxed hardened and experienced domestic jihadis such as Zawahiri, Fadl, Mustafa Setmariam Nasar, better known as Abu Musab al-Suri ("the Syrian"), a leading theoretician of jihadism, and even his own shura council. In those revealing interviews I mentioned earlier, Fadl revealed that al-Jihad's senior members set up al-Qaeda. According to former jihadis, Fadl planted several senior al-Jihad lieutenants within bin Laden's inner circle, such as Abu Hafs al-Masri and Abu Ubayda al-Banshiri, in the hope of influencing bin Laden's thinking and actions.[45]

It was, however, bin Laden who steered things, taking the organization in a radically different direction. The Egyptian contingent, as we have seen, wanted to deploy al-Qaeda as another weapon in the battle against the secular-leaning Egyptian regime and thus co-opt bin Laden. Bin Laden surprised his mentors by presenting them with a stark choice: union with al-Qaeda or separation.

Unlike their Saudi counterpart, who had resources and new recruits from the Gulf, Zawahiri and his men faced a grim future after their expulsion from Sudan in 1996. The war with the Egyptian regime had been lost. Many of Tanzim al-Jihad's field lieutenants and mid-rank members had been arrested and captured by the Egyptian authorities with assistance from the CIA and Western intelligence services. Zawahiri and his men had therefore become increasingly dependent on bin Laden for survival. After his arrival in Afghanistan in 1996, Zawahiri struggled, to no avail, to find alternative financial resources and greener jihad pastures. While on a funding mission to Dagestan, a federal republic of Russia in the North Caucasus region in 1996, he was imprisoned. He escaped only because the authorities did not know his true identity and because bin Laden sent large bribes to the police. Union with bin Laden was Zawahiri's only choice, though in his autobiography he maintains that his merger with al-Qaeda was designed to unify the Muslim ranks against Islam's enemies.[46]

According to Fadl, Zawahiri unilaterally aligned himself with al-Qaeda without prior consultation with al-Jihad's shura council, precipitating his expulsion from the organization, along with the few associates that joined him.[47]

Although it was a marriage of necessity, not love, the bin Laden–Zawahiri union marked the beginning of a more potent phase for al-Qaeda and for transnational jihad generally, a fusion of Qutbian ideas and Saudi Arabian *asabiya*. Zawahiri gave up all pretense of independence and converted heart and soul to bin Laden's transnational cause. He provided bin Laden with the conceptual and ideological justification and legitimization to attack the West. For a man who spent most of his life battling on the home front, his sudden transformation is indicative of the turmoil that engulfed the jihadist movement in the second part of the 1990s—following the disaster in Egypt—as well as bin Laden's ability to use that turmoil to hijack the movement and change its direction. He recruited the skilled and hardened lieutenants who had battled the Egyptian, Algerian, and Iraqi regimes in the 1980s and 1990s, and Soviet troops as well.

However, contrary to the dominant terrorism narrative, bin Laden had very limited success in co-opting domestic jihadis and broadening the social base of his new organization among Muslims in general. With the exception of Zawahiri's small inner circle within Tanzim al-Jihad, fewer than a dozen lieutenants, most domestic jihadis—including junior and senior members of al-Jihad and al-Gamaa al-Islamiya, the largest jihadist organization in the region, or the military wing of Algeria's Islamic Salvation Front (FIS)—joined al-Qaeda, fearing, rightly, that transnational jihad was a reckless venture that could bring ruin to the Islamist movement. After the leadership of al-Gamaa al-Islamiya found out that one of its mid-level lieutenants, Rifaa Ahmad Taha (alias Abu Yasir), a hardliner, was present at the ceremony announcing the formal launch of the World Islamic Front and was one of the signatories, it forced him to release a disclaimer about being a member of al-Qaeda, or speaking for the Islamic group. Taha released a statement in which he denied that al-Gamaa al-Islamiya was a founding member of the World Islamic Front: "We are not a party in any front that confronts Americans."[48]

In several classified memos to his cohorts after he joined al-Qaeda, Zawahiri made the case for transnational jihad by saying that the jihadist movement was at a crossroads and that it had failed to weaken Muslim rulers. Secular regimes had won the battle, Zawahiri argued, because jihadis had not made inroads into Muslim public opinion; they had lost the struggle for Muslim hearts and minds and had not been able to nourish and sustain a durable and viable social base. "The solution" was to drag the United States into a total war with the umma and in the process awaken Muslims from their political slumber.

From its very inception, al-Qaeda's strategy has been to embroil the United States in all-out confrontation with the world of Islam and to brand itself as the vanguard of the umma, its spearhead of armed resistance. As noted above, success and failure must therefore be assessed on this strategic level. To what degree has it won Muslim hearts and minds, and has it triggered a clash of cultures or religions between the Christian West and the world of Islam? Has it driven the West into bankruptcy by forcing it to expand the War on Terror?

What bin Laden achieved in Afghanistan between 1996 and 2001 was a remarkable operational and ideological feat. He translated his ideas into concrete action—a militarily operational hierarchical organization. Bin Laden's shura (ruling council) supplied theological legitimacy, organizational skills, and combat expertise. Despite skepticism from domestic jihadis toward bin Laden's transnational jihad, in less than four years he recruited a small private army of Saudi and Yemeni fighters, along with a limited number of young men of other nationalities. Khalid Sheikh Mohammed, the acknowledged architect of the September 11 attacks, estimates that in any given camp in Afghanistan, 70 percent of recruits were Saudis, 20 percent were Yemenis, and 10 percent were from elsewhere.[49] Saudi and Yemeni fighters, in other words, formed the backbone of al-Qaeda's striking force, they swore *baya* to Abu Abdullah, and were prepared to die for him and his cause.

Before bin Laden, "transnational jihad" had not been in the jihadist lexicon. For more than three decades, the jihadist movement was inward-looking, its rhetoric and action focused on the home front. No prominent ideologues and clerics advocated transnational jihad or theorized about its dialectics. Bin Laden was the impetus behind it. That achievement, though self-limiting and highly elitist, must be set against fierce internal and external opposition and in-surmountable challenges. He imposed his agenda on a skeptical, fragmented jihadist community and triggered a war that is still raging worldwide.

The transition to transnational jihad was neither automatic nor driven by rhetoric and discourse alone. Al-Qaeda led the way through its spectacular attacks and bombings, bringing new donors and recruits to bin Laden's new organization. Bin Laden tapped into a rising generation of mujahideen, indoctrinated and inspired by the rhetoric of a puritan, absolutist, and textualist Islamist ideology, radicalized by the Afghan war and the persecution of Muslim com-munities in Bosnia, Chechnya, and elsewhere, and ready to do battle on behalf of persecuted Muslims worldwide and against real and imagined enemies. Young, naïve, impatient, and uncompromising, members of this generation believed that they were God's warriors, and that they had a sacred obligation to lay their lives on the line for the umma.

Even before formally launching al-Qaeda in 1998, bin Laden and his lieutenants plotted "spectacular martyrdom operations" against the "head of the snake," as they famously labeled the United States, the idea being to force it out of its hole, to provoke a violent and irrational reaction. In August 1998 they carried out the twin bombings of the American embassies in Nairobi, Kenya, and Dar es Salaam, Tanzania, in which 291 people were killed and approx-imately 5,000 were wounded. After the Clinton administration retaliated with a missile strike at an al-Qaeda camp in Afghani-stan, Zawahiri used bin Laden's satellite phone to call a Pakistani journalist to say that he and bin Laden were safe. "The war has only just begun," he added ominously.[50]

In October 2000, following up on its threat, a boat with two suicide bombers on board rammed the *USS Cole*, a Navy destroyer, while it was refueling in the Yemeni port of Aden, killing 17 sailors and injuring 47. The goal was to force the United States to overreact and get bogged down in all-out war in Muslim lands, said al-Qaeda military commander Abu Hafs al-Masri, after the *Cole* bombing: "We did the Cole and we wanted the United States to react. And if they reacted, they are going to invade Afghanistan and that's what we want . . . Then we will start holy war against the Americans, exactly like the Soviets."

However, the *Cole* bombing was only a diversion. By 1998 bin Laden had concluded that the only way to kill a large number of Americans was by striking inside the United States itself: only a massive blood-letting of American blood would force the United States out of Muslim lands. Khalid Sheikh Mohammed, now bin Laden's top terrorism executive manager, was busy designing the architecture of the September 11 attacks, having received final clearance from bin Laden. Jealously guarding his secret, bin Laden kept Zawahiri and even his shura council—not to mention Mullah Omar, his generous, gullible host—in the dark about the substance of the strikes and their timing. Al-Qaeda finally took war to the US homeland.

2

The Growing Rift

As we have seen, al-Qaeda emerged as a result of the convergence of two developments—entropy of the local jihadist movement in the mid-1990s (not in the late 1980s, as many terrorism experts and security pundits claim) and the reverberations of the Afghan jihad. Transnational jihad spearheaded by al-Qaeda was a desperate effort to keep a ship from sinking by altering its direction, if not its final destination—in this case away from the near enemy and toward the far enemy. Bin Laden was the most powerful force behind the rise of al-Qaeda, a testament to his leadership and managerial skills. Turning the table on his ideological and theological mentors and patrons, he founded his organization on the ruins of a broken movement and absorbed some of its heavyweights, such as Zawahiri and Abu Hafs al-Masri, within the transnational network.

In this sense, al-Qaeda began as a mutation, the result of an implosion within a fringe social movement teetering on the brink of collapse. When bin Laden's group burst onto the Islamic scene in the early 1990s, the jihadist movement had largely spent itself—jihadism had failed. Al-Qaeda's decision to internationalize jihad was less an indicator of internal cohesion and strength of jihadism than of its inner turmoil.

In the 1990s some scholars conducting field research on social movements were fully aware of internal cleavages appearing among jihadis. When I arrived in Egypt in late 1998, for example, a fierce war raged between most jihadis who, after six years of armed struggle, lost the fight against Arab and Muslim rulers and a small group of the so-called Afghan Arabs led by bin Laden on one side and Zawahiri on the other. While domestic jihadis declared a unilateral ceasefire—a codeword for surrender—and began to reflect on their failed and costly jihad, a determined minority chose to keep fighting. They declared war against the world's last remaining superpower, with the hope of resurrecting militant jihadism among the rank and file and gaining credibility in the eyes of the umma.[1]

Bin Laden's al-Qaeda was therefore at odds with the great majority of local jihadis, who by the turn of the millennium had revisited and rethought the use of violence as a means of gaining political power. While incarcerated, top ideologues of the movement were putting the final touches on theological and ideological "revisions" that formalized and legitimized the end of armed jihad.[2] Long before September 11, the jihadist civil war had started, and it would spread throughout the Muslim world and determine the future of the entire movement.

It was not mere coincidence that the first shots in this civil war were fired in Egypt in the late 1990s, given that the jihadist offensive against the near enemy had started there. With eighty million people, it is the most populous Arab state and was, until recently, the Muslim world's cultural and intellectual epicenter. Egypt was the birthplace of the modern jihadist movement, and it remains to this day the best place to look to understand its complexities and to locate its fault lines. The movement's founding fathers were almost entirely Egyptian, as were the authors of many of its defining documents. The brain of contemporary jihadism is Egyptian.[3]

A few years before September 11, I spent some months interviewing the rank and file of the movement, to take stock of where it was going. A man named Kamal al-Said Habib seemed to stand out as being somehow representative of this generation. I knew him only by reputation. Many of those concerned about the future of Islamist militancy did as well. He was one of the top former leaders of al-Jihad, a paramilitary organization that had played a pivotal role in the assassination of Egyptian President Anwar Sadat in 1981 (Zawahiri was also then part of Habib's al-Jihad). Habib was a key figure in the first generation of Muslim militants, who in the 1970s had planted the seeds of armed jihad throughout Muslim lands. If I wanted to locate the starting point of the jihadist movement and its future prospects, I needed to understand the worldviews and thoughts of Habib and his generation.[4]

They had learned the hard way what happens when one tries to Islamize society through force. The resulting bloodshed was horrific; there were executions and lengthy prison sentences (Habib had spent ten years in an Egyptian prison); families were destroyed. He and other former "warriors of God" had now, I was told, reassessed their old ways—their misguided, offensive interpretation of jihad. They were charting a new course, one committed not to violent revolution but to political persuasion and *dawa*, or religious calling. They were older now. They were wiser. In late 1998 and early 1999 I spent six months with Habib and other militants profiling his generation and the new journey the jihadist movement was traveling.

Habib acknowledged that he and his peers had made a fatal mistake. Rather than trying to build support from the bottom up, they became fixated on capturing political power and imposing their religious order from the top down. Instead of galvanizing the masses, as they had imagined, their methods—such as the random killings of tourists and ordinary citizens—repelled most Egyptians. God-fearing and peace-loving by nature, the Egyptian public withdrew any sympathy they might have shared with the revolutionaries. "We were naïve, arrogant, and immature, fired up by the spirit of youth," Habib told me in one of our last conversations. It was early in the evening and we had gone to a political rally organized by a moderate Islamic party, the kind of gathering he would not have dreamed of attending thirty years ago. "We had big dreams but few resources, and there was a pronounced gap between the means at our disposal and our ambitions. Gradually, we lost sight of the balance between ends and means and fell into the trap of armed escalation with the government. We were no match for its powers."[5]

Every movement goes through phases, the jihadist movement no less than any other:

> We have come a long way since the 1970s, even though our journey has been painful and costly. We had to learn by trial and error. We were fortunate to be the pioneers. But we had no support network of wise men and spiritual mentors to guide us through the minefields. We were on our own, struggling against great odds and challenges. We read the inspiring works of Ibn Kathir, Ibn Taymiya, and Sayyid Qutb out of context and history. We superimposed our fears, aspirations, and immature interpretations on their complicated ideas. We horribly miscalculated.[6]

"What if you had succeeded?" I asked him. "Were you truly prepared to establish a viable Islamic government?"

> Thank God, we did not win, because we would have constructed a state along the same authoritarian lines as the ones existing in the Muslim world. We had no vision or an intellectual framework of what a state is or how it functions and how it should be

administered, except that it should express and approximate the Islamic ideal. While I cannot predict that our state would have been totalitarian, we had little awareness of the challenges that needed to be overcome.

The honesty of his reply left me dumbfounded. He was suggesting that he and his generation of domestic jihadis had been misguided; they had been more an elitist vanguard than a mass movement. This contradicted their initial claim that they had represented the umma's popular will and that their armed jihad was legitimate.

Of all the militants I have come to know over the years, Habib still stands apart. Privy to the innermost councils of the radical Islamist movement for more than a quarter of a century, he is perhaps the most open and candid of them all. His story also reveals the dramatic changes that have taken place within jihadism over the decades. Once a fierce proponent of armed resistance against pro-Western secular Muslim rulers, he is now struggling to reconcile himself to nonviolent political action. He has taken the lead in trying to chart a new course for those who are fed up with killing and getting killed but are still wedded to the dream of a Qur'anic-based state.

His jihadist journey seemed to have come to an end. Habib was not the only radical who questioned the raison d'être of his violent actions against secular-leaning Muslim regimes; many of his cohorts had reached a similar conclusion. He and others of his generation had been destroyed by their armed struggle: thousands perished and thousands more were still rotting in prison cells. "What do you tell the families of the martyrs, and how would you take care of their beloved ones?" he once asked with genuine emotion.

That was the 1990s, an era promising new beginnings for Habib and his generation. There was a consensus, both inside and outside jihadist circles in the region, that jihadis had reached the end of their rope, and that their fight against secular Arab regimes had been lost. Equally important, the executive or so-called historic leadership of the jihadist movement (al-Gamaa al-Islamiya or the Egyptian Islamic Group and to a lesser extent Egyptian Islamic al-Jihad) were penning revisions along Habib's lines, explicitly acknowledging failure and revisiting old sacred concepts that legitimized their armed insurgency.[7]

From its very inception in the mid-1990s, transnational jihad has been, as I have argued, a fringe phenomenon. Bin Laden always portrayed his actions as a last resort to defend the Muslim community, filling the void left by "apostate" rulers and pliant religious scholars who collaborated with Islam's enemies. In a message addressed to clerics in Saudi Arabia in the mid-1990s, he asked rhetorically whether they were prepared and willing to lead: "Our Islamic umma is confronting a very grave challenge and being subjected to terrible aggression, and her rulers and many of her scholars have forsaken her. Who will lead and direct her, if not [me]?"[8]

A year later, in August 1996, bin Laden released a juridical edict declaring defensive war, or jihad, against the Americans for their continued presence in Islam's birthplace, the Kingdom of Saudi Arabia, and positioned himself and his cohorts as a pioneering vanguard. Just as they had smashed "the largest infidel military force in the world," the Soviet Union, he vowed that "today, in the same peaks of Afghanistan, we work to do away with the injustice that has befallen our umma at the hands of the Judeo-Crusader alliance, especially after its occupation of Jerusalem and its appropriation of Saudi Arabia."[9]

Few people then and now appreciate that bin Laden's call-to-arms against "the Judeo-Crusader alliance" was primarily directed to Saudis and Yemenis who rallied to the battle cry of jihad. The presence of a potent American military force in Saudi Arabia caused considerable upheaval and opposition inside the Kingdom and polarized the country. Bin Laden's call to jihad resonated with key religious scholars in the Kingdom who legitimized and authorized his call. Volunteers journeyed to Afghanistan to train in bin Laden's camps and join his vanguard. The bulk of al-Qaeda's foot soldiers were, as we have seen, Saudi and Yemeni, indicative of the local, nationalist context of bin Laden's struggle, as opposed to the globalized, borderless public utterances. Stripped of its rhetoric and drama, bin Laden's call was aimed at inciting opposition against the House of Saud and destabilizing the regime. In a sense, transnational jihad was bin Laden's fig leaf, masking a desire to seize power in his native land. There was no better way to mobilize his people and Muslims in general than by summoning them to liberate Islam's holiest places in Saudi Arabia and Palestine. He advanced his nationalist ambition by appealing to higher interests than his own— the umma's. By appropriating the language of Islam, bin Laden hoped to attain greater legitimacy for his nationalist agenda.

Like Zawahiri, bin Laden was religiously hyper-nationalist, even though his jihad call is rhetorically transnational and does not recognize territorially based nationalist units. For bin Laden, the only way to level the playing field with the Saudi monarchy was to expel American troops from the Kingdom as the mujahideen expelled the Soviets from Afghanistan. Once Soviet troops retreated from Afghanistan in 1989, the client government they left behind fell like rotten fruit.

Nonetheless, after September 11 most observers ("security-based analysts," as they are sometimes called) have generally viewed al-Qaeda through a cultural and religious prism, and missed the utilitarian and political-strategic drivers. They take bin Laden's rhetoric at face value, while neglecting its historical-political context. Seen as the quintessential moment that changed the world, the attacks were invested with exaggerated and unnecessary cultural and religious meanings, conflating terrorism, a universal tactic, with "Islamic terrorism," an intrinsically cultural or expressive element of the conflict. The tendency to "ideologize" the use of terrorism—that is, to create a link between the raison d'être of radical Islamist groups and the tactics they employ—has led to ignorance of specific contexts and motives, and distortion and misunderstandings as well. A well-known Israeli observer asserted: "Motives are entirely irrelevant to the concept of political terrorism. Most analysts fail to recognize this and, hence, tend to discuss certain motives as logical or necessary aspects of terrorism. But they are not. At best, they are empirical regularities associated with terrorism. More often they simply confuse analysis."[10]

If contexts for and motives behind politically based violence "confuse analysis," then there is no reason to understand the sociopolitical and strategic logic behind the actions of al-Qaeda and other Islamist groups; if anything, it would be a waste of time. Instead of considering the use of terrorism by militant Islamists as a common tool in asymmetric warfare, these observers portray them as warriors in a cultural war against the West and the liberal rationalist narrative of history. Everything can be explained as part of timeless and irrational hatred of the West.[11] For example, Israeli diplomat-analyst Dan Gold has traced the historical roots of the violent tactics used by domestic and transnational jihadis to "the ideological motivation to slaughter thousands of innocent people."[12]

Gold and like-minded pundits do not seem concerned that until 1990 bin Laden was part of the US-led alliance pitted against "godless communism." They depoliticize violence and focus overwhelmingly on the tactics employed by groups like al-Qaeda—to the detriment of understanding and explaining the motives behind those tactics.[13] All *causus belli* are often overlooked in favor of a reductionist approach that views these organizations simply as "jihadi murderers," crazy Arabs; or Islam itself is presented as "the enemy."[14] As a result, these analysts tend to become propagandists for the War on Terror, trafficking in orientalist pseudo-explanations, and effectively ignoring the key questions: how and why did al-Qaeda and transnational jihad rise and why did they turn their guns against the United States?

In US policy circles, as well as those in the West (though to a lesser extent), there existed little appreciation of the fact that neither Islam nor its religious texts would be useful in unlocking the "al-Qaeda riddle." Bin Laden and Zawahiri thought in strategic and political terms, veiling their real ambitions in cultural and religious cloth. In his two most recent works, *Fursan tahta rayat al-nabi* [Knights under the prophet's banner] and "Exoneration: A Treatise Exonerating the Community of the Pen and the Sword from the Debilitating Accusation of Fatigue and Weakness," written in 2000 and 2008, respectively, Zawahiri acknowledges that al-Qaeda's strategy is designed to win Muslims' hearts and minds and become the leader and vanguard of the umma. To do so, he points out that the Islamist movement must raise the banner of liberation over the three most important holy sites, all of which are occupied by foreigners— Mecca and Medina in Saudi Arabia and al-Aqsa in Jerusalem: the Muslim masses would not rise up unless there is leadership that they can trust and a well-defined enemy. In particular, Zawahiri stressed that Palestine is the one issue on which the umma agrees and the Islamist movement must champion and take ownership of it.

Time and again, bin Laden and Zawahiri stressed that the expulsion of American and Israeli occupiers from Islam's holy sites remains their top priority. From the beginning of his transnational journey in the mid-1990s, bin Laden's pronouncements were littered with references to America and Israel or what he called the "Judeo-Christian alliance which is occupying Islamic sacred land in Palestine and of Saudi Arabia." When he formally launched al-Qaeda in February 1998, bin Laden prioritized his call to Muslims: "To kill the Americans and their allies—civilians and military—is an individual duty incumbent upon every Muslim in all countries, in order to liberate the al-Aqsa Mosque [Jerusalem] and the Holy Mosque [Mecca] from their grip."[15]

Bin Laden's detractors and supporters mistook his rhetoric for strategy and painted his terrorist tactics in terms of expressive cultural acts. But al-Qaeda is a vehicle for his nationalist empowerment inside the Saudi kingdom, along similar lines to Zawahiri's Tanzim al-Jihad in Egypt. The empowerment of the umma and the restoration of the Islamic caliphate is an ideal, impossible to attain, but a powerful tool of ideological and theological mobilization that resonated with thousands of young Saudis and Yemenis. In multiple testimonies, some of these recruits have said that they joined bin Laden because they were motivated by a desire to expel American occupiers from Muslim lands, particularly Saudi Arabia. Bin Laden targeted an important constituency, one that responded reflexively to specific religious and cultural symbols and references, and was willing to act upon them.

A qualification is in order here: one must guard against a reverse tendency to diminish the significance of September 11 or underestimate its consequences. There are few examples of non-Western insurgent groups striking the metropole in the way that al-Qaeda did, and this "global" element remains hugely significant, whatever exaggerated claims are made of the reach of transnational jihad. Throughout the Cold War, insurgents kept their struggles local, even though they fought as proxies of foreign powers. The same was true with most anti-colonial conflicts. Algeria represents an exception to the rule, but there, much of the mainland terrorism was perpetrated by homegrown right-wingers. A crucial and enabling factor of the attacks on New York and Washington was, therefore, globalization—in the mundane sense of enhanced interconnection and communications.

Analysts must, without ideologizing terror, still be attentive to what was fundamentally different about September 11. This also raises another critical question about bin Laden's strategic calculation: given his regional motives, why did he think it at all strategic to attack the United States and risk the blowback? Why not launch another attack on American troops in Saudi Arabia, as with the Khobar Towers operation? Central to bin Laden's calculation was that only the killing of a large number of Americans in their homeland would force US policy makers to rethink their presence in Arab lands. Most people with any knowledge of the United States would have predicted an extreme response, out of proportion to the provocation, and this is exactly what occurred. In a way, bin Laden unwittingly reinvigorated America's belief in itself as the moral force in the world—the world's policeman—and triggered an actual War on Terror, not a merely rhetorical one.

In the late 1990s bin Laden and Zawahiri faced stiff resistance from most domestic jihadis who declared a unilateral ceasefire in their fight against Muslim rulers. Most local jihadis viewed the call to internationalize jihad as reckless and suicidal, a recipe for catastrophe for the Islamist movement.[16]

From the outset there emerged a rift between domestic and transnational jihadis who, though a tiny minority, hoped to hijack the movement and internationalize jihad. Zawahiri, the emir of Tanzim al-Jihad, could not convince his shura council and some of his close lieutenants to sign on. In fact, a mutiny took place among al-Jihad lieutenants against Zawahiri, whose union with bin Laden caused a rupture within the organization and ultimately brought about its dissolution as an independent entity. According to Fadl and other close associates, Zawahiri was only able to persuade a handful of mid-level members of Tanzim al-Jihad to join bin Laden's al-Qaeda. Al-Jihad's shura council released a statement expelling them all.[17]

Al-Qaeda's transnational jihad was embraced by a tiny minority within the jihadist family and has never grown deep roots in Muslim societies. No internal unity or coherence has ever existed among jihadis who, while sharing a similar ideological viewpoint of the world, differ bitterly over tactics and strategy. From the beginning, divisions and rivalries between local and transnational militants limited al-Qaeda's military reach. As we will see, after September 11 these divisions and rivalries escalated into an open struggle.

In this unfolding drama, transnational jihad was at a great disadvantage because, unlike its domestic rival, it had no viable constituency to fall back upon, and after September 11, many publicly challenged the very theological foundation of transnational jihad. Far from courageous and selfless Islamic warriors, bin Laden and Zawahiri were accused of having huge egos and earthly ambitions. Young Muslims were urged not to fall victim to their schemes.

The rise and fall of transnational jihad must be placed within the context of jihadi and Muslim politics in general. September 11 was bin Laden's and Zawahiri's attempt to turn the wheels of fortune in their favor by claiming the mantle of discredited and vanquished local jihad and thus gaining credibility in the eyes of the umma. Muslims, not Americans, were the true target.

The jihadis I interviewed in 1998 and 1999 dismissed Zawahiri's invitation to join al-Qaeda as reckless and suicidal. "How could we take on America, the greatest power in the world after we had been vanquished by Muslim tyrants [rulers]," a former lieutenant of

Zawahiri's Tanzim al-Jihad told me in Yemen. "Opening a second front against the sole surviving superpower and its Western allies was suicidal." Many viewed the battle as strategically lost and said that the costs of continuing the fight could not match any likely benefits. Zawahiri implicitly acknowledged this reality, I was told, when in 1995 he decided to suspend attacks in Egypt and called on his followers to observe a "truce" and assess what went wrong and why almost a thousand members of al-Jihad had fallen into government hands. Former associates inquired, critically, how could Zawahiri turn around and declare war on the West?

There was fresh thinking among the senior echelon: was jihad against the near enemy licit in terms of Islamic law? How high are the costs to the umma? Are there not other nonviolent ways, such as *dawa* (religious calling), to Islamize society? Implicit in these questions is a utilitarian, rational calculation that differs from that of doctrinaire al-Qaeda jihadis who view gain and loss in absolute terms.

Other associates of Zawahiri pointed out that he had spent a lifetime plotting and carrying out attacks to overthrow the Egyptian government. "Jerusalem will not be liberated unless the battle for Egypt and Algeria is won and unless Egypt is liberated," he wrote in 1995—words used against him later. Jihadis of all persuasions criticized Zawahiri's paradigm rupture and the new merger with bin Laden. They feared that the so-called "World Islamic Front for Jihad against the Jews and Crusaders would unleash U.S. might against all jihadis and endanger the very survival of the movement, after it had already suffered crippling blows by the Egyptian authorities."[18]

At the heart of the great debate that unfolded in the late 1990s was the question of the efficacy of waging jihad against the far enemy and the pitfalls of joining bin Laden. What infuriated jihadis most was that Zawahiri had joined with the bin Laden group without prior consultation. Zawahiri's chief lieutenant in Yemen criticized the new shift in tactics and warned that bin Laden had a "dark past" and "tainted history" and therefore he "could not be trusted."[19] "Only a few, who could be counted on the fingers, supported it," recalled Hani al-Sibai, a close ally of Zawahiri, at an emergency meeting. Zawahiri did not convince those present that targeting America would reinvigorate and rejuvenate their cause; many warned of dire consequences.[20]

Another participant in the emergency meeting reported that Zawahiri repeatedly threatened to resign and accused his own brother Muhammad of squandering funds. Everyone agreed the alliance with al-Qaeda was a disaster, recalled Tariq Anwar, a veteran associate of Zawahiri. "I expected some members to start wrestling each other. I always felt this entity may dissolve in seconds."[21]

Zawahiri could not even enlist his own men. In the end eight lieutenants of Tanzim al-Jihad joined the World Islamic Front. The rest remained on the sidelines and subsequently joined the other thousands of decommissioned and deactivated jihadis.[22]

Yet, despite all the internal rifts and divisions, bin Laden and Zawahiri not only brought war to American shores but, for a short while, embroiled the lone surviving superpower in "a large-scale [military] front which it cannot control." Bin Laden in particular now took the lead. "He turned a personal vendetta against America into a matter of life-and-death, the umma's struggle," said a former mentor.[23] He latched onto individuals such as Khalid Sheikh Mohammed, who plotted to kill a large number of Americans and shake the foundation of the only surviving superpower. According to testimonies by former associates, bin Laden took direct charge of the planning for the September 11 operation. He reportedly pressured Khalid Sheikh Mohammed to expedite the execution of the attacks and maintained the strictest secrecy. When, three months before the attacks, bin Laden told his shura council that a "big operation" against America was in the pipeline, it cautioned him to seek permission from their host, Mullah Omar. Bin Laden managed to avoid doing this. In fact, neither Zawahiri nor his shura council was informed of the specifics or timing of the bombings (Zawahiri reportedly knew only twenty-four hours in advance).

Bin Laden had made up his mind to punish the "occupiers" of "Islamic sacred lands," regardless of the costs and repercussions. He ignored skeptics and doubters among domestic jihadis, as well as his inner circle of Afghan Arabs, including Abu Musab al-Suri and Abu Abd al-Rahman al-Canadi, who sought to persuade him against confrontation with America. He flouted the orders of the Taliban to refrain from using the country as a staging ground for hostile action against the West. He was a man on a mission, a mission that would turn al-Qaeda into a household name.

3

A Success and a Miscalculation

In an unguarded moment, bin Laden once conceded that the September 11 attacks had exceeded his wildest expectations. His goal had been to "terrorize" Americans, to kill hundreds, and to force them to rethink their military presence in the Islamic world. He had not expected so many people to die, or the World Trade Center Towers to collapse, though he shed no tears over either. Luck also played a big part in the stunning success of the operation.

Nonetheless the attack was his doing. Khalid Sheikh Mohammed planned it and saw it through, but responsibility for approving and financing it was bin Laden's; he owned it.

In mid-1996, Khalid Sheikh Mohammed traveled to Afghanistan to meet with bin Laden and his close companion Mohammed Atef for the first time. Khalid considered himself a sort of terrorist entrepreneur and freely touted his extensive jihadist credentials—particularly his successes and near-misses during his time in the Philippines—but in truth his track record never matched his own ambitions. Khalid considered bin Laden's al-Qaeda a business opportunity and he arrived in Afghanistan with an audacious proposal.

At his meeting with bin Laden, Khalid unveiled an extensive operation involving ten planes hitting cities on both coasts and targeting federal buildings and nuclear power plants. Khalid described how, on the tenth plane, after killing all the male passengers on board with his own hands, he would land the plane and then give a long speech about how America had deserved this. This operation would send shock waves around the world. He, Khalid Sheikh Mohammed, would be the most famous man on Earth.[1]

Bin Laden, who had a symbiotic and neurotic relationship with the media, not surprisingly reacted with little enthusiasm to this grandiose one-man show. He thought the plot impractical and worried about its impact on the future course of his organization. He had received numerous other proposals for attacks. He encouraged Khalid to stay in Afghanistan with al-Qaeda, but he stressed that he was not ready yet to commit to such a large-scale operation. Khalid politely declined bin Laden's invitation; he chose instead to travel around the world to work with other jihadist organizations.

Intoxicated with the success of the embassy bombings in East Africa two years later, in August of 1998, Mohammed Atef encouraged bin Laden to revisit Khalid's proposal. What had seemed overly ambitious two years earlier now seemed possible, but would require modifications to make it less about Khalid and more about bin Laden. According to former associates, after the bombing of the two US embassies and the retaliation by the Clinton administration against al-Qaeda, bin Laden had reached a point of no return—the only way to force the United States to withdraw from Muslim lands was to kill a large number of Americans by striking inside the United States. In the spring of 1999, bin Laden informed Khalid that al-Qaeda had accepted his proposal.[2]

In a series of meetings with Atef and Khalid in Kandahar (Zawahiri was noticeably absent from these meetings), bin Laden put his own personal mark on the plot, and transformed it. He narrowed the targets to the Pentagon, the White House, the World Trade Center, and the Capitol. He dismissed the use of one of the planes to make a media statement, as Khalid had originally envisioned. He designated Khalid as the mastermind of the operation, but he never ceded full control of the plot.

After the spring of 1999, Bin Laden's personal involvement deepened. From the outset, he and Atef micromanaged the planning and execution of the plot. Bin Laden selected the men who would pilot the planes in the attacks, never even consulting Khalid, who found himself in the position of having to make bin Laden's choices work. Bin Laden preferred those whose personal loyalty to him trumped all other considerations. The Yemeni jihadis whom bin Laden initially chose, however, could not obtain US visas.[3]

Of the initial four selected to be pilots, only those with Saudi passports, Khalid al-Mihdar and Nawaf al-Hazmi, were able to take part in the operation. Bin Laden told Khalid to send these two men to California to begin pilot training. On January 15, 2000, after tactical training in Afghanistan, they arrived in Los Angeles.

Bin Laden believed that the remaining pilots should be chosen from seasoned al-Qaeda members who had been with him in Afghanistan. But, in late 1999, a group of jihadis from Hamburg who arrived to train in Afghanistan changed his thinking. Mohamed Atta, Ramzi Binalshibh, Marwan al-Shehhi, and Ziad Jarrah's fluency in English, their technical education, and their long experience living in the West made them more suitable for the operation.

Shortly after their arrival in Afghanistan, Atef met with the Hamburg group and informed them of bin Laden's decision to include them in the mission. After receiving tactical training in Afghanistan, Atef instructed them to return to Germany to begin pilot training. Bin Laden designated Mohamed Atta the operational commander, again, without consulting Khalid, who had not yet met these new recruits. Bin Laden would inform him later of his decision.

Before returning to Germany in early 2000, Atta met several times with bin Laden to discuss the operation. Then he and his men began to prepare for their mission. Atta found the flight schools in Germany and Europe unsuitable for their training and did not like the length and cost of their programs. In March 2000, he began researching schools in the United States. Khalid assisted with their visa arrangements to enter the United States.[4]

Meanwhile, in California, the initial recruits, Hazmi and Mihdar, who lacked the education of the Hamburg contingent, found themselves struggling with the immense task set out for them. By May 2000, they had concluded that their inability to learn English (despite language courses and tutoring) prohibited advancement in their training. They were inept pilots. One trainer remarked that they showed no interest in take-offs or landings, but were only interested in flying the plane after it took off. They surprised their instructors when they asked if they could be trained to fly Boeing jets. On June 9, 2000, Mihdar left the United States after deciding that he lacked the necessary skills. He would later return as one of the "muscle hijackers."

With the abrupt departure of Mihdar, bin Laden sent Hani Hanjour to California to meet up with Hazmi. Hanjour arrived in San Diego in December 2000 and met Hazmi, who was working at a gas station at the time. Hazmi was assigned to accompany Hanjour for training in Arizona, but was no longer considered suitable for pilot training. Instead he was designated as a "muscle hijacker." After many hurdles, by the end of March 2001, Hanjour had completed his training and Hazmi and Hanjour arrived in Falls Church, Virginia, to await further instructions.[5]

The entire Hamburg contingent had arrived on the East Coast by the end of June 2000. They eventually settled on several flight schools in Florida. To avoid detection, they chose different schools.

In contrast to bin Laden's first recruits, they excelled in their training. By mid-August, Atta and Shehhi were able to make solo flights and earned their private pilot license tests. In mid-December, they received their commercial licenses and began practicing flying large jets on flight simulators. Jarrah also obtained a single-engine private pilot certificate and advanced to flying larger jets on flight simulators.

From December 2000 to February 2001, the hijackers took vacations in Europe and in the Middle East and returned to the United States in the spring of 2001. Atta, Jarrah, and Shehhi returned to Florida, while Hazmi and Hanjour eventually settled in New Jersey. They waited for the arrival of the "muscle hijackers," whom bin Laden had met with during the summer and early fall of 2000. He selected thirteen men, each of whom he met with personally. The majority were Saudi and included Satam al-Suqami, Wail al-Shehri, Waleed al-Shehri, Abdul Aziz al-Omari, Ahmed al-Ghamdi, Hamza al-Ghamdi, Mohand al-Shehri, Majed Moqed, Saeed al-Ghamdi, Ahmad al-Haznawi, Ahmed al-Nami, and Fayez Banihammad.[6]

Before sending them to the United States, bin Laden had them undergo a thorough training process that involved learning tactics and attending lectures led by him. They were then sent to Saudi Arabia to obtain visas and new passports and were ordered to return for yet further training. From late 2000 to early 2001 they received special instruction by Abu Turab al-Jordani at the al-Matar complex in Afghanistan. Afterward, they traveled via Pakistan and the UAE, and from there to the United States. By early summer 2001, they had all settled in Florida.

During the summer of 2001, the would-be pilots began taking additional classes and undertook cross-country surveillance flights to prepare for their pending operation. The date for the operation had not yet been set, but Atta knew that it was fast approaching. He and Hazmi met for the first time during the summer. Prior to this point, the two teams had operated, for the most part, independently of one another. Khalid had primarily interacted with the California and Arizona group, while bin Laden, through Ramzi Binalshibh, interacted with the Hamburg contingent. From this point onward, both groups were under the leadership of Atta, and therefore with al-Qaeda, though only a few of its senior leaders were briefed.

On July 8, Atta travelled to Madrid to meet with Binalshibh, to go over the final details of the operation and its timing. Binalshibh reconfirmed the target list with Atta, and told him that bin Laden wanted the attacks carried out as soon as possible. Atta had asked if it was possible to target a nuclear plant as well. Binalshibh replied that only targets approved by bin Laden would be allowed. Atta had not yet settled on a date for the attacks but told Binalshibh that he would let him know as soon as possible. Interestingly, bin Laden had first pushed for the attack to occur on May 12, 2001, seven months after the *Cole* attack, but Khalid made clear to him that they were not ready. Bin Laden then pressed for June or July, around the time of the visit of Israeli Prime Minister Ariel Sharon to the Temple on the Mount in Jerusalem. Binalshibh told Atta not to inform the other hijackers about the timing of the attack until the final days.[7]

Atta returned to the United States on July 30, 2001. He spent August finalizing the operation, and remained in frequent contact with Binalshibh. He ordered all the pilots to begin scoping out the selected targets. On August 4, Atta attempted to pick up Mohamed al-Kahtani, the last of the "muscle hijacker" contingent, but Kahtani was denied entry into the United States. By the third week of August, Atta had settled on the date, September 11, and confirmed the date of the attack with Binalshibh.

Binalshibh promptly reported the date to bin Laden, and he also sent a message to Khalid confirming the attack. Bin Laden only told Atef, though word had been spreading among the shura council and the Taliban leadership that an attack was imminent. Bin Laden told visiting guests that this was the case. Mullah Omar warned bin Laden that he remained opposed to any attack against the United States, and encouraged him to strike the enemies of the Taliban inside Afghanistan. Senior al-Qaeda leaders urged him to heed Omar's warning. "I will make it happen even if I do it by myself," he responded defiantly.

Bin Laden gave the green light for the attacks to take place on the 11th of September 2001. Atta began to assemble his men into teams to travel to their respective points of departure: Newark, Dulles, and Boston. From these points, they would launch the most significant terrorist attack against the American homeland in its history.[8]

Bin Laden counted on his conclusion that the United States was a paper tiger that would avoid waging a costly, prolonged war. Americans had become unwilling to sustain significant human casualties. Between 1996 and 2001 he often cited the cases of American troops in Beirut and Mogadishu, in 1983 and 1993, respectively, to demonstrate that the United States lacks the political will to do battle. It had retreated under the cover of darkness from Lebanon and Somalia, bin Laden was fond of saying. According to testimony by former close associates, he also believed those who had visited America as tourists and told him exactly what he wanted to hear— that Americans had lost their warrior mentality. One or two big attacks would break their will.

Weighed down by group think, a common enough phenomenon in decision-making, bin Laden dismissed dissenting opinions, in particular from his shura council, which, of course, had opposed attacks on the United States, lest that provoke the lone superpower and endanger the survival of the Taliban's Islamic emirate. The Islamic emirate was the only refuge for religious activists like themselves; it did not require them to obtain visas to enter Afghanistan. Why not give the Taliban the chance to consolidate its nascent government and apply that Islamic model to other Muslim countries?

Their counsel went unheeded. "Bin Laden was a one-man show," said a former insider who knew him well during the Afghan war and in Sudan. "One must either agree with [his] opinion or shut up; dissent is not tolerated."[9] Bin Laden ran al-Qaeda with "absolute individual leadership," acknowledged another senior associate who spent years with bin Laden and Mullah Omar. This makes bin Laden's al-Qaeda "the first private sector jihad organization in Muslim history," said Egyptian-born Abu al-Walid al-Masri.[10] Bin Laden had informed fewer than a dozen of his aides about the attack and thus narrowed the circle of opposition and debate. He closed his mind to any cognitive dissonance. If the Afghan mujahideen could defeat one of the most powerful armies in the world and bring down an empire, they could easily expel the United States from Muslim territories.

Bin Laden neglected several factors that in the long term proved decisive. First, there was a relative consensus among Muslims about the legitimacy of the Afghan resistance against Soviet occupation. The Soviets had invaded a Muslim country and occupied it. In contrast, al-Qaeda killed almost 3,000 noncombatant Americans at home without direct provocation by the United States. Moreover, he did so without prior consultation with the Taliban or the umma. In fact, as one of his former top cohorts commented, bin Laden turned a personal vendetta into the umma's cause. And the umma would not rise up to defend its renegade son. On the morning after the attacks, he and his uninformed hosts faced America's wrath on their own.

As we have discussed, if bin Laden had been more knowledgable about American history and foreign relations, he would have expected the United States to retaliate immediately and overwhelmingly to a direct attack. Lebanon and Somalia were the wrong yardsticks by which to measure the American response. It is doubtful if bin Laden would have instigated the bombings had he known what to expect.

Bin Laden said that if the United States dared to invade Afghanistan, a sea of Muslim recruits would rise up to resist them. His gamble on the umma and fellow jihadis coming to his rescue was a losing one. In his memoir, Zawahiri wrote that the Islamist movement (meaning he, bin Laden, and others) must strive to gain the confidence and credibility of the umma by raising the banner of jihad on its behalf. Yet neither the umma nor the bulk of decommissioned domestic jihadis joined bin Laden's transnational battle. Although September 11 was a stunning success operationally, it failed to achieve bin Laden's grand design. In one stroke, the Islamic emirate was no longer and Islamists and jihadis lost their safe refuge, leading to confusion within the Muslim movement as a whole.

When Soviet troops invaded Kabul, the calls for jihad echoed from nearly every corner of every mosque in the Arab and Muslim world. Tens of thousands of Muslim men, including jihadis, flooded into Afghanistan to resist the Russian occupation. They came with the blessings of the religious and the ruling establishment. In contrast, there was a deafening silence when the United States declared war on the Taliban and al-Qaeda. Although Muslims everywhere criticized America's impulsiveness and reliance on force, they stopped short of calling for jihad against it. No religious authority lent its name and legitimacy to repelling the US troops. The responses of Muslims to both September 11 and the overthrow of the Taliban were drowned out by their subsequent vocal opposition to the expansion of the War on Terror, particularly the American-led invasion and occupation of Iraq.

Contrary to received wisdom, September 11 did not turn out to be al-Qaeda's baptism by fire, a force multiplier, a game changer. There was no mass following, no river of young recruits to rise up against the "impious" pro-Western local rulers, as had happened with the Islamic revolution in Iran in the late 1970s.

After September 11, bin Laden gained notoriety, but for the wrong reasons. The Western media televised images of disfranchised Palestinian teens and children in refugee camps celebrating the attacks. This disturbing but instinctual reaction by some refugees testifies to America's bitter legacy in the Arab world, particularly along the Palestine-Israel front. There is a widespread belief that America's support for Israel is directly responsible for prolonging the Palestinian predicament and that this support has poisoned Arab-American relations since the late 1940s. On September 11, some Palestinians felt a brief moment of elation; finally Americans had had a little taste of Palestinian suffering, powerlessness, and shock. Other Arabs and Muslims doubted al-Qaeda was responsible.

By focusing on the "why do they hate us" issue—overinflated as it was—the Western media missed the more revealing story. There was little media coverage of the thousands of young Iranians who observed a candlelight vigil for the victims of September 11, or of the outpouring of public empathy worldwide, including in Muslim countries. Many ordinary Arabs and Muslims—from bank tellers to fruit vendors and taxi drivers to small shop owners with whom I talked immediately after the attacks—expressed compassion for the families of the dead. Even those who voiced strong anti-American foreign policy views concurred that the attacks were a crime. Islam proscribes the killing of noncombatants, particularly indiscriminate targeting of children, women, and the elderly. This moment of sympathy also offered a brief moment of opportunity, a catalyst to recalibrate America's relations with the Muslim world.

More devastating to bin Laden was the response by mainstream Islamists, some of whom have been mentioned earlier, such as Hassan al-Turabi, formerly head of the Islamic National Front and now of the People's Congress in Sudan (which hosted bin Laden from 1992 to 1996); Sayyid Muhammad Husayn Fadlallah, the spiritual founding father of Lebanon's Shiite Hizbullah; Salman al-Awdah; and of course Fadl, the former mufti of al-Qaeda; as well as Yusuf al-Qaradawi, an Egyptian-born conservative cleric now based in Qatar. Far from embracing al-Qaeda's "blessed terrorism," as bin Laden termed it, they condemned it as un-Islamic.

The diverse theological and ideological backgrounds of these men testify to al-Qaeda's failure to convince Muslims, particularly politically radicalized religious activists, that targeting civilians is religiously legitimate. While this may be cold comfort to the families of the victims, it posed a significant theological challenge to bin Laden. Yet Western media took little notice of the fierce debate that was unfolding in the Muslim world after September 11. Instead, it focused almost exclusively on reductionist, historical questions about "why they hate us so much, and where are the Muslim moderates?"

There are tens of thousands of domestic jihadis scattered around the Muslim world. Had bin Laden and Zawahiri succeeded in re-activating this army of local jihadis into the al-Qaeda network, they might have fielded and deployed several brigades. The current conflict would be far deadlier if more domestic jihadis had joined the fray. This goes to the heart of the question of whether al-Qaeda speaks for and represents the bulk of jihadis (much less the umma) or, as I have argued, only a fringe. After 1996 bin Laden and Zawahiri had already launched an ambitious campaign to take control of the remnants of the jihadist movement and change its direction. Unable to rally the disparate factions and put an end to the internal rivalries, they had plunged into a confrontation with the United States, hoping that it would serve as a galvanizing and unifying experience.

Rallying the umma requires an external enemy—a clear, specific enemy. The goal was to generate a major world crisis, provoking the West and America in particular "to come out of its hole," as Sayf al-Adl, al-Qaeda's senior military commander, wrote, and to attack Muslim countries.

After the initial shock and a self-imposed period of silence, the chiefs of the main jihadist groups publicly denounced what bin Laden had done. Some of these leaders were legendary figures in mujahideen circles. Abu al-Walid al-Masri, who was close to bin Laden and was the first non-Afghan to swear allegiance to Taliban leader Mullah Omar, saw the attacks as a calamity. He was among the most senior of the Afghan Arabs to break with bin Laden, and to take his grievances public, publishing a series of articles in the Cairo-based Arabic newspaper, *al-Sharq al-Awsat*, in 2004 and 2005 entitled "The Story of the Arab Afghans: From the Entry to Afghanistan to the Final Exodus with Taliban."[11] He lambasted what he saw as bin Laden's "catastrophic leadership" and his underestimation of American willpower. As Abu al-Walid writes with characteristic bluntness, matters after September 11 "took an opposite turn compared to what bin Laden had imagined. Instead of buckling under his three painful blows, America retaliated and destroyed both the Taliban and al-Qaeda."[12]

Nonetheless, al-Qaeda members knew better than to openly challenge bin Laden, as we discover through Abu al-Walid. "You are the emir, do as you please!" he reported them telling their leader. That attitude encouraged recklessness and caused disorganization, "characteristics that are unsuitable for this existential battle in which we confront the greatest force in the world, U.S.A." Abu al-Walid believed that it was necessary to "to consider the real nature and the size of this battle," and to prepare the mujahideen and the Muslim masses for an "extended, long-term battle that requires great sacrifices." September 11 was a dream of "an easy victory."[13]

By stifling internal debate and underestimating the enemy, bin Laden was rendering al-Qaeda's final years in Afghanistan "a tragic example of an Islamic movement managed by a catastrophic leadership." Driven by his appetite for attention—his "extreme infatuation" with the international media—bin Laden was "leading them to the abyss and even leading the entire country to utter destruction, but they continued to bend to his will and take his orders with suicidal submission."[14] What seemed to fuel Abu al-Walid's anger was his view that bin Laden "was not even aware of the scope of the battle he had opted to fight, or was forced into fighting. Therefore," he concluded, bin Laden "lacked the correct perception and was not qualified to lead." He cited an old Arab proverb: "Those who work without knowledge will damage more than they can fix, and those who walk quickly on the wrong path will only distance themselves from their goal." The disaster in Afghanistan demonstrated one essential principle, according to Abu al-Walid: "that absolute individual authority is a hopelessly defective form of leadership, an obsolete way of organization that will end in nothing but defeat." Bin Laden's authoritarian style of leadership was responsible for pitting jihadis against America in a struggle that, in his opinion, was "beyond the present capabilities of the whole [Islamist] movement."[15]

But in fact, matters went deeper than this. What happened in Afghanistan demonstrated the intellectual bankruptcy of the jihadist project. "It may be that the Islamic movement had already suffered from an intellectual as well as an organizational defeat before it had even started its battle against America. Jihad is a broad and serious issue that should not be left to the jihadist groups alone. Jihad is more than just an armed battle."[16]

September 11 demonstrated the utter failure of al-Qaeda's transnational jihad, concluded Abu al-Walid, a damning indictment of bin Laden and Zawahiri. His withering criticism of al-Qaeda revolves not only around tactics but ideology and philosophy; it challenges the theological foundation of the global jihad project and raises questions about its legitimacy and viability. According to one of the most senior leaders of the Afghan Arabs, there were structural faults with the discourse and conduct of the Islamist movement as a whole.

Abu al-Walid's assessment has been echoed by others, including the Egyptian al-Gamaa al-Islamiya. Whereas at the height of its strength in 2001, al-Qaeda's membership ranged between 3,000 and 4,000 fighters, al-Gamaa fielded tens of thousands of activists in the 1990s. Of all the Islamists, al-Gamaa senior leaders (most of whom were imprisoned in Egypt in the 1980s and 1990s and have only recently been released) presented the most comprehensive critique of bin Laden's transnational jihad and conceded that armed jihad against the near enemy and the far enemy was a failure. Their self-critique goes much further than Habib and Abu al-Walid's. Since early 2002 al-Gamaa has released approximately twenty-five books authored by its top leaders, two of which are critiques of al-Qaeda's ideology and tactics. These are vital historical documents that shed light on the thinking of the largest and most influential jihadist organization in the region. These have not been translated into English and thus have not received the attention they deserve in the West. The first, authored by Muhammad Essam Derbala and reviewed and approved by the entire leadership, is titled "Al-Qaeda Strategy: Mistakes and Dangers" and the other, authored by Nagih Abdullah Ibrahim, is "Islam and the Challenges of the Twenty-First Century." Both were serialized in *al-Sharq al-Awsat*, a London-based Arabic paper.[17]

Derbala, a senior leader of al-Gamaa and serving a life sentence for his role in the 1981 Sadat assassination, draws on religious texts to show that al-Qaeda's attacks violate Islamic law, which bans killing civilians of any religion or nationality. What is fascinating about the document is the way in which Derbala uses the very terms bin Laden and Zawahiri adopted to justify their jihad to point to its illegitimacy. He accuses them of violating the sharia itself, waging jihad by superimposing their own views over those of the Prophet, and comes close to calling them apostates. Still, bin Laden and Zawahiri could cut their losses, Derbala concludes, if they halted their jihad and conceded their errors; otherwise, they would meet a fate similar to that of the Algerian Armed Islamic Groups (GIA), a criminal cult that forsook Islam and met defeat at the end of the 1990s.[18]

Echoing Abu al-Walid, Derbala insists that jihad must not be waged without an honest assessment of costs, benefits, and capabilities. "Al-Qaeda has to understand that jihad is only one of the Muslims' duties. Jihad is a means, not an end." Making jihad for the sake of jihad, as al-Qaeda has done, produced the opposite of the desired results—the downfall of the Taliban regime and the slaughter of thousands of young Muslims. Surely, the umma is much worse off now, Derbala points out, as a result of al-Qaeda's foolish and reckless conduct.[19]

Derbala and his associates denounced al-Qaeda for preaching that American and Muslim interests would never meet and that "the enmity is deeply embedded and the clash is inevitable." They cited several cases in the 1990s when the United States helped to resolve international conflicts with results that benefited Muslims: American military and financial assistance in the Afghan war tipped the balance in favor of the mujahideen against the Russian occupiers; from 1990 to 1991 the United States helped Kuwait and Saudi Arabia expel Iraqi forces from Kuwait; in 1995 American military intervention put a stop to the persecution and massacre of Bosnian Muslims by Serbs; and in 1999 the United States led a NATO military campaign to force Serbia to end ethnic cleansing in Kosovo.[20]

American and Muslim interests can and do meet; history has proven that there is nothing inevitable about a clash of cultures between Islam and the West, because Islam is a universal religion, fully integrated with other civilizations. They reprimand bin Laden for advocating war between *dar al-iman* ("house of belief"), and *dar al-kufr* ("house of unbelief") based upon a misreading of the umma's capabilities. "The question is, where are the priorities? Where are the capabilities that allow for all of that?" Al-Qaeda was trying to ignite a clash of civilizations without possessing the means to wage—*let alone prevail in*—a global struggle.[21] Thus, if al-Qaeda proved capable of mastering anything, it was in making enemies rather than following the Prophet Muhammad's example and neutralizing them. Al-Gamaa's leaders call for engagement with the West based on mutual respect and peaceful coexistence.[22] "Some claim that there is a crusader war led by America against Islam," writes Derbala. "However, the majority of Muslims reject the existence of crusader wars." Religious motives may influence American policy toward Muslim nations, he adds, "but these are not crusader wars." Rather, "interests remain the official religion of America, and those interests determine its international relations."[23]

Acknowledging failure, the main author of al-Gamaa's second manifesto, Nagih Abdullah Ibrahim, also sentenced for life for Sadat's assassination and released after September 11, writes that Muslims must relinquish myths maintained by extremists (such as himself) for decades. According to Ibrahim, the attacks and their reverberations exposed the need for Muslims to face reality head-on and make difficult decisions if they wanted to catch up with the rest of humanity. Muslims could no longer afford to postpone reforms in a world whose social, political, and economic interactions are evolving quickly, leaving them further and further behind. "Standing still would mean suicide."[24]

A real renewal of Islamic thought, Ibrahim posits, would enrich the education of young Muslims and make them less vulnerable to easy conspiracy theories, such as those that were spun around September 11. "Conspiracy theories retard the Arab and Muslim mind, restricting its ability to rationally resolve problems." Ibrahim laments the fact that instead of viewing foreign affairs in terms of state interests and power relations, Arabs see them through a lens of conspiracy theories that scapegoats the West for "all of our tragedies and neglects our own strategic errors."[25] Those strategic errors—*not the West*—he writes, are the real villains behind the decline of the umma. Islamists and nationalists are equally responsible for conspiracy mongering and leading young Muslims astray.[26]

Ibrahim, Derbala, and the others cited their own experience fighting the Egyptian government to show the pitfalls of engaging in jihad without considering conditions at home and abroad; jihad not only failed to achieve their goals, but, more importantly, it lost them public support. They had forgotten "that armed struggle or jihad was never an end in itself, and Islam did not legislate fighting for the sake of fighting or jihad for the sake of jihad." Jihad is only one duty in Islam; Muslims must not overlook other choices, such as *al-sulh*, "peacemaking," practiced by the Prophet Muhammad throughout his life. By neglecting *al-sulh* as a strategic choice, all jihadis— themselves included—made grave mistakes that endangered their movement's very survival.[27] Even as he preached the value of piety and faith, bin Laden should have listened to his own internal counsel and tried to understand his adversaries. In the end he fell victim to hubris. Because it lost touch with reality, rationality, and the essence of the principles of Islam, al-Qaeda caused the downfall of two Muslim regimes—in Kabul and in Baghdad. Ibrahim sees little difference between bin Laden's al-Qaeda and Saddam Hussein's dictatorship: one leader destroyed his own network; the other destroyed the Iraqi state.[28]

Religious coexistence is a strategic, not a tactical, goal in Islam, particularly when Muslims migrate to foreign lands. What makes the crime of the suicide bombers of September 11 uniquely un-Islamic, Ibrahim writes, is that the US government had admitted them as guests. This was a betrayal of the most fundamental spiritual obligation, the one practiced in shops, cafés, and homes throughout the Arab world. Had the bombers read the Sunna (the corpus of the deeds of the Prophet, the second source of Islam after the Qur'an), they would have respected peaceful coexistence.[29]

Speaking from his prison cell, Karam Zuhdi, the emir of al-Gamaa, gave a series of interviews to the Egyptian weekly magazine *al-Mussawar* and to *al-Sharq al-Awsat* in which he accused al-Qaeda of dragging the umma into a confrontation it neither desired nor had the capability to pursue. Bin Laden became "obsessed with killing Americans, Christians, and crusaders without distinctions," stated Zuhdi. He went further by saying that the late President Sadat, whom he and his cohorts assassinated, was a "martyr," a rare acknowledgment of criminal and moral responsibility for his murder.[30] What is the alternative, the imprisoned leaders ask. Jihad should only be activated against foreign occupiers, and only legitimate leaders should be in charge of the call to jihad.[31]

Al-Gamaa's critique of September 11 is all the more powerful because the credibility and legitimacy of its leaders cannot be questioned, even by al-Qaeda. Zuhdi, Derbala, Ibrahim, Usama Hafiz, Asim Abd al-Magid, and the rest who signed and blessed the two documents from which I have quoted extensively, were the founding fathers of a major wing of the jihadist movement. While students at Asyut University in the late 1970s, they published one of the first manifestos of violent jihad, entitled *Chapters from the Charter of Islamic Political Action*.[32] They paid their dues in blood and sweat and have languished in prison for decades. Like Habib and Abu al-Walid Kamal, they were the pioneers of contemporary jihadism. Their critique of both al-Qaeda's transnational jihad and their own misguided armed insurgency amounts to a wholesale repudiation of contemporary jihadism. Its importance lies in reclaiming the ethical foundation of the institution of jihad and accepting the dominant theological interpretation, a radical transformation of local jihadist doctrine. This marked the beginning of a widespread revolt against al-Qaeda.

The majority of key Islamists and jihadists have echoed al-Gamaa's view that September 11 was a catastrophic blunder. In his diaries, serialized in *al-Hayat*, a leading Arabic newspaper, Hani al-Sibai, a former close associate of Zawahiri, who resides in exile in the United Kingdom (the Egyptian government has sentenced him to death), is bluntly critical. Since its birth in the 1990s, he writes, the global jihad movement led by al-Qaeda has proved disastrous to the Islamist movement and the umma alike. Sibai calls the decision to shift operational priorities and attack the United States unwise, based neither on rational analysis nor on consultation with the rank and file.[33]

While al-Gamaa's leaders stressed moral and ethical aspects in their condemnation, most Islamist criticism is based on utilitarian and pragmatic considerations. Usama Rushdi, who was in charge of al-Gamaa's media committee and a senior member of its consultative council, comes closest to coupling the moral with the political. In several interviews with the Arab media, Rushdi argues that although al-Qaeda justified its attacks on the United States in religious terms, those terms had nothing to do with Islam, which does not sanction killing civilians or violating legal and moral precepts, because it would threaten international harmony and coexistence.[34] Criticizing American foreign policy is easy, Rushdi acknowledges; however, hostility to America does not justify attacking it. "Do the ends justify the means in this struggle, or should the means be as justifiable as the end?" The greatest threats facing the jihadist movement are self-inflicted wounds—a direct indictment of his own journey, not just al-Qaeda's.[35]

Even before the smoke cleared over the September 11 attacks, internal dissension had already begun to take its toll on al-Qaeda. The umma did not respond the way bin Laden had expected, and like-minded jihadist groups accused him of heresy and treachery. The instantaneous and spontaneous censure of bin Laden and Zawahiri turned into a torrent of pointed criticisms. Yet most in the West and in the United States simply did not hear it, focusing instead on launching a global War on Terror, a war that, paradoxically, has sustained bin Laden and his ilk. President Bush and his administration used the September 11 attacks as a justification to engineer fundamental change in the Middle East. Part of that justification involved inflating the threat posed by al-Qaeda.

4

Decline and Fall

Operationally, after bin Laden and his cohorts were expelled from their safe haven in Afghanistan, together with the Taliban, al-Qaeda was effectively decapitated. The leadership was on the run or captured. Dispersed haphazardly into various countries, most of which were unwelcoming, bin Laden's men were rounded up by vigilant local security services that competed with one another to show Americans that they were cooperating with them against al-Qaeda.

From Yemen to Syria, and from the United Arab Emirates to Pakistan, the hunt for al-Qaeda's operatives netted scores of significant arrests. Iran, for example, arrested or extradited hundreds of bin Laden's men who had fled there, including senior military commanders and members of his family. Yemen rounded up hundreds of former jihadis and imprisoned them en masse. President Ali Abdullah Saleh flew to Washington and showed his support by allowing the CIA to use an unmanned drone to kill Abu Ali al-Harithi, then leader of al-Qaeda in Yemen, along with five other suspects, as he was driving in the desert east of the capital, Sana'a, in November 2002.[1]

Since Barack Obama entered the White House, there has been a steady deterioration in US-Pakistan relations, culminating with the killing of bin Laden in a special operation ordered by the US president on his compound in Abbottabad near the capital, Islamabad. Despite the double game that Pakistan has played toward the Taliban in Afghanistan—going after them and supporting them—in the wake of September 11 the Pakistani authorities offered valuable and tangible assistance to the United States, helping it arrest more than 400 of bin Laden's top lieutenants and operatives, including Khalid Sheikh Mohammed and Abu Zubayda, who some consider the third-ranking figure in al-Qaeda.[2] There is increasing evidence that just two years after the attacks bin Laden and Zawahiri had been vulnerable, constantly on the move from one rural location to another between Pakistan and Afghanistan, fully preoccupied with avoiding capture. Western intelligence authorities say they had reliable information on bin Laden's movements, though the information was not recent enough for "actionable intelligence." Soon afterward, bin Laden went deeper underground, leaving no trace left behind until the tracking of his trusted courier beginning in August 2010.[3]

Between 2001 and 2003 there existed a window of opportunity: al-Qaeda was in disequilibrium and there was genuine goodwill worldwide toward the United States. The period from September 11 until the 2003 invasion and occupation of Iraq was rich with possibilities and opportunities regarding the campaign against bin Laden's men. Lacking any public Muslim support and with very few safe shelters, the noose was tightening around their necks. On the run and defensive, al-Qaeda faced a decidedly bleak future. Instead of capitalizing on this by building up a genuine transnational coalition, particularly of Muslim societies, to capture the remnants of al-Qaeda, the Bush administration shifted gears.

Bush's decision to invade and occupy Iraq in 2003 was a godsend to al-Qaeda, allowing it to regroup, reorganize itself militarily, and decentralize its decision-making process. The expansion of the War on Terror prolonged al-Qaeda's survival. Were it not for the war in Iraq, the fight against bin Laden and his men would have been shorter, less costly, and more conclusive. Certainly, America's occupation of Iraq, which lies in the heart of Arabian Islam, enraged millions of Arabs and Muslims, whose negative neutrality was transformed into visceral hostility. Iraq became a rallying cry for jihad against America, a foreign invader, together with its "coalition of the willing."

Far from welcoming US and Western troops as liberators, Muslim opinion viewed the subjugation of Iraq through the prism of the colonial legacy, which has neither been forgotten nor forgiven. Had it not been for logistical and operational obstacles, hundreds of thousands of young Muslims would have journeyed to Iraq to fight the foreign occupiers. In my travels between 2003 and 2006, I met hundreds of Arab youth from Libya, Morocco, Algeria, Libya, Yemen, Lebanon, Jordan, and elsewhere, many of whom said they were desperately attempting to go to Iraq and join the jihad there. While most were not members of al-Qaeda, they seemed disposed to its message of defending the umma against foreign occupation. Despite the extraordinary pressure the United States exerted on Iraq's neighbors to seal their borders, thousands managed to get in.

A limited clash against a struggling and declining al-Qaeda was thus turned into a greater struggle with the world of Islam, precisely as bin Laden and Zawahiri had hoped. The war in Iraq provided a recruitment bonanza and an opportunity to gain credibility in Muslims' eyes, to be perceived as an armed vanguard of the umma. Ironically, in his speech to Congress given nine days after September 11, President Bush accurately diagnosed al-Qaeda's isolation and existential predicament: "The terrorists practice a fringe form of Islamic extremism that has been rejected by Muslim scholars and the vast majority of Muslim clerics . . . the terrorists are traitors to their own faith, trying, in effect, to hijack Islam itself."[4]

Yet the Bush national security team disregarded its own diagnosis of al-Qaeda and treated it more as a potent strategic adversary than a precarious "fringe" group—precisely allowing it to become that adversary. After the initial invasion and success, America became an occupying force in Iraq, and al-Qaeda used the breathing space this created to smuggle fighters into the country and to recalibrate its message and focus preponderantly on Iraq. Within a few months, a small band of thirty Afghan Arab fighters led by Abu Musab al-Zarqawi, a Jordanian-born high school drop-out who had previously fallen out with Zawahiri and bin Laden over tactics and strategy, set up a lethal organization called al-Tawhid wa-l-Jihad, modeled along the lines of al-Qaeda. At the height of its power from 2004 to 2006, al-Tawhid wa-l-Jihad exceeded bin Laden's organization in numbers and strength, and superseded it in brutality. Zarqawi fielded one of the largest arsenals of suicide bombers in history and deployed them indiscriminately. His goal was to kill as many Iraqis, particularly Shiites, as possible, triggering an all-out sectarian war between the two leading communities—Sunni Arabs and Shiites—which he almost single-handedly brought about.

In October 2004, Zarqawi announced that he was formally changing the name of his group to "al-Qaeda in the Land of the Two Rivers," a reference to the Tigris and Euphrates, and declared his allegiance to bin Laden. Two months later, in an audiotape broadcast by Al Jazeera satellite television, bin Laden endorsed Zarqawi as his deputy and anointed him the emir of al-Qaeda in Iraq, praising his "gallant operations" against the Americans.[5]

But the relationship between bin Laden's al-Qaeda and Zarqawi's was much more complex. Each possessed differing agendas and oversized egos. According to accounts by close associates, from the beginning of their relationship in the late 1990s, bin Laden and Zawahiri kept the younger Zarqawi at arm's length, and Zarqawi, in turn, criticized his elders for not being fierce enough with the enemy. It is reported that bin Laden was initially reluctant to agree to a merger between al-Qaeda and Zarqawi's al-Tawhid wa-l-Jihad because of his excessive sectarianism and violence; communal strife between Sunnis and Shiites would distract from the focal confrontation against the far enemy.[6]

By the end of 2004 bin Laden had put his reservations aside and embraced Zarqawi, whose stardom had eclipsed bin Laden's own. Zarqawi spearheaded al-Qaeda's fight in Iraq and thousands of young volunteers rallied to his call. Hiding in Pakistan, bin Laden was becoming isolated and more and more marginal, while Zarqawi's suicide bombers captured world headlines. Yet bin Laden swallowed his pride. A union with Zarqawi offered him a "golden and unique opportunity" to expand the confrontation against the United States and convince his jihadist cohorts and Muslims in general that his organization was still relevant despite setbacks in Afghanistan, Pakistan, Saudi Arabia, Yemen, and elsewhere.[7]

Bin Laden's gamble on Zarqawi proved costly. Zarqawi consciously attacked Iraqi civilians, including women and children, and plotted mass killing of Shiites. Despite repeated written requests by al-Qaeda's senior leadership to strike only at the Americans, he sent wave after wave of suicide bombers at Shiites. Zarqawi was on a murderous crusade to foment bloody communal strife and bring the temple down on everyone's head. Nothing would stand in his way—neither bin Laden, Zawahiri, nor Sunni Arabs, a segment of whom initially provided him with shelter and support. When Sunni tribal leaders challenged his tactics and his attempt to impose a Taliban-like regime on their neighborhoods, he cracked down viciously, frequently ordering the assassination of Sunni politicians who dared to participate in the nascent political order. By 2005 the hundreds of bombings, kidnappings, and beheadings had turned the vast majority of Iraqi and Muslim opinion against al-Qaeda in Iraq and al-Qaeda Central in general.

Zarqawi's spiritual mentor, Abu Muhammad al-Maqdisi, a prominent Salafi-Jihadi ideologue who had groomed Zarqawi while both were in prison in the 1990s, publicly reprimanded him for his terrorism against civilians. In several interviews, Maqdisi said that violence that targeted civilians was wrong. Such extremist tactics harmed the interests of the umma and tarnished the image of Islam. Maqdisi reminded his former pupil that so-called martyrdom operations should be carried out only under stringent and exceptional conditions. He cautioned him against alienating Iraqis by losing sight of the nature of the struggle in Iraq, and of the fact that Iraqis knew what was best for their country.[8]

Similarly, in a letter to Zarqawi in July 2005—seized by US authorities and made public—Zawahiri chastised his ally for excessive violence, which alienated the Muslim masses and turned them against al-Qaeda: "You shouldn't be deceived by the praise of some of the zealous young men and their description of you as the shaykh of the slaughterers."[9] The strongest weapon which the mujahideen enjoyed, wrote Zawahiri, was the support of the Muslim masses in Iraq and neighboring countries. Without it, al-Qaeda would be crushed. "So, we must maintain this support as best we can, and we should strive to increase it."[10]

Both Maqdisi and Zawahiri stressed to Zarqawi that attacking the Shiites was counterproductive to the greater goal of expelling the Americans, the foreign occupiers, from Muslim territories. Zawahiri noted that while it was true that Shiite Iran had collaborated with the US invaders and that the "rejectionist" Shiite sect represented a danger to Salafi Islam, the sectarian factor was secondary in importance to the fight against the far enemy. Many who were sympathetic to the jihadist cause in Iraq had serious reservations about the sectarian bloodletting. Therefore, al-Qaeda in Iraq was to avoid any action that the Muslim masses do not understand or approve.[11] "We are in a battle, and that more than half of this battle is taking place in the battlefield of the media. And that we are in a media battle in a race for the hearts and minds of our ummah."[12]

But Zarqawi was beyond redemption. He surrounded himself with extremists who offered him "complete allegiance" and faithfully carried out his orders, according to Maqdisi. Instead of broadening his social base among Iraqis, Zarqawi alienated his most important allies, the Sunni-dominated insurgency; eventually they turned against al-Qaeda. Many tribal Sunni insurgents even joined the so-called Awakening Councils, sponsored by the United States, and expelled Zarqawi's men from their areas. When in June 2006 American warplanes dropped two 500-pound bombs on a house in which Zarqawi was meeting with aides and killed him, al-Qaeda in Iraq was almost a spent force.

The reverberations of Zarqawi's death and the subsequent fracturing of his organization were felt far beyond Iraq. Bin Laden and Zawahiri had lost more than an overzealous ally; they had lost any hope of gaining traction with Muslim public opinion. Zarqawi's mass slaughter of civilians had created a public outcry against al-Qaeda; and as much as he might have tried, bin Laden could not distance himself from Zarqawi, whom he had, after all, deputized as the emir in Iraq and whose actions he had praised as "gallant operations" against the enemies of Islam. In the eyes of Muslims, Zarqawi was bin Laden's lieutenant in Iraq. For the first time ever, bin Laden offered a public apology—for the mistakes of his men in Iraq. He asked for tolerance and forgiveness. It was, however, too little and too late. Public polls and surveys showed a steep decline and high mistrust in Muslim attitudes towards al-Qaeda (see the finding of the polls below).

Bin Laden and Zawahiri's high expectations in Iraq were crushed by Zarqawi's suicide bombings, kidnappings, and beheadings. They had hoped to leverage the war in Iraq to spread their call and influence near and far. Indeed, in his 2005 letter to Zarqawi, Zawahiri sketched out al-Qaeda's strategy to set up a Muslim state in Iraq that would be a stepping stone to the entire region:

> It has always been my belief that the victory of Islam will never take place until a Muslim state is established in the manner of the Prophet in the heart of the Islamic world, specifically in the Levant, Egypt, and the neighboring states of the Peninsula and Iraq; however, the center would be in the Levant and Egypt.[13]

Zawahiri had recommended that Zarqawi pursue an incremental strategy to re-establish the ancient caliphate rule:

> First, expel the Americans from Iraq.
> Second, establish an Islamic authority or emirate on whatever liberated territory and expand it throughout Sunni areas.
> Third, extend the jihad wave to Iraq's secular neighbors.
> Finally, confront Israel because the Jewish state was established only to challenge any new Islamic entity.[14]

Zarqawi, however, had pursued his own violent goals, independently of his elders. Contrary to the received wisdom in the West, local branches of terrorist organizations have their own peculiar characters and agendas. Al-Qaeda in Iraq is a case in point. Its methods were disastrous for al-Qaeda in Mesopotamia and al-Qaeda Central as well. Sunni tribes had become fed up with its sectarian fanaticism, and worked with US troops, killing and expelling hundreds of its militants from their areas, particularly from Anbar province.

Although the American "surge" of 2006–7 is commonly credited with improving security in Iraq, al-Qaeda's terrorism played a key role. The surge capitalized on public disaffection with al-Qaeda and with the outright armed revolt by the same Sunni Arabs who had previously provided its members shelter and recruits. They could do so again. The recent surge of al-Qaeda's attacks is in fact a product of rising dissatisfaction among Sunni Arabs who had been promised integration into the government. Around 100,000 members of the Awakening Councils had been told that they would be given jobs in Iraq's security and bureaucratic services. Such integration has not yet happened.

In Iraq, al-Qaeda lost more than a battle and country; it lost a historic opportunity to integrate itself with an aggrieved Sunni community that initially had tolerated its presence, and it lost the opportunity to make inroads into neighboring Arab countries. Al-Qaeda could have become a legitimate wing of the Sunni-dominated insurgency had Zarqawi and his men exercised restraint and respected local culture and tradition.

The lost opportunity goes to the very heart of al-Qaeda's character. It bears repeating: far from being an institutionally coherent social movement, al-Qaeda is a loose collection of small groups and factions that tend to be guided by charismatic individuals. Zarqawi was the rule, not the exception. He disregarded the council of his elders and superiors, sacrificing the future of an Islamic state in Iraq at the altar of his fanaticism. Bin Laden and Zawahiri are at the mercy of followers of the late Zarqawi, and of the Palestinian Fatah al-Islam in Lebanon—men who have their own agendas. Al-Qaeda's inability to dissuade them from attacking the near enemy endangers the survival of the entire transnational jihad enterprise.

Since 2006 the balance of forces has shifted from al-Qaeda's transnational and local jihad in favor of repentant radicals like

Fadl—Islamists who are struggling, often against great odds and under enormous pressures, to accommodate themselves to gradual social and political change in their societies. Al-Qaeda may dominate American thoughts and headlines, but its members constitute a small minority.

Al-Qaeda's new leadership faces a serious shortage of skilled recruits in the Muslim heartland. In Saudi Arabia, Iraq, Lebanon, Jordan, Indonesia, and elsewhere, most of the intelligence about al-Qaeda suspects comes not from surveillance and intelligence services but from relatives and friends, a testament to the changing political and social landscape, as well as public disillusionment with bin Laden's men. For many Muslims, al-Qaeda is a liability whose very presence causes instability and insecurity; bin Laden and Zawahiri do not offer any solutions to pressing social and political challenges—only blood and tears.

Since 2007 public polls conducted in Muslim countries show a plurality of citizens deeply concerned about terrorism and the image of Islam abroad. A growing majority of Muslims view al-Qaeda negatively and endorse active measures to limit its activities in their societies. For example, between 2001 and 2007, Gallup conducted tens of thousands of hour-long, face-to-face interviews with residents of more than thirty-five predominantly Muslim countries. They found that, contrary to the prevailing perception in the West that the actions of al-Qaeda enjoy wide support in the Muslim world, 93 percent of respondents condemned, on religious and humanitarian grounds, the killing of noncombatants.[15] According to a public opinion survey carried out in late November and early December 2007 by Terror Free Tomorrow, a non-profit group seeking to establish the reasons people support or oppose extremism, fewer than one in ten Saudis had a favorable opinion of al-Qaeda and 88 percent approved of the Saudi authorities' pursuit of al-Qaeda operatives.[16]

A poll conducted by the same organization in Pakistan in January 2008 showed that support for al-Qaeda, the Taliban, bin Laden, and other militant Islamist groups had dropped by half from the previous August. In August 2007, 33 percent of Pakistanis supported al-Qaeda; 38 percent supported the Taliban. By January 2008 al-Qaeda's support had dropped to 18 percent, the Taliban to 19 percent. When asked if they would vote for al-Qaeda, just 1 percent of Pakistanis polled answered in the affirmative. The Taliban had the support of 3 percent of those polled.[17]

Despite the war in Pakistan's tribal areas and the revival of the Taliban, most ordinary Pakistanis say they have no confidence in either the Taliban or al-Qaeda. Contrary to terrorism reports in the West, Pakistan is not under imminent threat by the Taliban or al-Qaeda. Ordinary Pakistanis display much more common sense and realism than terrorism "experts" would have it. A 2009 Pew Global Attitudes Survey on Pakistani Public Opinion concluded that only 9 percent of those surveyed had a positive view of al-Qaeda. This finding represents a significant decrease in favorability from 2008, when 25 percent of those surveyed had a positive view of al-Qaeda. The poll also found that 79 percent of those surveyed were concerned about extremism in the country.[18]

Pew surveys in 2007 reveal a substantial decline in the percentage of those who believe that suicide bombings and other forms of violence against civilian targets are justified to defend Islam against its enemies. Wide majorities say such attacks are rarely acceptable.[19] The shift has been especially dramatic in Jordan, where 29 percent of the population now view suicide attacks as often or sometimes justified, down from 57 percent in May 2005. In Indonesia, the largest majority Muslim nation, 74 percent of respondents agree that terrorist attacks are "never justified"; this is a substantial decline from the 41 percent level to which support had risen in

March 2004; in Pakistan, that figure is 86 percent; in Bangladesh, 81 percent; and in Iran, 80 percent.[20]

A Pew Global Attitudes Survey in 2009 indicates a continued upward trend in those respondents who conclude that suicide bombing was "rarely/never justified." In Indonesia, 85 percent of those surveyed agreed that suicide bombing was "rarely/never justified." Of those surveyed in Pakistan, 90 percent said the same thing, 82 percent in Jordan, and 31 percent in the Palestinian territories.[21] The minority that says suicide bombing is justified under exceptional circumstances tends to refer to the Palestine-Israel conflict and not to al-Qaeda's transnational jihad.

Compare those figures with a recent study that shows only 46 percent of Americans think that "bombing and other attacks intentionally aimed at civilians" are "never justified," while 24 percent believe these attacks are "often or sometimes justified."[22]

Confidence in al-Qaeda has also fallen in most Muslim countries in recent years. A December 2007 poll conducted in Saudi Arabia shows that bin Laden's fellow countrymen had "dramatically turned against him, his organization, Saudi volunteers in Iraq, and terrorism in general."[23] In Pakistan's North West Frontier Province, where al-Qaeda has a foothold, the percentage of those with a favorable opinion of bin Laden dropped from 70 percent in August 2007, to just 4 percent in January 2008—a spectacular decline over a short period.[24] In a 2009 Pew Global Attitudes Survey of the Palestinian territories, confidence in Osama bin Laden had dropped from 72 percent in 2003 to 52 percent in 2009. Similarly, in Jordan, confidence in bin Laden halved from 56 percent in 2003 to 28 percent in 2009, and in Turkey, confidence dropped from 15 percent in 2003 to 2 percent in 2009.[25]

And still, all of these surveys and polls do not reflect the gravity of al-Qaeda's crisis and isolation. Indeed, al-Qaeda has become so unpopular that some believe bin Laden to be an American agent. For a majority, al-Qaeda's efforts to foment sectarian strife brought fatal repercussions to Muslim society. As almost every opinion survey shows, the issue of security ranks extremely high on the priority list of Muslims, an indication of the extent to which al-Qaeda's violence has colored public attitudes.

The theological critiques of the organization, coupled with its wholesale attacks on civilians, have had a ruinous impact on al-Qaeda's operational capacity. Testimony by jihadis returning from al-Qaeda's "havens" in Pakistan's tribal areas paint a picture of an organization in complete disarray. These volunteers say they were made to pay for their own equipment and weapons, given desultory basic training, then patronized and ignored.[26]

Yet this dismal portrait of al-Qaeda's "core" in the Pakistani frontier zone pales in comparison to its like-minded elements elsewhere. Former jihadis and Islamists in Egypt, Palestine, Jordan, Lebanon, Saudi Arabia, the Persian Gulf, Britain, France, Germany, and Spain tell me that al-Qaeda's attacks on civilians, particularly in Muslim countries, coupled with the mayhem these attacks wrought, have relegated it to the margins of Islamic society. The social and political space that once provided refuge for al-Qaeda and its affiliates has diminished to almost nothing, with even Sunni Muslims pursuing such groups in several countries, including Saudi Arabia, Iraq, Jordan, and Lebanon, and providing most of the information about al-Qaeda operators to local intelligence and security services.

Al-Qaeda's local branches there and elsewhere have suffered military setbacks and are rapidly fading. For example, overwhelming public support allowed the Lebanese government to bring down Fatah al-Islam, which subscribes to al-Qaeda's ideology and was active in the Palestinian refugee camp of Nahr al-Bared in northern Lebanon, though unfortunately hundreds of people were killed in the process. In Saudi Arabia, according to a recent intelligence report, about 70 percent of information about al-Qaeda suspects now comes from relatives, friends, and neighbors, not from security agencies and surveillance.[27] Bin Laden's loss of Saudi Arabia must have been particularly painful to him, given that he had promised to make his last stand in his native land and the birthplace of Islam.

In Algeria, a bastion of Islamist militancy since the early 1990s, the public has recently been active in opposing extremists who subscribe to al-Qaeda–style ideology and tactics, and who have carried out devastating suicide bombings and assassinations in the Maghreb and the Sahara. In September 2006 Zawahiri formally approved the formation of al-Qaeda in the Islamic Maghreb (AQIM) from the breakaway factions of two violent Algerian jihadist organizations— the Salafist Group for Preaching and Combat, and the GIA. The indiscriminate attacks of AQIM against civilians have alienated Algerians and North Africans in general and caused dissent among some of bin Laden's lieutenants. In an interview with a Qatari newspaper in February 2008, Abu Turab al-Jazairi, an Algerian and al-Qaeda lieutenant in northern Iraq, expressed his anger at AQIM's attacks at home. "The attacks in Algeria sparked animated debate here in Iraq," he said. "By God, had they told me they were planning to harm the Algerian president and his family, I would say, 'Blessings be upon them!' But explosions in the street, blood knee-deep, the killing of soldiers whose wages are not even enough for them to eat at third-rate restaurants . . . and calling this jihad? By God, it's sheer idiocy!"[28]

Al-Qaeda's appeal has also faded in Indonesia, with the demise of Jemaah Islamiya, a loose affiliate of al-Qaeda. All this seems to bolster the conclusion of the 2006 National Intelligence Estimate on Trends in Global Terrorism: Implications for the United States, that "the Muslim mainstream emerges as the most powerful weapon in the war on terror."[29]

Historically, organizations that alienated their base of support were eventually abandoned, even when they continued to operate. The post–World War II history of ultra-leftist terrorism in Europe provides a case in point. The neo-Marxist political agendas of these small middle-class groups—the Red Army Faction in Germany, the Red Brigades in Italy, Action Direct in France, and others—had little appeal among the citizens they hoped to mobilize. Similarly, the Islamist armed insurgency against the Egyptian and Algerian regimes in the 1980s and 1990s failed because the public became fed up with the violence and instability caused by the militants. In his memoirs, Zawahiri acknowledges this—and this is why he advises his cohorts to win Muslim hearts and minds, to foster a positive public image of the jihadist movement. According to Zawahiri, one of the lessons he learned in his lifelong struggle to establish a Qur'anic-based state is that without public support among Muslims, jihadis will be crushed in the shadows by "secular apostate rulers." Not only has al-Qaeda lost the hearts and minds of local Muslim populations, it has also lost the support of those with the greatest influence over their populations. A cultural revolution has been occurring within Islam, with key Muslim clerics, civil society leaders, and even former militants, stressing above all the ethical and moral foundations of the institution of jihad.

Moreover, al-Qaeda faces a revolt from within. Former high-ranking leaders within the bin Laden group blamed him directly for the turmoil engulfing the Muslim world and called for his quarantine. As I mentioned in the first chapter, the preacher and scholar Salman al-Awdah, a prominent Saudi mentor of bin Laden, reproached him publicly—on his website[30] and in comments on MBC, a Middle Eastern television network. "How many people were forced to flee their homes and how much blood was shed in the name of al-Qaeda?"[31] The reaction of his former pupil is not known, but the angry denunciation of Awdah by bin Laden's supporters left no doubt that it must have stung. The significance of this admonition can only be fully appreciated in the context of Awdah's position—he is an influential Salafi preacher with a large following in Saudi Arabia and abroad. In the 1990s the Saudi regime imprisoned him, along with four other leading clerics, for criticizing the kingdom's relationship with the United States, particularly the stationing of troops there after the 1991 Gulf War. Throughout the 1990s bin Laden defended Awdah and other incarcerated clerics and championed them as fellow Salafi travelers who shared his strict religious principles and worldview. In his Declaration of Jihad in August 1996, bin Laden listed the incarceration of Awdah by the Saudi authorities "on the advice of America" as one of his grievances against the United States.[32]

Awdah's critique stresses the moral failure of al-Qaeda more than any other, in part because of its timing. Theologically, his public reproach of bin Laden symbolizes a rejection by some of the most pivotal figures who powered revolutionary Islam. "You are responsible—brother Osama—for spreading *takfiri* [excommunication of Muslims] ideology and fostering a culture of suicide bombings that has caused bloodshed and suffering and brought ruin to entire Muslim communities and families."[33] "Is Islam only about guns and war? Have your means become the ends themselves?"[34]

Never before had bin Laden's legitimacy been subjected to such direct, withering censure by a respected Salafi scholar whose credibility as a radical cleric and defender of Muslim rights worldwide is unassailable. Adding insult to injury, Awdah praises those "brave hearts" and "courageous minds" that have defected from al-Qaeda and distanced themselves from its terrorism. "Many of your brethren in Egypt, Algeria and elsewhere have come to see the end of the road for al-Qaeda's ideology," he states. "They now realize how destructive and dangerous it is."[35]

Seeking to limit further damage, bin Laden felt obliged to apologize to Muslims over the murderous conduct of his associates in Iraq, Jordan, and Saudi Arabia. In an audiotape broadcast by Al Jazeera in October 2007, he conceded that his like-minded militants in Iraq and elsewhere "made mistakes."[36] He laid his personal authority and credibility on the line. In a rare moment of self-criticism, he advised "himself, Muslims in general, and brothers in al-Qaeda everywhere to avoid extremism" and to put the interests of the umma above those of tribe, party, and nation, including Shia/Sunni orientation. In addition, bin Laden openly scolded his followers in Iraq for their "fanaticism," using the Arabic word *taassub* (or extremism in allegiance to a parochial group or tribe that excludes others).[37]

Never before had bin Laden been so willing to air al-Qaeda's dirty linen. In the past, he and Zawahiri had privately urged individuals, such as Zarqawi, to avoid triggering sectarian violence.[38] By going public he was implicitly acknowledging his powerlessness over the local affiliates that may prove to be al-Qaeda's own worst enemy. Al-Qaeda's leaders do not exercise meaningful command over their far-flung followers and freelancers who pledge allegiance to the franchise but remain independent of it.

In his 2007 "message to the people of Iraq," bin Laden's openly expressed misgivings about his supporters reflect the gravity of al-Qaeda's crisis in Iraq and elsewhere.[39] Stressing unity over the current division and disarray, he urged Sunni tribes and other armed Iraqi Sunni groups to uphold their "tradition" of resisting foreign occupation, just as they resisted British colonialists in the last century. He called on them to stop fighting al-Qaeda members and unite against the real enemy—the US-led coalition.[40] Bin Laden even invoked the Prophet Muhammad to drive home his message of unity and forgiveness:

The Prophet, peace be upon him, said once: no one is perfect. We all make mistakes and we should seek forgiveness for these mistakes. Human beings commit wrongs, and wrongs always lead to conflict and dispute. Having acknowledged that we have made mistakes . . . [w]e can now seek to rectify these mistakes.[41]

Yet this self-anointed leader of all mujahideen failed to sway the Sunni Awakening Councils. Having expelled so many al-Qaeda members from their quarters at such great cost, Sunni communities appear unwilling to let them back into the fold.

It is not only Sunnis that have rejected the tactics of al-Qaeda in Mesopotamia. A 2007 ABC News/BBC/NHK poll revealed that 100 percent of those surveyed in Iraq—Sunni and Shia alike— found al-Qaeda attacks on civilians "unacceptable"; ninety-eight percent rejected the militants' attempts to gain control over areas in which they operated; and 97 percent opposed their attempts to recruit foreign fighters and bring them to Iraq.[42]

It has therefore fallen on other al-Qaeda lieutenants to do what bin Laden, in the end, could not. Abu Turab al-Jazairi, an al-Qaeda lieutenant in northern Iraq, conceded that his group suffered a major public relations problem because it "has been infiltrated by people who have harmed its reputation." He said that only about a third of the fighters who call themselves members of al-Qaeda in Iraq are trustworthy.[43]

Al-Qaeda's troubles transcend Iraq, Saudi Arabia, and Algeria. In November 2007 none other than Fadl went public in a series of articles serialized in two leading Arab newspapers, in which he criticized bin Laden and Zawahiri (cited before more than once). "Al-Qaeda committed suicide on 9/11 and lost its equilibrium, skilled leaders, and influence," Fadl announced. "September 11 was a failure."[44] For two weeks, Fadl's lengthy revisions dominated news cycles and engendered a fascinating debate among former and current militants. The overwhelming majority of those who rejoined the public debate agreed with Fadl.[45]

"Rationalizing jihad"—the title given to the assemblage of articles—is a pointed theological rebuttal of al-Qaeda transnational ideology and strategy. Fadl publicly called bin Laden and Zawahiri "false prophets" and "extremely immoral"; he accused them of being untrustworthy, treacherous, liars, and tyrants. As mentioned before, having spent years in the trenches with Zawahiri and bin Laden in Pakistan, Afghanistan, and Yemen in the 1980s and 1990s, Fadl knew whereof he spoke. Nonetheless, Fadl, currently in an Egyptian jail, responded to anyone who might question his credibility by saying that the litmus test is the theological legitimacy of his arguments, not whether he is incarcerated. Most of Zawahiri's imprisoned and exiled lieutenants and associates signed Fadl's rebuttal of al-Qaeda, thus further undermining the legitimacy and authority of bin Laden and Zawahiri. Clearly Fadl is not simply one more pundit spouting anti–al-Qaeda rhetoric. Although Fadl, who crafted what became known as "Al-Qaeda's Guide to Jihad," reserved his harshest criticism for Zawahiri, his former ally, he dismissed bin Laden as religiously illiterate and al-Qaeda as an empty shell which lacks a popular base of support and a religiously sanctioned mandate.[46]

In addition to questioning the moral character of his two former allies, Fadl delivered an assault on the ideology and practice of transnational jihad. The former mufti of militant jihad called on young Muslims to learn their religion, be wary of "false prophets," and desist from terrorism.[47] Fadl demystified bin Laden and Zawahiri, and brought them down from their moralizing perch.

Fadl is something of a legend among jihadis. He is the author of the two most often-cited core jihadist manifestos—"The Collector in Pursuing the Noble Science" and the "Pillar of Preparation for

Al-Jihad in the Way of God." He systemically cites Qur'anic verses and religious edicts to make his points. His is the most comprehensive indictment of transnational jihad and those who practice it.

In March 2008, Zawahiri published a rebuttal of Fadl's attack on al-Sahab Islamist media—in the form of a "letter" called "The exoneration." In this nearly 200-page letter, he accuses his former mentor of being in the service of US intelligence and a traitor to the cause. The response was designed to shift focus away from Fadl's theological challenge. He accuses his former mentor of writing his book "in the spirit of the Minister of the Interior," serving the Crusaders, Zionists, and apostate Arab leaders by attempting to anesthetize the mujahideen and force them out of the jihadi battlefield.[48]

Like bin Laden before him, Zawahiri continues to acknowledge that jihadis have made mistakes: "I neither condone the killing of innocent people nor claim that jihad is free of error. Muslim leaders during the time of the Prophet made mistakes, but the jihad goes on . . ."[49] However, Zawahiri quickly reassures his audience that nothing will "stand in the way of the fierce wave of jihadi revivalism that is shaking the Islamic world to its very foundation."[50] Far from being defeated, the jihadist movement is marching toward victory. He cites the September 11 attacks, as well as the battles in Iraq, Afghanistan, and Somalia as examples of progress being made in the war against America. All Fadl's critique reveals, Zawahiri tells his readers, is his own weakness.

At the end of 2008, Fadl penned a sequel, "The exposure," replying to Zawahiri's rebuttal; he also granted several interviews with top Arab news organizations.[51] In addition to assailing bin Laden and Zawahiri yet again with a barrage of insults, he made a number of overarching claims: that transnational jihad was merely a vehicle driven by an overambitious and ignorant bin Laden to punish the United States for stationing its troops in Saudi Arabia;

that Zawahiri's migration to transnational jihad was purely designed to keep him in the limelight after he destroyed Tanzim al-Jihad because of his recklessness and shortsightedness; that bin Laden ruled al-Qaeda like a personal fiefdom and tolerated no dissent; that on September 11 al-Qaeda had sowed the seeds of its own destruction and that, in his estimate, al-Qaeda is finished as a coherent and functioning organization; that al-Qaeda is a theological wasteland, because neither bin Laden nor Zawahiri possesses theological knowledge to interpret religious texts nor do they rely on prominent clerics and scholars to help them understand the rules and regulations of the institution of jihad.

One of the many things that Fadl reveals during this exchange was that he penned most of Zawahiri's manifestos and articles, including widely cited books. Similarly, he recalls an incident in Sudan in the early 1990s, when bin Laden inquired about a theological matter. He said that he recommended that bin Laden consult a particular text. He reports that bin Laden replied: "I can never get through a book."

And perhaps the most damning conclusion reached by Fadl is that politically motivated violence, whether against the near enemy or the far enemy, is counterproductive. Like all revolutions, jihadism ended up devouring its own children. Accordingly, he spends much time and space warning young Muslims against falling for the so-called Internet shaykhs who distort and manipulate religious texts to incite the young to join the fray.

To limit the damage Fadl had caused, Zawahiri was forced to stage an "online town hall meeting" to answer queries about al-Qaeda's conduct and future. Some of the thousands of questions by supporters expressed unease about the killing of civilians attributed to al-Qaeda and wanted assurances that bin Laden and Zawahiri did not violate theological principles, particularly targeting noncombatants, except under extreme conditions. Zawahiri chose to respond to one question: "Excuse me, Mr. Zawahiri, but who is killing, with your Excellency's blessing, the innocents in Baghdad, Morocco and Algeria? Do you consider the killing of women and children to be jihad?" "We have not killed innocents," replied Zawahiri. "In fact, we fight those who kill innocents. Those who kill innocents are the Americans, the Jews, the Russians, the French and their agents. Were we insane killers of innocents, it would be possible for us to kill thousands of them in the crowded markets, but we are confronting the enemies of the Muslims and targeting them, and during this, an innocent might fall."[52]

Knowing the debilitating damage that the loss of Muslim public support has exacted on his organization, Zawahiri has recently attempted to distance al-Qaeda from this shedding of civilian blood. In a largely overlooked statement marking the ninth anniversary of the September 11 attacks, Zawahiri urged Muslims to embrace jihad but avoid indiscriminate slaughter: "We disown any operation which a jihadi group carries out in which it doesn't show concern for the safety of the Muslims," he said in an audio message, a message designed to respond to critics and change how Muslims view al-Qaeda.[53]

Far from stemming the rising tide of Muslim opposition to al-Qaeda and its loose affiliates, the inquiries exposed bin Laden and Zawahiri's predicament not just among ordinary Muslims but also among fellow jihadis. They have reached a conceptual dead end. Lacking the strength to rejuvenate their fading cause, the best they can do is hope that one or a few of these disillusioned and radicalized young Muslims who live in the West, such as the failed Christmas Day bomber or the Times Square plotter, get to their bunkers and acquire the explosives training to carry out an attack back home. That is now the extent of al-Qaeda's strategic reach.

It would seem to be the end of a long road. Beginning in the late 1970s, the first wave of jihadis targeted the near enemy and fought prolonged and costly battles in Egypt and Algeria. By the mid-1990s it was over. Pro-Western Arab authoritarian governments had defeated the militant Islamists, killing, capturing, and expelling most of them. Picking up from where the first generation left off, the second wave (the so-called Afghan Arabs) shifted focus to the far enemy (the United States and its Western allies) in a desperate effort to gain Muslim public support. By 2003 that strategy was already in tatters. The irony is that the American invasion of Iraq occurred just when the second wave of attacking the far enemy was failing. Now al-Qaeda's military operations blur the lines between the near enemy and the far enemy, but it is all too clear—to most Muslims at least—that they have killed many more fellow Muslims than they have Westerners. Despite public denials, al-Qaeda no longer makes a distinction between attacks on Muslims and Westerners. Regardless of the reasons for the momentous conceptual-operational shift since 2003, it shows that al-Qaeda faces a deepening existential crisis, a moment of reckoning. In contrast to the theological debates that accompanied the launching of the first and second waves, neither bin Laden nor his propagandist and now apparent successor (no formal announcement has been made on the new emir to succeed bin Laden yet) Zawahiri has been able to rationalize this radical change of strategy. Transnational jihad, the raison d'être of al-Qaeda, is not a cause but a civil war.

5

Legacies and Aftershocks

There is plenty of evidence to suggest that defections, internal cleavages and leadership crises, military setbacks, theological assaults by leading radical clerics, as well as a sharp decline in public support among Muslims, have all sapped al-Qaeda's strength. This should not come as a surprise to anyone. We have seen that the global or transnational jihad of the al-Qaeda variety never had a viable social constituency or a popular base of support among Arabs and Muslims. Most Muslims do not subscribe to its rhetoric and ideology and have not joined its ranks. Declining public support in the Muslim world and the loss of legitimacy mean fewer skilled recruits and fewer shelters. As I show in this chapter, it has become clear that ordinary Muslims provide most of the intelligence about al-Qaeda suspects—a development that further illustrates the degree to which public opinion has shifted against it.

There might be a time lag before these factors take their final toll on al-Qaeda; it is difficult to set a time limit. But if history serves as a guide, revolutionary movements alienate public opinion at their own peril. Once the social foundation cracks beneath them, these movements slowly but steadily tumble into oblivion.

Equally important, al-Qaeda Central has suffered a catastrophic military defeat and now, of course, the loss of its founding leader. At the height of its power in the late 1990s, as we have seen, al-Qaeda comprised about 3,000 to 4,000 armed fighters. Today, its ranks have dwindled to around 300, if not fewer. According to former CIA Director and now Defense Secretary Leon Panetta, there are probably between 50 and 100 al-Qaeda fighters in Afghanistan.[1] But internal deliberations among US officials show that for all practical purposes there is no al-Qaeda in Afghanistan. In *Obama's Wars*, Bob Woodward cites the minutes of a meeting between Vice President Joe Biden and General David McKiernan, the commander of US forces in Afghanistan and International Security Assistance Force (ISAF), that took place during Biden's visit to the country. Biden reportedly asked McKiernan about al-Qaeda's presence in Afghanistan. "We haven't really seen an Arab here in a couple of years," McKiernan replied. Biden later asked front-line soldiers about the whereabouts of al-Qaeda, the main reason the Americans were in this country, and their responses were generally "I don't know."[2]

Local factions that subscribe to al-Qaeda's ideology and tactics exist in Pakistan, Yemen, Iraq, the Maghreb, Somalia, and elsewhere, though these factions are both liabilities and assets, and more local than transnational in outlook. Most victims are therefore Muslim civilians. The material links and connections between local branches and al-Qaeda are tenuous at best.

Only al-Qaeda in the Arabian Peninsula (known as the Yemen-based branch "AQAP") has shown any determination to plot attacks against the US homeland. In addition to the foiled ink bomb plot, AQAP succeeded in co-opting and arming a self-radicalized freelancer—the aforementioned Christmas Day bomber—allowing bin Laden to claim responsibility for the failed bombing. Senior officials of the Obama administration also accused the Pakistani Taliban (known as Tehrik-i-Taliban Pakistan, or TTP) of joining forces with al-Qaeda—some of whose senior leaders it may be hiding—and of facilitating, directing, and probably financing the failed car bombing in Times Square.[3]

Local factions give a false impression that al-Qaeda Central possesses the reach and capability to wage a borderless, global war despite exercising little operational control over them. They are nonetheless a force multiplier, a kind of strategic reserve, and an effective public relations tool that reaffirms the existence and relevance of al-Qaeda's transnational jihad.

In Yemen, Somalia, and al-Qaeda in the Islamic Maghreb (AQIM), these local factions seem to have given the organization a new lease on life. That lease is extremely tenuous and limited, yet its very existence reinforces widely held Western perceptions, or misperceptions of al-Qaeda's omnipotence, once again reinforcing the terrorism narrative and creating an overreaction. Moreover, these local factions are not an extension of al-Qaeda Central. They might share a similar ideological worldview, a similar rhetoric, and sometimes plot attacks against Western targets, but they are intensely local and dedicated to the overthrow of "renegade" Arab and Muslim rulers rather than external enemies. They would fight on both fronts if they could, but they cannot; when they do, they face an avalanche of internal and external resistance that puts their very survival at risk.

AQAP currently numbers between 50 and 300 core operatives in Yemen—as many as those in Pakistan, though they are younger and greener and lack the operational skills and training of members of al-Qaeda Central. Most are rookies with little combat experience. As I learned in my interviews with a dozen or so Yemeni al-Qaeda members in 2007 and 2008, most are only semi-literate and disfranchised; they lack the knowledge and sophistication of their predecessor generation, which fought in Afghanistan.

AQAP is something of a shadowy fringe group with no mass following. Nevertheless, led by Nasser al-Wahishi, a former private secretary to bin Laden and a disciplined and experienced operative, and by its military commander, Qassim al-Raymi, this Yemeni branch of al-Qaeda has become more organized and coherent. Its recent resurgence—that lease on life I mentioned—is closely linked to deteriorating social, economic, and political conditions in this benighted Arab country, as well as the dismantling of its neighboring Saudi group. Indeed AQAP was formed by a 2009 merger between the Saudi and Yemeni branches. The arrival of approximately two dozen seasoned and skilled fighters fleeing the lost cause in Saudi Arabia, some of whom had fought in Iraq and Afghanistan, provided operational expertise (for example, in bomb-making and media outreach) and a sense of purpose and initiative.

For example, Ibrahim Hassan al-Asiri, a Saudi operator of AQAP who studied chemistry at King Saud University, is believed to be the top technical expert and bomb-maker. American intelligence officials assert that he designed the foiled mail bombs in October 2010, as well as the underwear explosives. Asiri, the son of a Saudi military officer who grew up in Riyadh, is also suspected of having designed the body cavity bomb that killed his younger brother, Abdullah al-Asiri, in a failed attempt last year to assassinate Prince Muhammad bin Nayef, the top Saudi counterterrorism official.[4] The case of Ibrahim al-Asiri—who never made it to Afghanistan or Iraq and who acquired his bomb-making skills after he had joined AQAP—shows how one technical expert can serve as a force multiplier in a small group. He thrust AQAP into the spotlight and has rattled Obama's national security team.

AQAP has also gained notoriety because of Anwar al-Awlaki, a Yemeni-American cleric who received a great deal of media coverage for his purported ability to influence young Muslims living in Western societies, such as the Christmas Day bomber and the US army major who shot thirteen of his comrades in Fort Hood, Texas.

Despite that coverage Awlaki is unknown in Yemen and neighboring countries, and his importance is overblown by Washington—the Obama administration designated him as a legitimate target for assassination in April 2010. He does not possess any social constituency either inside or outside Yemen.

Despite a concerted campaign by the Yemeni authorities and the US military to destroy AQAP, the results have been mixed. Beginning in June 2010 AQAP carried out several attacks on security facilities in the south, killing about 100 members of the army and security forces and injuring many others. In one particular attack on June 19, 2010, AQAP displayed operational boldness and sophistication by launching simultaneous and coordinated raids on a Yemeni intelligence headquarters in Aden, freeing prisoners and killing eleven people; it also attacked two police stations in Zinjibar, killing three officers.[5]

Attacking security personnel and government officials represents a radical departure for al-Qaeda. After an American strike that killed Yemeni civilians and children in December 2009, its operators joined a protest rally broadcast live on Al Jazeera, in which a speaker, shouldering an AK-47 rifle, appealed to Yemeni counterterrorism officers: "Soldiers, you should know we do not want to fight you!" he shouted. "There is no issue between you and us. The issue is between us and America and its agents. Beware taking the side of America."[6]

For a brief moment, AQAP seemed to have learned from al-Qaeda's past, avoiding the trap of attacking the near enemy. Since the founding of AQAP, Wahishi and Raymi struggled to appeal to the people of Yemen, especially to the tribes that offered them shelter and protection, using an Internet magazine, videos, and interviews with local journalists. They encouraged al-Qaeda members to marry tribal women and mediated tribal disputes. In early 2007,

Zawahiri issued an audiotape addressed to "the noble and defiant tribes of Yemen," urging them to imitate the defiant Afghan Pashtun and Baluch tribes and to "support your mujahideen brothers."[7] Al-Qaeda learned a painful lesson in Iraq, that public support among Muslims, especially those of the dominant tribes, is vital to survival.

That moment did not last long. Marking a recent shift in its tactics, AQAP has declared all-out war against what it called the "tyrant" government of President Saleh and its soldiers "who terrorize Muslims, support the crusade against our country, and are the first line of American defense in Yemen."[8] In an audio message made in August 2010, AQAP also threatened to overthrow the Saudi monarchy "for its participation in the US-led crusade against Islam," and called on Saudi armed forces to attack Israel.[9] Now the al-Qaeda branch is waging a hit-and-run guerrilla insurgency campaign against the very Yemeni officers against whom it had vowed not to fight. In an audio message, al-Qaeda military commander Raymi declared his intent to establish the so-called Aden-Abyan Islamic Army (AAIA), a militia that aims to overthrow the Saleh regime—a tall order and one fraught with hubris, but nevertheless revealing of al-Qaeda's new tactics.[10]

Regardless of how al-Qaeda rationalizes it, the bloodletting is bound to turn ordinary Yemenis against them. Killing Yemeni soldiers will not endear AQAP to the people nor empower it. Once al-Qaeda's presence becomes too costly for its tribal hosts, it will not be welcome there. There is increasing evidence that in the Shabwa province the situation between the tribes and al-Qaeda is "tense." Al-Qaeda operators were forced to leave some villages and flee to the mountains after locals became weary of their presence and the unwanted attention and risk they had brought.[11]

Nevertheless, the growing brazenness and activism of al-Qaeda's Yemen branch and how this relates to the country's problems—deepening social and political crises, lawless tribes, and sclerotic state institutions—is alarming. For example, AQAP manipulates and leverages its tribal connections in the south to gain a foothold in the rising secessionist movement there. This strategy comes at a critical time in Yemen, a country engulfed in social and revolutionary upheaval designed to topple its ruling autocrat, currently being treated in a military hospital in Saudi Arabia for wounds sustained in an assassination attempt on his life on June 3, and transition to a more representative government. A separatist movement with a sizable segment of public opinion has gained momentum in the south, demanding a divorce from the union imposed by the north in the early 1990s. Jihadist chiefs, such as Khalid Abd al-Nabi, who in 1994 joined the Saleh government and battled the Socialists, have now turned against their former allies and directly support the secessionist forces in southern Yemen. Although Abd al-Nabi's goal is to establish a sharia-based state in southern Yemen, he is willing to ally himself with the devil—southern nationalists and Socialists—to defeat a greater evil, the Saleh regime. He travels widely and with impunity, along with a large armed escort.[12]

The al-Qaeda Yemen branch has tried to embed itself in these raging internal conflicts—particularly in the south, as mentioned, and mainly in the Shabwa and adjacent Abyan provinces, and the Marib province, east of Yemen's capital—and to position itself as the spearhead of opposition and armed resistance to the weak and hated central government in Sana'a. Since August 2010, government forces have battled the opposition and al-Qaeda elements to regain control over the city of Loudar in Abyan province; they have left dozens of dead in both camps and forced thousands from their homes.[13] Examining statements by the authorities and the rebels, it is difficult to tell whether the government is confronting only the secessionists, the jihadis, or both, though the separatists have denied joining forces with jihadis. Yemeni reporters in Abyan say that separatists and jihadis cooperate indirectly, facilitating each other's attacks against security forces despite their ideological differences.[14]

Yemen is a fragile state whose institutions have nearly reached their breaking point. In addition to the secessionist movement in the south, a rebellion in the north between the government and the Houthis has raged off and on since 2004, a conflict that has killed thousands and displaced hundreds of thousands.[15] Feuding tribes—some abetted by the authorities—have taken their toll on the central government's authority and credibility. The social and political upheaval is driven by the same reasons as in the south: economic grievances, massive unemployment, abject poverty, declining oil revenues, pervasive corruption, unsustainable water consumption, an incompetent bureaucracy, and a closed authoritarian political system. Al-Qaeda has found a fertile ground in the south in particular, because it has a large population of unemployed young men who are angry at the government's broken promises. In my interviews with these young Yemenis in the period since 2007, many have told me that they were drawn to al-Qaeda because of its radical allure and defiant rhetoric, and because the protracted autocratic system had failed them, abandoning them to a bleak life in the desert.

Statistics do not convey the extent of the social and economic misery in Yemen. Almost 40 percent of the country's 23 million people are unemployed. More than a third of the population is undernourished, and almost 50 percent live in abject poverty. Though it is the poorest Arab country, Yemen has one of the highest fertility rates in the region—upward of 3.7 percent. This means that today 60 percent of the population is under the age of 20. And while the population has increased at a very fast pace, resources have declined at an even faster rate. In the next few years, Yemen's oil—its major source of hard currency—will meet only the country's domestic consumption needs.

Despite pledges of support by Yemen's oil-producing Gulf neighbors and the international community, little progress has been achieved on the social and economic fronts. Less than 10 percent of the aid pledged by regional and international donors has been delivered to Yemen, because of the country's weak infrastructure and donor fatigue, and thus the living conditions for the majority of the Yemeni population continue to deteriorate.

The Saleh government—for that's what it still is—can no longer deliver social goods and patronage, historically the underpinnings of his rule, or manipulate tribal disputes that allow it to maintain an upper hand. After more than three decades in power, Saleh's ability to co-opt adversaries and maintain friends has shrunk considerably. US diplomatic cables leaked through WikiLeaks show a calculated effort by Saleh to use the country's daunting challenges as a kind of threat to coax the Americans into providing more aid. In a meeting with John Brennan in September 2009, Saleh pressed the American envoy to offer "deeds, not only words," to help ameliorate Yemen's social, economic, and political crisis. "Referencing the high poverty rate and illicit arms flow into both Yemen and Somalia, Saleh concluded by saying, 'if you don't help, this country will become worse than Somalia,'" reported the American ambassador, Stephen A. Seche, who attended the meeting.[16]

Given Yemen's weakening institutions, the status quo is unsustainable. The powerful democratic wave that shook the very foundation of Arab countries in 2011 threatens to end Saleh's 31 year rule. It is not only the survival of his regime at stake, but also the survival of the Yemeni state as a whole. Despite an effort to appoint himself president for life, Saleh said he would neither seek reelection nor hand over authority to his son once his current term ends in 2013. "No extension, no inheritance, no resetting the clock," Saleh stated. But those concessions failed to quell a widespread public revolution and a concerted effort to get rid of him following the ouster of Egyptian President Mubarak.

This grim scenario, however, does not mean that Yemen will disintegrate in the way that Somalia did, and hence risk becoming dominated by al-Qaeda. Despite the country's myriad problems, a frequent visitor to Yemen recognizes that the state still guides ordinary peoples' daily lives, either in the form of jobs, subsistence, health, education, or patronage. Although the government's resources have declined, it still provides employment and status (though with sometimes meager salaries) to many tribes, securing the state's hold over society.[17] Saudi Arabia's money and patronage sustain influential tribes and give them a stake in the existing order, as well as an incentive to prevent al-Qaeda from gaining a foothold. The problem is that by giving financial support directly to the tribes, the Saudis further weaken the hold and reach of the central government.[18]

If Saleh does not step down, Yemen will very likely plunge into all-out civil war, a scenario which perfectly suits AQAP's purposes. As Saleh recovers from his wounds, fighting between his loyalist troops and tribal opponents rages in the capital and some of the provinces. AQAP has already exploited the escalating violence to spread its tentacles, particularly in the restive south. Should Saleh return to Yemen, as his close aides say he will, Yemen would face a grim future.

Nevertheless, again, it is misleading to simplify Yemen's challenges or to portray it as a new headquarters of al-Qaeda and therefore of transnational jihad. Although AQAP is extremely dangerous—as shown by its offensive against the Yemeni authorities, the failed underwear bomber, and the foiled mail bombings—it poses a relatively slight challenge to Yemen and a limited security menace to the West. It does not possess the material, human means, or endurance to sustain a transnational campaign, nor does it have the assets or resources to build viable alliances with Yemeni tribes and a social welfare infrastructure.

In fact, AQAP is inherently dependent on the generosity and protection of tribes that are notorious for their shifting loyalties and allegiances. Tribal conduct is governed by pragmatism and survival in a harsh environment rather than by ideology. By the end of 2010, Awlaki's own tribe, together with more powerful tribes, reached a deal with the government to chase AQAP operators from its neighborhood. Now AQAP is militarily confronting the authorities and Western powers, a risky venture that will most likely degrade its capability. Regarding the Christmas Day attempt, President Obama said the Nigerian suspect had acted under orders from the al-Qaeda branch in Yemen, which "trained him, equipped him with those explosives and directed him to attack" the United States. Vowing to hold accountable all those involved, Obama sent a letter to Saleh, delivered by none other than General Petraeus, then head of the US Central Command, in which he pledged to double the $70 million in counterterrorism aid to the poverty-stricken country in 2009, a figure that does not include covert programs run by American special forces and the CIA.[19]

According to the American ambassador (as revealed in a leaked cable), although Saleh rejected General Petraeus's proposal to send US advisers along on Yemeni counterterrorism operations, he did not have any objection to that of moving away from the use of cruise missiles and instead allowing US fixed-wing bombers to circle outside Yemeni territory, "out of sight," and engage AQAP targets when actionable intelligence became available.[20]

The United States has already ramped up counterterrorism assistance to Yemen to $155 million in fiscal year 2010 and as much as $250 million in increased security support, from just $4.6 million in 2006.[21] Yemen now receives as much aid as Pakistan, a clear indication that the United States perceives AQAP as an increasing and "very serious threat," according to Mike Mullen, the Chairman of the Joint Chiefs of Staff.[22] Indeed, CIA analysts reportedly see al-Qaeda as a greater threat in Yemen than in Pakistan.[23] Before the failed Christmas Day bombing in 2009, the Obama administration had escalated its military operations in Yemen and since that time it has carried out at least four missile and air strikes in the mountains and deserts of the country, killing dozens of civilians along with a few alleged militants.[24]

There are some doubts as to how effective these attacks are. For example, in December 2009, a US Navy ship off the coast of Yemen fired a double cruise missile, according to a report by Amnesty International, hitting what was supposed to be an al-Qaeda training camp in the southern Abyan province. The first report from the Yemeni government claimed that its air force had killed "around 34" al-Qaeda fighters there and that others had been captured elsewhere in coordinated ground operations. The next day, Obama called Saleh to thank him for his cooperation and to pledge continuing American support, then he sent General Petraeus to Yemen to deliver personally to Saleh a package of enhanced counterterrorism and security assistance.

In the meeting with Petraeus mentioned previously, while Saleh praised the December strikes, he said that "mistakes were made" in the killing of civilians, according to leaked American diplomatic cables. Saleh lamented the use of cruise missiles that are "not very accurate" and welcomed the use of aircraft-deployed, precision-guided bombs instead. Having publicly claimed that they were

Yemeni strikes, Saleh's major concern was to keep up the ruse and prevent public backlash at home."We'll continue saying the bombs are ours, not yours," Saleh told Petraeus.[25]

The Yemeni press quickly identified the Americans as responsible for the attack; Yemenis gathered to express their outrage. Al-Qaeda joined the rally and tried to capitalize on public anger. An inquiry by the Yemeni parliament found that the strike had killed at least forty-one members of the Haydara family in one of two Bedouin encampments living near the makeshift al-Qaeda tent. Three more civilians were killed and nine were wounded four days later when they stepped on unexploded munitions from the missile. According to an investigation by Amnesty International, the missile had been loaded with cluster bombs, which disperse small munitions, some of which do not immediately explode, increasing the likelihood of civilian casualties. Human rights groups condemn their use.[26]

The December strikes may have killed fourteen al-Qaeda fighters, according to the Yemeni parliamentary commission, but they also instigated a public outcry against the Saleh regime and his American allies, and provided al-Qaeda with a propaganda opportunity. Further undermining the authority of the Saleh regime, a cruise missile was fired at a suspected gathering of al-Qaeda in Marib province, east of Sana'a in May 2010, killing Deputy Governor Jabir al-Shabwani (and four escorts). Shabwani had reportedly been seeking to persuade the militants to lay down their arms. Once again Amnesty International found evidence that cluster munitions were used in the attack. The killing of Shabwani, who was also a shaykh of the powerful Abeida tribe, almost triggered another rebellion against the Saleh regime. The Abeida—including Shabwani's father Shaykh Ali al-Shabwani—attacked oil installations, bombing an oil pipeline and cutting the lines of an electrical power station that provides a portion of power to the capital, causing blackouts lasting for several hours.[27]

Saleh, whom American officials described as "angry," agreed to tribal arbitration and paid blood money to Shabwani's family and tribe, a concession that prevented a bloodbath. According to several Yemeni opinion-makers with whom I spoke, the killing of Shabwani sent shock waves through the Saleh regime; it undermined the legitimacy of the hard-pressed government in the eyes of the tribes and the public at large. Saleh did not eject US forces from Yemen or call for a halt to its clandestine operations because he so desperately covets US assistance—as long as it does not destabilize his rule.

Leaked US diplomatic cables show Saleh laboring hard to leverage the fight against AQAP and internal enemies and to extract financial and material support from the United States, but on his own terms—imposing strict limits on American operations in his country, even as he helped disguise them as his own. For example, in the meeting with Brennan, Saleh repeatedly requested more funds and equipment to fight AQAP and the Houthi insurgency in the north as well. According to a cable by the American ambassador, Saleh told Brennan that "this war we're launching [against the Houthis] is a war on behalf of the United States . . . the Houthis are your enemies too," citing videos of Houthi followers chanting, "Death to America." America's failure to view the Houthis as terrorists and to support the Yemeni government, added Saleh, undermines its claims of friendship and cooperation. In his cable, the ambassador noted that the Houthis have not attacked US interests in the fighting between and the government forces that broke out in 2004.[28]

For Saleh, the US strike that killed Shabwani and his four escorts reinforced his worst fears about the danger inherent in unilateral American military tactics. Attempting to preempt internal criticism,

Yemen's foreign minister, Abu Bakr al-Qirbi, told Saudi-owned Arabic newspaper *al-Hayat* that while the United States has carried out attacks in the country, the air strikes ended in December because the "Yemeni government ascertained they weren't achieving results." Qirbi added that combating al-Qaeda is the responsibility of Yemen's security forces and that his government would not extradite the US-born Awlaki to the United States if he were captured.[29]

By fall 2010 it was widely reported that Obama's national security team had called for an escalation of operations in Yemen, including the use of armed drones: "We are looking to draw on all of the capabilities at our disposal," a senior official told the *Washington Post*. He described plans for "a ramp-up over a period of months."[30] An American counterterrorism official told the *Wall Street Journal* that Special Operations forces and the CIA were positioning equipment, drones, and personnel in Yemen, Djibouti, Kenya, and Ethiopia, in an effort to step up operations against AQAP and al-Shabab.[31]

Furthermore, the air cargo bomb plot of October 2010 added a sense of urgency to the Obama administration's review of expanded military options, which included putting elite assassination squads under CIA authority.[32] The *Wall Street Journal* cited unnamed officials as saying support was growing within the administration to shift operational control to the CIA, a move that would allow the Agency to strike at suspected targets in Yemen with greater stealth and speed, and without the explicit blessing of the Saleh government. Moreover, the White House was already considering adding armed CIA drones to its arsenal in Yemen, mirroring the Agency's Pakistan campaign.[33] This proposed escalation supplemented the presence of Special Operations teams already in place in Yemen that had played an expanded role in the country, including an effort to kill suspected al-Qaeda members such as Asiri and Awlaki.[34]

Underlying the American strategy are assumptions that do not fully recognize the complexity of the situation in Yemen, or the inherent risks of deepening US military involvement there. A rash American response might complicate matters further for the Yemeni government as well. In fact, AQAP's persistent efforts to attack the United States seem designed to force its military intervention in Yemen. That scenario would fuel rising anti-American sentiment there and supply al-Qaeda with additional recruits and public support. Saleh has warned senior American interlocutors that deepening military involvement in Yemen might prove costly in terms of casualties. In a previously cited meeting with Obama's counterterrorism adviser, Brennan, Saleh pledged unfettered access to Yemen's national territory for US operations against AQAP. "Highlighting the potential for a future AQAP attack on the US Embassy or other Western targets, Saleh said, 'I have given you an open door on terrorism, so I am not responsible,'" concluded a cable by the American ambassador.[35]

Since the 1990s, Yemen has provided a fertile breeding ground for jihadis. The Saleh government has, in turn, used them intermittently to destabilize its adversaries, including the Socialists and separatists in the south. After September 11, most jihadis accepted a tacit deal offered by the authorities that prohibited them from carrying out attacks within Yemen but which was vague about activities outside the country.

The co-existence deal recently collapsed due to the convergence of several factors: (1) the inability (or unwillingness) of the Saleh government to provide jobs and benefits promised to former jihadist chiefs such as Khalid Abd al-Nabi; (2) the deteriorating socioeconomic and political conditions throughout Yemen and the ensuing growth of armed insurgencies; (3) and the merger between the Saudi branch and the Yemen branch of al-Qaeda into the AQAP.

Despite the present dangers posed by AQAP, it seriously threatens neither the survival of the Yemen government nor vital Western security interests. There is a consensus among scholars who study Yemen, such as Sheila Weir, formerly of the London Museum; Sheila Carapico at the American University in Cairo; Nora Colton at the University of East London; Martha Mundy at the London School of Economics; and Steve Caton at Harvard University, that al-Qaeda is one of Yemen's least serious challenges. Instead of squandering precious resources on combating AQAP, a toothless and viscous entity, these prominent scholars counsel investment in institution-building, political economy, and good governance as more effective remedies for extremism.

The danger of a reinvigorated al-Qaeda hinges on whether Saleh decides to retain power and confront his people, as did his Libyan counterpart Qaddafi. The likelihood of armed clashes and civil war would provide AQAP with a fertile environment to strengthen its position as a spearhead of resistance against the Saleh regime.

American counterterrorism analysts assert that AQAP is now collaborating more closely than ever with allies in Pakistan and Somalia to plot attacks against the West, but their evidence is sketchy and is based more on risk assessment and inference than it is on hard facts. The few plots instigated by AQAP, such as the attack on the Saudi counterterrorism chief, the underwear bomber, and the air cargo bomb plot, seem to be the handiwork of the main bomb-maker in the group: Asiri. Indeed, some of the same officials who claim that there are links and connections between AQAP and Somalia's al-Shabab qualify this by adding that the "trajectory" points in "that direction," and that this is "hard to measure in an absolute way."[36] Somalia has not had a functioning government or economy for two decades, and rival warlords continue to battle for supremacy. There is a real danger that al-Shabab may overrun

Somalia and establish Taliban-like governance. But this is a different challenge altogether unless Yemen descends into all-out civil war.

One does not have to be a specialist on jihadist groups to appreciate the difficulties inherent in operational collaboration between local branches and al-Qaeda Central. Neither bin Laden nor now Zawahiri has been in a position to coordinate tactics and specific attacks. They have played almost no operational role in plotting specific terrorist activities; instead they act mainly as preachers and ideologues of transnational jihad. This conclusion has been buttressed by the "aspirational" nature of the various plots discovered in bin Laden's compound in Pakistan. According to CIA Director Leon Panetta, bin Laden's few surviving lieutenants in Pakistan were so demoralized that they had pleaded with him to resurface. Bin Laden ignored the plea, according to Panetta, choosing personal safety and security—at least for a time—over organizational survival. Surely if bin Laden and Zawahiri could not come to the aid of their own struggling lieutenants and coordinate war plans, they were and are unlikely to coordinate attacks with allies in distant lands.

Regardless of how dangerous AQAP might become, it remains first and foremost a Yemeni problem, one that must be tackled from within. Yemen itself must take the lead in educating and mobilizing public opinion, including the tribes, about the danger of al-Qaeda. Fortunately, there is very little public sympathy and support for al-Qaeda; the few tribes that provide it with shelter do so from adherence to a tribal code of hospitality and honor rather than ideology, and out of a shared sense of opposition to the Saleh regime. If these tribes are engaged and rewarded, they would send al-Qaeda's fighters packing back to the mountains.

But that is more easily said than done and will require greater support from the international community. Although US officials pay lip service to the benefits of socioeconomic and political development, they act as if confronting al-Qaeda requires mainly counterterrorism measures. In June 2010 the White House announced it was tripling its humanitarian assistance to Yemen, to $42.5 million—a paltry sum, given the country's urgent need and given that the United States may provide as much as $250 million in increased counterterrorism security assistance. As shown previously, there is increasing evidence that the Obama administration has put CIA and Special Operations troops in charge of the Yemen station. Western visitors at the American Embassy in Sana'a have noticed that it is increasingly crowded with military personnel and intelligence operatives—the so-called shadow warriors.[37]

Yemen has become a testing ground for the approach designed by Brennan, who says that America will rely on the "scalpel" instead of on Bush's "hammer." According to the *New York Times*, under the Obama administration, the CIA has been transformed into a paramilitary organization; even the Pentagon is becoming more like the CIA. Across the Middle East and elsewhere, Special Forces have expanded and widened their operations, with little congressional oversight. Some former top CIA and military officers say they are concerned because "there are not clear rules."[38]

Beyond the legal issues involved, over-reliance on unilateral counterterrorism exacerbates America's security dilemma in Yemen and beyond. While such measures might kill AQAP fighters, they also alienate Muslim opinion, opening the door to extremist groups. Edmund J. Hull, US ambassador to Yemen from 2001 to 2004, cautioned that American policy must not rely too heavily on force against al-Qaeda: "I'm concerned that counterterrorism is defined as an intelligence and military program. To be successful in the long run, we have to take a far broader approach that emphasizes political, social and economic forces."[39] Barbara Bodine, US ambassador to Yemen from 1997 to 2011 and a shrewd observer of the country, said that drone attacks "most assuredly do far more harm than good."[40] "If George W. Bush is remembered by getting America stuck in Afghanistan and Iraq," said Awlaki in an Internet statement, "it's looking like Obama wants to be remembered as the president who got America stuck in Yemen."[41]

In January 2010, nearly 200 prominent clerics in Yemen signed a statement pledging to lead a jihad against any foreign forces that occupied their country, sending a clear message that the United States should not expand military and intelligence cooperation with the Saleh regime.[42] Firsthand reports from Yemen indicate that such cooperation has turned more Yemenis against the embattled Saleh regime.[43] Of all Arabs, Yemenis currently voice the strongest anti-American sentiment. Any policy that neglects the local context and social conditions will help al-Qaeda.

So far, this has been the case. The terrorism narrative views Yemen through a narrow prism, as a kind of battlefront, along lines similar to Afghanistan, Pakistan, and Somalia. Everything is an extension of bin Laden's transnational jihad against the West; the local context is submerged within the global, and differences are overlooked or subordinated. The narrative follows a one-size-fits-all model that elevates al-Qaeda to the ranks of the major powers. AQAP has indeed actively plotted attacks against Western targets; but this does not make it an extension of al-Qaeda Central. Moreover, it is now pitted in a military confrontation with the Yemeni authorities, a clash that will likely take a heavy toll on the small organization, particularly if Saleh relinquishes power, as he says he will. That would herald the beginning of the end of AQAP.

Finally, there is Awlaki, who has emerged as a central conspiratorial figure in the eyes of American and British intelligence. In April 2010, as I mentioned, the Obama administration designated him as a legitimate target for assassination, despite the fact that he is an American citizen. That designation has taken on a greater degree of menacing credibility. Three days after American commandos killed bin Laden, a US drone launched a missile strike in a remote region of Yemen. Awlaki was the target. According to US officials, the strike, the first known attack in the country by the American military for nearly a year, does not appear to have killed Awlaki but may have killed members of AQAP.[44] Awlaki is the West's Public Enemy No. 1, declared Jonathan Evans, head of Britain's MI5 domestic security service: "The operational involvement of Yemen-based preacher Anwar al-Awlaki with al-Qaeda is of particular concern given his wide circle of adherents in the West, including in the UK," said Evans in a rare speech.[45] Increasingly, Awlaki is being depicted by Western intelligence officials as a threat on the same scale as bin Laden and Zawahiri. He was the only militant leader singled out in October 2010 in the first public speech given by Sir John Sawers, and the first speech ever made by a head of Britain's MI6. Sawers described "reading, every day, intelligence reports describing the plotting of terrorists who are bent on maiming and murdering people in this country" and cited Awlaki and Yemen as increasingly dangerous. "From his remote base in Yemen," he said, Awlaki "broadcasts propaganda and terrorist instruction in fluent English, over the Internet."[46]

Awlaki has been implicated in several terrorist plots in the United States and Britain, but he is no Osama bin Laden. He has few followers in Yemen and in the wider Arab and Muslim world; his message is specifically directed to a few young, disaffected Muslims living in Western societies. These young men turn to Awlaki and other clerics for confirmation of their anger and alienation. He fills an ideological vacuum for those who feel their Islamic identity is under threat.

Killing Awlaki would transform the fugitive preacher into a martyr and likely further poison Yemeni public opinion against the

United States. A more effective measure would be to shut down Awlaki's propaganda shop by convincing the tribe that gives him shelter, the Awalik in southern Yemen, to turn him over to the Yemeni authorities. In an interview with the *Guardian*, Sultan Farid bin Babaker, the leader of the tribe, was asked why he allowed a wanted man such as Awlaki to live among them. Bin Babaker replied that the cleric had committed no crimes in the community. Moreover, the Yemeni government had not asked him to hand Awlaki over. Were they to do so, Babaker noted, "we will think about it."[47]

Babaker is a close ally of the Yemeni government and a deal might be reached by which Awlaki would be accorded a chance to defend himself and receive due process inside Yemen following tribal tradition. This may prove Awlaki's best chance. After the failed air cargo bombings in October 2010, Yemen officially charged Awlaki with inciting the killing of foreigners and with membership in an armed gang, and plans to prosecute him in absentia.[48]

Indeed, there is growing determination on the part of the Yemeni authorities to bring Awlaki to justice, though that won't happen so long as Saleh clings to power. For Saleh, Awlaki's presence is a bargaining chip with the Western powers. This fact was not lost on AQAP, which had already warned kinsmen of the Awlaki tribe against collaborating with the government in a statement posted on an Islamist website. "Whoever decides to stand with [the West and the government] and be subservient to their demands should be wary of God's punishment," it read ominously.[49]

Before the air cargo plots, Yemeni security forces and local tribes had combed the mountainous Said district in Shabwa, looking for al-Qaeda operatives, according to a senior security official there; members of the Awlakis' own tribe helped with the search. The Shabwa governor and the Awlaki clan have signed an agreement, according to which they would "expel al-Qaeda elements from their territories and mount a joint operation with the army (to do so)," he added.[50] Moreover, mediation by tribal chieftains facilitated the surrender of more than a dozen al-Qaeda fighters and lieutenants to Yemen's security agencies in the Abyan province, an indication of the government's intention to co-opt the tribes and pressure al-Qaeda.[51] After the air cargo plot, more al-Qaeda fighters turned themselves over to the Yemeni authorities with the help of tribal mediation.[52] In November 2010, a tribal coalition led by the Dakhil tribe, one of the two biggest tribes in Yemen, pledged to join the authorities in the fight against al-Qaeda members—"deviants who ruin the reputation of the Yemeni tribes and state."[53]

The tribes hold the key to deactivating the al-Qaeda minefield in Yemen. Any strategy that does not fully involve them will most likely fail. To spite the government, the tribes have provided AQAP with shelter and refuge, but there is no substantial support for al-Qaeda in Yemen and, if history offers any guide, the tribes will side with whoever can offer them more. The post-Saleh government needs to construct a broad national coalition, one that includes the vibrant opposition and the tribes, an alliance that must be fully backed by Yemen's Gulf neighbors, particularly Saudi Arabia, and the international community, including the United States and Britain.

Although the current turmoil in Yemen works to the benefit of Awlaki and AQAP, there is no ideological affinity between them and the tribes. The anti-Saleh opposition—which consists of a broad spectrum of nationalist and Islamist voices—must be empowered to negotiate directly with the tribes, in order to persuade them to cease providing shelter to Awlaki and AQAP. Left to his own devices, Saleh, in whatever time he has left, will not act to institute reforms. He is the major obstacle to enacting change in this poorest Arab country. According to my interviews with reformists and activists from Yemen, only a national unity government without Saleh at the helm, one which represents most segments of society and political colors, will be able to begin to tackle the country's deepening structural social crisis and al-Qaeda as well; there is no other safe way out of the tunnel.

Although complicated and messy, long-term measures—as opposed to short-term counterterrorism measures—will ultimately turn the people of Yemen against Awlaki and his associates. Fearful of unilateral US military action, Yemeni officials have called for international assistance in their battle against al-Qaeda (and complained that the United States does not fully share intelligence with them).[54] It would be naïve to expect Saleh's government to wage all-out war against al-Qaeda; it does not possess the political will or the resources to do this. His survival is at stake. One of the significant insights that emerges from leaked American diplomatic cables is Saleh's effort to use the fight against AQAP to his own advantage and to set strict limits on American military tactics.

In late May 2011, days before the attempt on his life, as pressure built upon Saleh to sign a deal to step down that had been brokered by a regional bloc called the Gulf Cooperation Council—a deal that granted him immunity from prosecution if he left within 30 days of signing. He condemned the proposal as "a coup" and warned Yemen's American and European "friends" that his departure would open the door for al-Qaeda. "To the Americans and Europeans, al-Qaida is coming and it will take control," he said in a televised address to members of the security forces. "The future will be worse than the present."[55]

Driven by speculation and assessment, a risky business, the terrorism narrative focuses on the immediate. Every plot is ascribed to an all-powerful al-Qaeda Central, whose tentacles reach everywhere. While top US intelligence officials brief lawmakers that al-Qaeda is operationally and militarily in disarray, politicians continue to stress the gravity of its strategic threat. The risk of another attack, regardless of how small, inhibits American leaders, including President Obama, from leveling with the American people about the nature of challenge posed by al-Qaeda and like-minded factions. A decade after September 11, overreaction is still the hallmark of the US War on Terror.

There remains a disconnect between the consensus within the intelligence community and the foreign policy team, which still considers terrorism the number one enemy. For example, the 2008 National Defense Strategy approved by former Defense Secretary Robert M. Gates states that even winning the conflicts in Iraq and Afghanistan will not end America's long war against violent extremism. He embraced the long war idea that his predecessor, Donald H. Rumsfeld, invoked to equate the fight against terrorism with the fights against Soviet communism and Nazi fascism. One would have expected him to offer a less ideological, more nuanced, and more analytically thoughtful assessment of transnational jihad in general and of the changing nature and seriousness of al-Qaeda's challenge in a highly hostile geopolitical context in particular.

Two months after Secretary Clinton pronounced al-Qaeda a potent strategic threat to US national security—the pronouncement with which I began this book—former CIA Director Leon Panetta said that the bin Laden group is in disarray. "It's pretty clear from the intelligence we are getting that they are having a very difficult time putting together any kind of command and control, and they are scrambling."[56] Panetta drew a portrait of a leaderless organization that does not possess the capacity to coordinate attacks outside its narrow base along the Pakistan-Afghan border. Of all officials in charge of waging the so-called War on Terror, Panetta came closest to admitting that al-Qaeda is no longer a force to be reckoned with.[57] The materials seized in the raid on bin Laden's compound confirm a portrait of al-Qaeda as a militarily crippled organization with hardly any operational capability to coordinate attacks outside its narrow base along the Pakistan-Afghan border.

But, inevitably, even Panetta could not abandon the narrative completely. While al-Qaeda's leadership and resources have been greatly diminished, it will continue to look for ways to strike inside the United States, he said, using individual recruits who lack criminal records or known ties to terrorist groups. He cited the usual suspects.[58] The State Department's 2009 Country Reports on Terrorism echoed Panetta's conclusion: Although al-Qaeda's core in Pakistan suffered "significant setbacks," it was "actively" engaged in operational plotting against the United States and continues to recruit individuals from western Europe and North America.[59]

The cases cited by Panetta and the State Department are the ones that I've mentioned throughout this history—the failed Christmas Day bombing, the underwear bomber, and the air-cargo attempt. Let me now turn to them in detail to see what further light they and other attempts shed on the changing nature of transnational jihad.

The bin Laden group developed in the 1990s in a particular context and with a highly centralized and hierarchal structure. Now it has morphed into a fluid, globalized ideological label that rests on two interrelated claims—first, that the West, particularly America and Britain, is waging a crusade against Islam and Muslims and blocking the restoration of the Islamic caliphate; and second, that it is the personal duty of every Muslim to join in jihad against the enemies of Islam and assist in establishing Qur'anic-based states.

Some still believe this because al-Qaeda's ideology sanctions the killing of the enemies of Islam, including civilians, and therefore adapts easily to different temperaments, backgrounds, and concepts of victimhood. Al-Qaeda's top-down recruitment of would-be terrorists has been, for the most part, replaced by a bottom-up process, a product of rising tensions and hostilities.

The recent cases show clearly how al-Qaeda has bridged class, educational barriers, and location. Faisal Shahzad, the Times Square bomber, was a solid member of the middle class with a master's degree in business administration who seemed fully integrated into American life; Najibullah Zazi, who pleaded guilty in February 2010 to plotting a number of bombings in New York, an Afghan immigrant and a Denver-area airport shuttle driver, was a US resident; the Nigerian Abdulmutallab, the underwear bomber, was an engineering graduate of London University; Fort Hood's Major Nidal Malik Hasan; five American Muslims from Northern Virginia; the Jordanian doctor Humam al-Balawi, an informant-turned-suicide-bomber who killed seven US intelligence agents on the CIA base in Khost Province, near the Afghan-Pakistan border; and the Stockholm suicide bomber, Taimur Abdulwahab al-Abdaly, who blew himself up in Sweden, studied in Britain, and was happily married with three children.

Most of these individuals had in one characteristic in common: they had radicalized themselves—enraged by a specific grievance, and they were also fully integrated into life in the West. They seem to have internalized the kind of religious-political worldview that justified their taking matters into their own hands—in short, a license to kill.

After his Times Square attempt, Shahzad reportedly told investigators that he acted out of anger over the CIA's Predator strikes in Pakistan, especially a drone attack that took place while he was visiting in the country.[60] According to his family, Dr. Balawi had been enraged by Israel's 2008 war in Gaza and this had driven him to militancy.[61] Fort Hood's Major Hasan, a US-born army psychiatrist, publicly raged against the American invasion of Iraq and Afghanistan.[62] The war in Afghanistan-Pakistan led the five Muslims from Northern Virginia to Pakistan's battlefields.[63] In March, a Pakistani-American named David C. Headley pleaded guilty to helping plan the 2008 terrorist attacks in Mumbai.[64]

They eventually turned to al-Qaeda's mentors, such as Awlaki, for guidance and reassurance. They initiated the contact. For example,

Shahzad reportedly told investigators that he had sought out extremist factions in Pakistan to acquire bomb-making techniques and, most probably, religious legitimacy. When he made his guilty plea in US District Court in Manhattan, he told Judge Miriam Goldman Cedarbaum that he was "avenging" the war in Afghanistan and US intervention in Pakistan, Iraq, Yemen, and Somalia. "I am part of the answer to the U.S. terrorizing the Muslim nations and the Muslim people."[65]

When pressed by Judge Cedarbaum as to why he would target civilians if his goal was to retaliate against American troops, Shahzad answered, "Well, the drone hits in Afghanistan and Iraq, they don't see children, they don't see anybody. They kill women, children, they kill everybody. It's a war, and in war, they kill people. They're killing all Muslims."[66]

Shahzad is a classic example of bottom-up recruitment, yet while US officials and terrorism experts focus exclusively on Shahzad's connection with the Pakistani Taliban, they ignore how the War on Terror fuels homegrown radicalization in Western societies. Of the hundreds of media reports on Shahzad, only a *New York Times* article entitled "Fighting Terrorism, Creating Terrorists" drew a link between the bombing attempts and the War on Terror. According to the *Times*, "in case after case, plotters have cited America's still-growing military entanglement in the Muslim world as proof that the United States is at war with Islam."[67] Several homegrown suspects found guilty by US courts—and whom I met as part of their defense team—specifically mentioned America's "aggression" and "occupation" of Muslim lands in Iraq and Afghanistan as their justification; they seemed more driven by grievances stemming from the War on Terror than by theological and ideological considerations—above all, they felt a sense of solidarity with their persecuted Muslim brethren. "One has to understand where I'm coming from," Shahzad said in an unusual departure from tightly scripted guilty pleas, while sitting with his defense attorney and prosecutors sitting in federal court. "I consider myself . . . a Muslim soldier."[68] Four months later, after Judge Cedarbaum sentenced Shahzad to life in prison, he said Muslims have been defending their people and their lands. If that makes them terrorists, "then we will terrorize you." When the judge urged him to reflect on his actions and "whether the Koran wants you to kill lots of people," Shahzad replied, "The Koran gives us the right to defend, and that's what I am doing."[69]

Shahzad is not unique. Najibullah Zazi, who pleaded guilty to plotting to detonate a bomb in a New York subway, is also an example of bottom-up recruitment. Like Shahzad, Zazi told the court that in August 2008 he decided to go with friends to Pakistan to join the Taliban in fighting the US invasion of Afghanistan. He went to the Taliban, not the other way around, and while in Pakistan he was persuaded by al-Qaeda operatives to return to America to be a suicide bomber.[70] "I would sacrifice myself to bring attention to what the United States was doing to civilians in Afghanistan by sacrificing my soul for the sake of saving their souls," Zazi told the court.[71]

Officials and experts have focused exclusively on the al-Qaeda plot organized by Saleh al-Somali, Rashid Rauf, and Adnan G. el-Shukrijumah, the leader and a US citizen—who were then leaders of al-Qaeda's "external operations" program. "They've reconstituted. They have a new cadre of people. They're younger, just as motivated," former FBI agent Jack Cloonan said of al-Qaeda.[72] Cloonan and others do not have anything to say about the reasons—such as about Zazi's journey from the United States to Pakistan. Before that journey, al-Qaeda had no access to or hold over Zazi. He voluntarily went to Pakistan to fight with the Taliban against Western troops in Afghanistan and fell into the lap of Shukrijumah, who sent him back to the United States on a suicide mission.

Similarly, the five Virginia men traveled to Pakistan: Abdulmutallab flew to Yemen and there made contact with the al-Qaeda branch and Awlaki. There were warning signals. The families of the five Virginia men—and Abdulmutallab's father—warned the US authorities about their sons' radicalization.[73] Major Hasan had indirectly pleaded to be medicated and treated before he murdered his comrades.[74]

Likewise, the Pakistani-born suspect charged in an alleged plot to blow up the Washington subway system in October 2010 had come to the FBI's attention because he had asked people about ways to fight US troops in Afghanistan and Pakistan, according to unsealed court records.[75] Farooque Ahmed, a 34-year-old naturalized US citizen, reportedly hoped to journey to his native country and to fight there. The Taliban and al-Qaeda did not recruit him. He was lured by an e-mail from an FBI agent to a first meeting in April 2010 in the lobby of a hotel near Washington Dulles International Airport and entrapped in a conspiracy. Over the next seven months, Ahmed reportedly told undercover FBI operatives posing as terrorists that he was ready to martyr himself in battle and "wanted to kill as many military personnel as possible," the affidavit said.[76]

Ahmed is another example of bottom-up radicalization. Although it is too early to establish definite motivation, the 12-page sworn affidavit clearly indicates that Ahmed, an engineer with a bachelor's degree from the City College of New York, was radicalized by the conflict in Afghanistan-Pakistan. His ultimate goal, according to the affidavit, was to travel "to Afghanistan to fight and kill Americans."[77] Lacking access to or contact with either the Taliban or al-Qaeda, Ahmed and an associate allegedly tried to contact a terror group to help them travel to Afghanistan or Pakistan, the FBI said.[78] Investigators orchestrated a fake terror plot that allegedly ensnared him—the latest sting operation hatched by the

FBI—and Ahmed fell into it, implicating himself in an amateurish manner in the terror plot.[79] The detailed account provided by the FBI shows that he was a major part of the plot, providing surveillance and reconnaissance and offering his opinion on how to produce the most casualties.[80]

University student Roshonara Choudhry, 21, provides yet another example. According to the transcripts published in the British *Guardian*, Choudhry, a promising young student at King's College, attempted to assassinate former British minister Stephen Timms by stabbing him twice in the stomach because she held him personally accountable for voting in favor of the Iraq war. After being disarmed by Timms' assistant, Choudhry told detectives the stabbing was "to get revenge for the people of Iraq."[81]

Similarly, friends of Sweden suicide bomber Taimur al-Abdaly, 28, describe him as someone who enjoyed playing basketball and a good party, yet who had become increasingly angry over the past few years. Qadeer Baksh, chairman of the Luton Islamic Centre (also known as the al-Ghurabaa mosque) where Abdaly prayed for a short while, said that the bomber believed Western governments had no right to intervene militarily in Iraq and Afghanistan and urged others to "take matters into their own hands" because traditional mosques were not proactive enough.[82] Three weeks before the attack, Abdaly vanished from his home with no explanation to his wife and three young children. British security and intelligence sources said there was no evidence or indication that he was directed by any al-Qaeda leader and that Abdaly had probably planned his own attack.[83]

The phenomenon of bottom-up radicalization raises serious questions about whether al-Qaeda has "reconstituted" itself and has "a new cadre of people," as the dominant terrorism narrative claims, or become dependent on a few deluded, angry Muslim men and women. If anything, bottom-up, homegrown recruitment shows the gravity of al-Qaeda's structural crisis. It appears to be more of a side effect of the War on Terror than an indication of the organization's "adaptation" and "resilience."

Bottom-up recruitment is a marginal phenomenon and has not helped al-Qaeda's strategic operational predicament, or helped it to emerge from its crisis of legitimacy. After the Christmas Day bombing attempt, bin Laden issued an audiotape claiming responsibility and vowing further attacks, an assertion that exposes his shrinking assets and options.[84] Bin Laden's claim matters less than the fact that he was (at that point) still alive and transmitting, and still consumed by a relentless, systematic drive to promote al-Qaeda's transnational ideology and to kill a large number of American civilians.

Abdulmutallab, Zazi, Shahzad, and Abdaly keep al-Qaeda in the limelight and give a false sense of durability and potency. Much of the confusion stems from the lack of conceptual differentiation and distinction between al-Qaeda Central and various independent local branches, fellow travelers, and freelancers. Alarming as it is, the riddle of homegrown radicalization can only be solved by critically examining existing evidence and the changing social contours of militancy—not by lumping it all together.

The terrorism narrative, of course, recognizes no such distinctions. For example, the most recent US National Security Strategy, together with the State Department's annual report on terrorism, explicitly recognizes homegrown terrorism as a threat. Commenting on the new strategy, Obama's chief National Security Adviser, John Brennan, said that al-Qaeda is recruiting individuals with little training, attempting relatively unsophisticated attacks and seeking people already living in the United States to launch such attacks. "They are seeking foot soldiers who might slip through our defense,"

Brennan adds. "As our enemy adapts and evolves their tactics, so must we constantly adapt and evolve ours."[85] Like the National Security Strategy, the State Department report on terrorism paints a bleak picture of homegrown radicalization, noting an increase in the number of cases of Americans becoming operatives for foreign terrorist organizations.[86]

Similarly, some terrorism pundits argue that al-Qaeda poses as potent a threat to the US homeland as it did on the morning of September 11. As proof, they offer the rapid evolution of homegrown terrorism in the United States, a trend that, in their opinion, affects radicalized Americans from all walks of life. In a report assessing the terrorist threat, Bruce Hoffman and Peter Bergen assert that today al-Qaeda is more complex and more diverse than at any time over the past nine years, and that it possesses the capacity to kill dozens, even hundreds, of Americans in a single attack. More alarming in their view is the increasingly prominent role in planning and operations that American citizens and residents play in the leadership of al-Qaeda and its allies, and the higher numbers of people joining these groups.[87]

Hoffman and Bergen emphasize what they call the "Americanization" of al-Qaeda's leadership.[88] This heralds a new phase in the War on Terror: "the new frontiers have become the streets of Bridgeport, Denver, Minneapolis, and other big and small communities across America."[89] To keep them apprised of the changing face of terrorism, Hoffman and Bergen call on the nation's 50,000 public-safety agencies—the national security–industrial complex—to implement a significant training and information-sharing program, one that might meet the challenge "that America neglects at its peril."[90]

One gets the impression after reading Hoffman and Bergen's report that America is facing a veritable army of radicalized homegrown teens whose "only common denominator appears to be a newfound hatred for their native or adopted country, a degree of dangerous malleability, and a religious fervor justifying or legitimizing violence."[91] There is no attempt to provide any historical and sociological background to the recruits, or any context or sense of proportion. Buried in Hoffman and Bergen's text is the admission that the number of radicalized US citizens and residents "remains extremely small." Nevertheless, these people—mostly disaffected teenagers—apparently imperil the republic.

Bottom-up radicalization has less to do with al-Qaeda Central and more with the side effects of the raging War on Terror in the greater Middle East. I interviewed several homegrown suspects who were found guilty in US courts and almost all of them specifically mentioned the conflicts in Iraq, Afghanistan, and Pakistan as the main cause for their radicalization; of course they railed against the US War on Terror, which they viewed as a crusade against Islam and Muslims, but identity politics was the real driver behind their migration to militancy. Many said that they had become caught up in the heat of the moment and took up the fight, mostly online, against the United States. Most sounded like radical graduate students, adept at theory but ignorant of the real consequences—long prison sentences in very tightly controlled supermax-like jails. In many cases, they made foolish statements and implicated themselves in far-fetched conspiracies.

Nevertheless, there have also been homegrown plots that could have killed Americans, an alarming development the causes of which must be critically examined. In order to understand the migration of young Muslims in the West from moderate views to extremism we must widen the narrow prism of terrorism experts. There is more to the phenomena than reflexive hatred of their native or adopted countries, or "radicalization through the Internet."

Anecdotes and fear-mongering will not advance our understanding. Instead, Muslim communities must take the lead—and some have already done so—in making a systemic effort to account for and explain the intense alienation of some of their young members, a task made more difficult because most of the latter do not inform their own families.[92]

Mohamed Osman Mohamud—a 19-year-old Somali-American man accused of allegedly plotting to blow up a car bomb at an Oregon Christmas tree lighting ceremony in Portland—is a case in point. In a recorded video statement in the presence of undercover FBI agents, Mohamud briefly mentioned his parents and suggested that they had tried to steer him on another path in life: "To my parents, who held me back from jihad in the cause of Allah. I say to them [by Allah] if you—if you make allies with the enemy, then Allah's power [the glorified and exalted] will ask you about that on the day of judgment, and nothing you can do can hold me back," according to an FBI transcript of the statement.[93] Ironically, the Associated Press reported that someone concerned about Mohamud tipped the FBI, a recurring trend in homegrown radicalization.[94]

A 38-page FBI affidavit paints Mohamud as highly determined and deadly serious. Charged with attempted use of a weapon of mass destruction, which carries a maximum sentence of life in prison, he has pleaded not guilty. "The threat was very real," said Arthur Balizan, special agent in charge of the FBI in Oregon. "Our investigation shows that Mohamud was absolutely committed to carrying out an attack on a very grand scale."[95]

But Mohamud's attorneys and some local Muslims have raised questions about whether the FBI operatives who posed as co-conspirators played their role too well. Defense attorney Steve Sady questioned whether the operatives were "basically grooming" Mohamud to try to commit a terrorist attack. "The information released by the government raises serious concerns about the government manufacturing a crime," according to a statement released by Sady and Steven Wax, public defenders assigned to represent Mohamud.[96] Echoing the defense attorneys, John Pike, a mainstream security expert, says Mohamud's arrest seems to be the result of "1% his inspiration and 99% FBI perspiration," though he hastily added that the FBI's efforts to disrupt and deter attacks seem to be working.[97]

"I am confident there is no entrapment here," said Attorney General Eric Holder. "There were . . . a number of opportunities . . . [in which] the defendant in this matter was given to retreat, to take a different path. He chose at every step to continue." Other local officials praised the Justice Department's and FBI's handling of the case.[98] Still, Imtiaz Khan, president of the Islamic Center of Portland and Masjed As-Saber, a mosque where Mohamud worshipped, said several people at the mosque had questioned why law enforcement helped orchestrate such an elaborate plan for a terrorist act. "They're saying, 'Why allow it to get to this public stunt? To put the community on edge?'" Khan told the *New York Times*.[99]

Regardless of whether the FBI entrapped Mohamud—the latest in a series of sting operations that have involved FBI undercover informants posing as terrorists to help make a case against would-be bombers—he seems to be self-radicalized from the bottom-up, not from the top-down, as al-Qaeda operates. Beyond rhetoric or incitement, bin Laden's al-Qaeda had hardly anything to do with Mohamud and like-minded homegrown radicals. Friends called Mohamud "Mo," and one remembered him as the class clown. He drank beer, followed the Portland Trail Blazers and liked hip-hop music. He sometimes worshipped at a local Muslim center but was not devout. "He's a chill kid," Mo Kim, 23, an Oregon State student, told the local *Democrat-Herald* newspaper. "He was Black Friday shopping with friends the night before. It's kind of crazy. No one saw this coming. Some people think he was framed."[100]

Neighbors said Mohamud's parents separated in summer 2009. That was when the FBI said Mohamud began sending e-mail messages to a suspected al-Qaeda recruiter in Pakistan, drawing the bureau's attention. Like most bottom-up radicals, Mohamud took the initiative and tried to make contact with militants. According to an FBI transcript, for weeks in 2009 Mohamud tried in vain to connect with an alleged militant named Abdulhadi whose e-mail address was given to him by a former Oregon University student living in Pakistan. But Mohamud repeatedly mixed up the Hotmail address with the password, and the e-mails bounced back.

An FBI undercover agent contacted Mohamud and pretended to be Abdulhadi, providing an e-mail address that the FBI controlled. In all, FBI operatives met Mohamud on seven occasions and helped him find components needed to construct a bomb and schooled him in how to set off the explosives. The FBI undercover agents asked him to buy the bomb components and gave him $2,700 in cash to rent an apartment where they could all hide, and $110 to cover the cost of the bomb parts. On November 4, 2010, Mohamud and two agents drove to a remote location near the coast west of Corvallis, supposedly to test the homemade bomb design. In reality, federal agents remotely detonated a device. Mohamud was arrested after he and an agent drove into downtown Portland in a white van that carried six 55-gallon drums with detonation cords and plastic caps (all inert). Authorities said they allowed the plot to proceed to obtain evidence to charge the suspect.[101]

Although the drivers behind Mohamud's radicalization are still unknown, neither ideology nor upbringing appears to shed light on the tipping point that caused a rupture in his conduct. According to relatives and close friends, Mohamud came from a progressive family, leaders of the small Somali community in Portland, and never expressed extremist views. Mujahid El-Naser said he attended middle school in Portland with Mohamud and that he did not believe his friend would have become involved in the plot without the encouragement of the FBI. "If you talk with someone enough, they'll be convinced they need to do something. That's what I think the FBI might have done with him," said El-Naser.[102]

Nevertheless Mohamud joined a small segment of Muslim homegrown radicals in the West, including America, particularly from Pakistan, Afghanistan, and Somalia, who plotted to carry out attacks against their adopted countries. There is increasing evidence that the conflicts in these countries are militarizing important elements of the urban middle class there, as well as a few young Muslims who live in the West. The blowback of the wars in Afghanistan, Pakistan, and Somalia has reached Western shores and will likely persist as long as the battle rages.[103]

It is almost certain that one of these homegrown plots will succeed at some level. Given the degree to which al-Qaeda continues to exert its hold over the imagination of Americans and Westerners, one successful attack will inflame public fears and exert pressure on leaders to escalate militarily, starting a deadly cycle that may trigger a blowback. As long as war is being waged in Muslim lands, there will likely be armed resistance and calls for vengeance. Al-Qaeda and like-minded factions and individuals, such as the Pakistani Taliban and Awlaki, will continue to exploit the presence of Western troops to incite young Muslims to take arms against foreign invaders.

Nonetheless, there are fewer terror plots than one would have expected, given all the ideological mobilization and the conflicts raging across the greater Middle East. Homegrown extremism is a limited phenomenon and must be kept in perspective. Exaggerated public reports create unnecessary fear.

There is credible evidence that al-Qaeda and others continue to plot terror attacks against Europe. Al-Qaeda does retain some appeal in Europe among a few disillusioned and ghettoized young Muslims. For example, a month after the German interior minister Thomas de Maiziere publicly expressed skepticism of US terror warning about the October 2010 Mumbai-style plots against European targets, he said there was reason for concern of a terrorist attack in Germany and raised the country's threat assessment. But, despite the alarm, daily life progressed as usual for Germany's 82 million citizens. "There are situations in which calm is actually a civic duty and has nothing to do with apathy," wrote the conservative daily *Die Welt*. "It is not a sign of carelessness but of strength if life goes on as normal in dangerous situations."[104]

Western governments worry that extremist networks prey on radicalized young Muslims and facilitate recruitment for volunteers willing to stage urban attacks, such as those in 2004 in Madrid and the 2005 London bombings. Although European officials cite scores of their citizens training in Pakistan and elsewhere, exact numbers are difficult to ascertain because the flow is very small and cannot be measured precisely. Nevertheless, the radicalization of European citizens and residents has sent tremors throughout both Muslim and non-Muslim communities.[105]

In my interviews with young activists in France, Spain, Britain, and Italy, I came away with the distinct impression that they were out of touch with recent developments in Afghanistan and Pakistan, particularly with al-Qaeda's loss of public support and its deepening crisis of legitimacy and authority. Their views of bin Laden and Zawahiri—"defenders of the umma"—are frozen in time and space.

This will likely change when al-Qaeda's appeal disappears altogether in the Arab heartland of the greater Middle East.

There are already encouraging indicators that support for al-Qaeda's transnational ideology among European Muslims is waning. Although Awlaki's message resonates among a few radicalized individuals, there has been a "significant decline" in the number of Islamist attacks, according to EUROPOL director Robert Wainwright.[106] Peter Clarke, a former head of the anti-terrorism branch of the Metropolitan Police, told a conference organized by the New York University Law School in Florence in late May 2008 that successful convictions of terrorist plotters using normal legal processes had led to "constructive discussion in communities" of Muslims in the United Kingdom—communities that had been skeptical about the threat earlier. "People can no longer deny [the existence of plots by extremists] because they can see the number of convictions there have been before the courts using recognized legal process."[107]

Armando Spataro, Milan's deputy chief prosecutor and anti-terrorist coordinator, also speaking at the NYU Law School conference, said the terrorism threat would be difficult to sustain because the majority of immigrants did not "accept the terrorists' ideas."[108] Muslim opinion-makers and leading clerics in Europe and North America have become more proactive about challenging and de-legitimizing the ideology and tactics of transnational jihad.

For instance, in a landmark fatwa written by one of the Muslim world's most respected scholars, Muhammad Tahir ul-Qadri, a Pakistani scholar based in Canada, fundamentally refutes the theological arguments and justifications for al-Qaeda's ideology of transnational jihad. In his fatwa on terrorism, published by his influential worldwide organization, Minhaj-ul-Quran International (which has offices in several European cities but its headquarters in Lahore), Qadri refutes the division of the world into *dar al-Islam* (the abode of Islam) and *dar al-harb* (the abode of war), and instead, states that there is no separation between the two camps. This false and artificial division, argues Shaykh Qadri, has been manipulated and abused to justify un-Islamic acts in the name of Islam. His fatwa explicitly condemns terrorism, and pointedly shows such actions are a deviation from Islam.[109]

Despite this, both in Europe and the United States, the darker view of the threat persists. It rests upon three conclusions: that Al-Qaeda's strength remains undiminished along Pakistan's tribal border with Afghanistan; that the al-Qaeda branch in Yemen has revived; and that homegrown terrorism is an important and emerging threat to US and Western national security. The darker view acknowledges that al-Qaeda has lost so many skilled operatives that very young people with little training had to assume leadership positions; it does not give credence to the argument that al-Qaeda faces a crisis of massive proportion in terms of recruitment, finance, and legitimacy: While of course bin Laden is gone, Zawahiri, al-Adl, Awlaki, and others have not only escaped capture but are alive, well, and in charge of an expanding pool of potential suicide bombers worldwide; it is only a matter of time before they kill thousands of Americans.[110]

After AQAP claimed responsibility for the two attempts on US-bound cargo planes and threatened to bleed the enemy by a thousand cuts, a rhetorical device to spread fear, Ben Venske, terrorism expert and chief executive of IntelCenter, an intelligence-gathering group financed mainly by the US government, sounded the alarm: "AQAP is a dedicated, unwavering and sophisticated group. It will continue to strike at the US in creative new ways and it is only a matter of time until one of their attacks results in thousands dead and/or severe economic damage."[111]

Moreover, US politicians and terrorism experts still point to Pakistan's tribal areas along the Afghan border where bin Laden was believed to have his headquarters as the "heart of al-Qaeda" and center of gravity. During a visit to Kuala Lumpur, Malaysia, in November 2010, former Defense Secretary Gates told reporters that while al-Qaeda leaders continue to operate out of the Pakistan-Afghan border area, "they provide the guidance, they provide the priorities, they provide legitimacy to other al-Qaeda affiliates that are developing in other places, including in the Arabian peninsula, in Yemen in particular and in northern Africa, in the Maghreb."[112]

Some analysts have established that militants operating out of Pakistan's tribal belt, known as the Federally Administered Tribal Areas, or FATA, can be divided into four major groups: the Pakistani Taliban (TTP); the Afghan Taliban; al-Qaeda–affiliated Arab and Central Asian fighters; and, finally, the Punjabi Taliban. The Pakistani Taliban and the Punjabi Taliban have developed links with al-Qaeda, though their organizational structures are separate from bin Laden's transnational group. The core elements of al-Qaeda may have lost their power and infrastructure in the FATA region, but new organizations, influenced and inspired by its ideology, have filled that vacuum. The darker view asserts that al-Qaeda continues to direct and manage its cells and branches worldwide, and that its leaders need little more than a mobile phone (or a messenger) to instruct their followers and to select targets.[113]

During the Bush administration, this view held that the so-called long war against al-Qaeda would be America's top military priority over the coming decades. Other threats paled by comparison. The same has held true for the Obama national security team, which has made bin Laden's successors a higher strategic priority than nuclear-armed North Korea and a belligerent Iran, according to Secretary Clinton.

Appointed to lead a policy review of the AfPak strategy for the Obama administration in early 2009, Bruce Riedel, a former CIA official, now affiliated with the Brookings Institute, issued a pessimistic view of the threat posed by al-Qaeda and its allies in Afghanistan and Pakistan. According to insider accounts among national security officials, Riedel aggressively promoted his policy-oriented monograph, *The Search for Al Qaeda*. He reportedly told Obama that his book provided answers to understanding and dealing with al-Qaeda and its extremist allies in Pakistan and Afghanistan.[114] It is also a clear expression of the dark view and its ancillary, the long war.

Written in the final year of the Bush administration, *The Search for Al Qaeda* presents an alarming picture of al-Qaeda, one whose final chapter has yet to be written, though of course the subject of bin Laden's legacy and successors is or will be the subject of feverish speculation in forthcoming books (commentators have already spilled considerable ink speculating on new potential successors to bin Laden). Riedel argued that bin Laden's transnational organization was still an expanding threat that challenges American and Western interests worldwide. Instead of defeating al-Qaeda in 2001, the Iraq war and Pakistan's internal social and political turmoil have helped sustain al-Qaeda, which through its franchises, affiliates, and its symbiotic relationship with the Taliban has become deadlier and more viral than it was a decade ago. Riedel recommends a grand US strategy to defeat al-Qaeda, a strategy that is more ambitious and comprehensive than the current one, and which would take years, if not decades, to take effect.[115]

As I argued at the beginning of this book, when Obama came to the White House, he made it clear that he intended to change the language and discourse that had informed the policy debate on al-Qaeda and terrorism in general during the Bush years. As he told Bob Woodward, "I said very early on, as a senator, and continued to believe as a presidential candidate and now as president, that we can absorb a terrorist attack . . . This is a strong, powerful country that we live in, and our people are incredibly resilient."[116]

Obama's original thinking did not last long. Riedel, together with other terrorism experts, warned him that al-Qaeda was as dangerous as it was on the morning before September 11, if not more so. As Woodward reconstructs one conversation, which took place in March 2009 aboard Air Force One, Riedel reminded the president that he had told him during the campaign that al-Qaeda remained deadly. "After a review of intelligence, he said, it turns out that I was underestimating the danger. Though my first recommendation is an integrated civilian-military counterinsurgency for Afghanistan, you, Mr. President, have to be focused on the real, central threat—Pakistan."[117]

Seconding Riedel's bleak prognosis, Peter Lavoy, the top official on Pakistan in the Department of National Intelligence (DNI), said that al-Qaeda was "embattled" and beleaguered, but not yet finished. The drone attacks and other counterterrorist operations in Pakistan had damaged bin Laden's organization considerably, but because of its weakened condition al-Qaeda had grown more dependent on local extremist groups for support. "'They're the leech riding on the Taliban, and strength for the Taliban gives strength to the leech riding it,'" he concluded. A victory for the Taliban strengthened al-Qaeda.[118]

Riedel and Lavoy's analysis lumped al-Qaeda with the Taliban together and lent support to a military hierarchy that saw US intervention in Afghanistan as a strategic imperative. Woodward's extensive interviews with Obama's officials reveal that the president was boxed in by his generals and pressured to escalate militarily and support a surge in the Afghanistan-Pakistan theatre.

Vice President Joe Biden has been a lone dissenting voice within the administration on al-Qaeda and the Taliban. He made the case that al-Qaeda and the Taliban were not synonymous and that they should not escalate the fight in Afghanistan. Instead, Biden advocated a limited military approach that focused on bin Laden's men and his associates in Pakistan. According to first-hand accounts of the passionate debate that unfolded among Obama officials, Biden disputed the claim that al-Qaeda and the Taliban were so intertwined that the success of one meant the success of the other. "No, they're actually very distinct," Biden said, again according to Woodward. "We're assuming that if al Qaeda comes back into Afghanistan, where it wasn't, it would be welcomed by the Taliban. Is that a correct assumption? We have no basis for concluding that.'"[119] Like Biden, the late Richard Holbrooke, Obama's then special envoy to Afghanistan and Pakistan, believed that even if the Taliban retook large parts of Afghanistan, al-Qaeda would not come with them. That might be "the single most important intellectual insight of the year," Holbrooke apparently remarked hours after the meeting had concluded.[120] Pitted against Biden and Holbrooke, Panetta argued in an NSC meeting that they were "struggling to separate the groups that are relatively linked."[121]

Biden, as I've noted, lost the debate. Once again the terrorism narrative—equating al-Qaeda with the Taliban—had triumphed. As a result, the United States is not only waging war against bin Laden's few hundred survivors, but also against the Taliban. There is no doubt that al-Qaeda has served as a force multiplier to militant groups, particularly those operating in Pakistan. Taliban rebels have deployed al-Qaeda–style suicide attacks with deadly effect and appear to share its ideological worldview. The veteran Pakistani journalist Ahmed Rashid notes that the production of suicide belts has become a cottage industry in the tribal Pashtun region, similar to local handicraft production. "One household makes the detonator, another sews the belt, a third molds ball bearings, and so on. These are then collected and paid for by the Taliban."[122]

In particular, the Pakistani Taliban (TTP), a force that emerged from the underdeveloped tribal regions (FATA) that have suffered poverty and injustice in addition to being ruled by an archaic and dysfunctional system of administration inherited from the British, has adopted al-Qaeda tactics and aspects of its transnational ideology as well.[123] When the TTP is compared with the Afghan Taliban, however, a marked difference emerges. The practice of indiscriminate bombing against civilian targets, particularly Shiites and Sufi shrines in Pakistani cities, and largely implemented by sectarian groups based in Punjab, appears to be sponsored by the TTP. Elements of sectarian organizations, such as Lashkar-e Jhangvi and Sipah-e-Sahaba Pakistan, seem to have been co-opted by the TTP, in order to mount a terrorist campaign in Pakistan that initially focused on military and police targets and then, increasingly, on civilians. In contrast, in Afghanistan, the Taliban rarely target civilians indiscriminately. The TTP is also often reported to recruit young people, including as suicide bombers, a practice as yet undocumented in Afghanistan.[124]

Determined to bring down the present Pakistani state, the main Pakistani Taliban rebel grouping, together with its Pakistani and foreign allies, has waged all-out war against the government. In 2009 there were no fewer than eighty-seven suicide attacks in major Pakistani cities, in many cases targeting the most sensitive of military and intelligence facilities, such as the military headquarters in Rawalpindi; a mosque where military families prayed; and the offices of Pakistan's intelligence agencies in three cities—killing thousands and wreaking havoc.[125] That year the number of Pakistani civilians killed in Taliban attacks exceeded civilian deaths even in Afghanistan.[126]

The Pakistani authorities responded by adopting a policy of zero tolerance towards the TTP and other Pakistani Taliban and launching an unprecedented military campaign against their sanctuaries in the FATA and Swat Valley area in the adjoining North West Frontier Province (now called Khyber-Pakhtunkhwa) that displaced some three million people and destroyed much of what was left of the tribal structures.[127] Overplaying their hand, the Pakistani Taliban faced the full brunt of the security apparatus, particularly the army and public opinion that is increasingly turning against them.[128] Nevertheless, the TTP retains some strength, as is evident from their suicide attacks across Pakistan. Today the TTP's main sanctuaries are in Orakzai and Kurram agencies in FATA in North Waziristan, where the Pakistani army has not carried out any major offensive.

Like their Arab jihadist counterparts, particularly in Iraq, the Pakistani Taliban might have committed suicide. These militants have largely alienated the populations where they had succeeded in imposing their heavy-handed, arbitrary rule.[129] "People are very angry," said Beena Sarwar, a human rights activist and filmmaker in Pakistan.[130]

Unable to broaden their power base of support, the Pakistan Taliban have therefore failed to spread their jihadist ideas and influence. Today the TTP does not threaten the survival of the Pakistani state.[131]

Militant Islamists in the southern Punjab, increasingly being called "Punjabi Taliban," pose a potentially more dangerous threat to the state than do the Taliban from the frontier. Pakistani security officials worry about a nexus between the Taliban in North Waziristan and the Punjabi Taliban, which would give the latter a greater reach.[132] The TTP's main problem is that they did not heed the more powerful actors in the area; it is not surprising, then, that they remain the only Taliban group seriously targeted by the government.

Although in the short term victory might prove elusive for the Pakistani authorities, given that the Taliban groups have suicide recruits ready to strike, in the long term the balance of power favors the government, particularly since the militants have not formed alliances and coalitions with more powerful radical groups inside the country like Lashkar-e-Taiba, though a breakaway faction from within LeT has joined the TTP.[133] Even the relationship between the TTP and the Afghan Talibanis seems increasingly tenuous; Mullah Omar tried for some time to maintain a working relationship with the TTP when the late Beitullah Mehsud was at its head, but this seems to be doubtful now. Mullah Omar, who argued that all Taliban should make the Afghan front their priority, might have played a role in negotiating a truce between the TTP and the Pakistani army. A combination of American pressure and drone raids, however, caused the truce to collapse. Despite repeated demands from the Pakistani authorities, the Afghan Taliban still hesitate to denounce the TTP formally. An agreement regarding the formation of a new alliance between the Afghan Taliban, Hizb-i Islami, and Lashkar-e-Taiba, focused on fighting in Afghanistan, is reported by Pakistani sources to be in the making but has not, as of writing, been confirmed by Taliban sources.[134]

If these al-Qaeda splinter groups have survived, it is because of American activities in the region. Although drone attacks have killed militants, they have also killed hundreds of civilians, including children. Predator strikes in the tribal areas have inflamed Pakistani and Afghani nationalism and anti-American sentiments. In particular, the drone attacks have radicalized a critical segment of the Pakistani middle class, from whose ranks emerge new recruits. A panel of five leading journalists of varying political orientations agreed that deepening US military involvement in Pakistan has radicalized the middle class in urban cities, an alarming development. "Many Pakistanis feel impotent in the face of preponderant American power; that has had a terrible impact on society," said Mustafa Qadri, an independent journalist based in Pakistan who has written widely for Pakistani and foreign press. "Many Pakistanis feel the need to strike back because Islam is under attack, [and they seek] a sense of empowerment."[135] The recent violation of Pakistani territory by NATO helicopters, culminating in the killing of three paramilitary border guards, is a symptom of military escalation and has intensified anti-American sentiments in the country. Even the pro-US government in Islamabad retaliated by closing a vital link for NATO supplies to the war in Afghanistan, in order to show its displeasure and respond to public anger. Pakistani leaders threatened to stop providing protection for NATO convoys if the military alliance's helicopters attacked targets inside the country again.[136]

There is a widespread perception among Pakistanis that the United States is violating the sovereignty of their country, a perception that has become far more pronounced and openly, even officially, expressed since bin Laden's killing. According to interviews with senior military officers in Pakistan, suspicion of the United States has deepened among junior officers. "In the lower ranks, anti-Americanism is at its highest," one officer in the country's north told the *Washington Post*. Like others interviewed, he spoke on the condition of anonymity because he was not allowed to discuss the matter publicly.[137]

There is a "trust deficit" with the United States, warned Pakistani Prime minister, Yousaf Raza Gilani, a pro-US politician. "Traditionally the ISI worked with the CIA," he told *Time,* but "what we're seeing is that there's no level of trust."[138] In a rare appearance before the nation's parliament, Pakistan's spy chief, Lt. Gen. Ahmed Shuja

Pasha, denounced the American raid as a "sting operation."[139] Parliament then passed a resolution declaring that the drone attacks violated Pakistan's sovereignty in the same way the secret attack on bin Laden's compound did. The lawmakers warned that Pakistan could cut the supply lines to American forces in Afghanistan if there were more attacks. US policy makers do not seem to appreciate the intensity of nationalist feelings among the military ranks in Pakistan and the potential security repercussions.

But even before the humiliating incursion on Pakistani sovereignty on May 1, tensions ran high. Quatrina Hussain, a charismatic young woman and the host of a popular political talk show, has expressed her fear that America's unilateral military actions undermine the credibility of the current government in Islamabad in the eyes of Pakistani and feed anti-Americanism. "Many Pakistanis feel betrayed by the Pakistani state and the urban elite is being very radicalized," reported Quatrina. "Anti-American sentiment is at its highest point."[140]

Manipulating these rising anti-American feelings, the Pakistani Taliban and other militants have called for vengeance and pledged to carry out suicide bombings in major American cities. Law enforcement officers say that the US war in Pakistan—rather than cultural differences or personal problems—lay behind Shahzad's transformation from suburban respectability to alleged terrorist, though ideology played a role in his conversion to terrorism.[141]

There is no doubt that Pakistan-Afghanistan has replaced Iraq as the new source of homegrown radicals. Pakistani recruits have traveled as far as Yemen and Somalia. Yet senior officials of the Obama administration seem unwilling to draw a causal link between the escalation of the US military commitment in Pakistan-Afghanistan and the new wave of extremists. Nonetheless, following the lines of the terrorism narrative, the dark view, Obama has embraced the claim that the Afghan Taliban and al-Qaeda function more or less as a single entity. In short, Obama foreign policy views the Taliban through the lens of al-Qaeda and the global War on Terror.

Yet one of the key goals of the Afghan Taliban movement is to get off the terrorist list and gain international recognition as a legitimate national force. Although elements of the Taliban under the command of Sirajuddin Haqqani in eastern Afghanistan have limited ties to al-Qaeda, it is clear that Haqqani is not interested in al-Qaeda's transnational agenda and is opposed to waging war against the Pakistani state.[142] Some Arab militants reportedly continue to be hosted by the Haqqanis in northern Waziristan, but they keep a very low profile. The Haqqanis are responsible for a disproportionate share of suicide attacks in Afghanistan, one of the hallmarks of al-Qaeda, but they are not as indiscriminate as the TTP. The Haqqanis are probably the best-funded of the Taliban groups and at the same time dependent on the Pakistani security forces for financial and military support. The Haqqanis tend to do what their Pakistani patrons tell them to do, and are rewarded accordingly.

In other words, the conflict in Afghanistan is far broader and complex than an entity called "al-Qaeda," rather it involves a formidable coalition of Pashtun tribesmen and a non-aligned Islamist movement against what they see (rightly or wrongly) as a foreign threat to their identity and way of life. A case can be made that the Taliban are a "peasant army" on the Afghan side.[143] The war has drawn a few hundred militant Islamists from Kashmir, the Arab world, and even from Central Asia. Al-Qaeda is but a very small element in this coalition, a side effect, a parasite nourished on lawlessness and instability. The twenty to fifty al-Qaeda operatives in Afghanistan cannot drive, let alone lead, a potent insurgency, notwithstanding all the speculation of al-Qaeda being a force-multiplier. The Taliban have reportedly made it clear that there is no need for foreign fighters because they have plenty. Over the last three or four years, the Afghan Taliban nearly quadrupled their numbers, going from 7,000 to more than 25,000, according to US intelligence; they have gained more followers within the Pashtun tribes, who are a majority in Afghanistan, as well as other ethnic groups in the north, such as the Uzbeks and Tajiks, who also resent the presence of foreign troops in their country.[144] In April 2010 Afghan military intelligence estimated the presence of 4,000 foreign fighters in Afghanistan, overwhelmingly from Pakistan. Bin Laden's men therefore account for only 1 or 2 percent of international volunteers fighting alongside the Taliban.[145]

Yet President Obama framed his decision to deploy an additional 30,000 soldiers and marines to Afghanistan by early 2010 (bringing the number of US troops in Afghanistan to almost 100,000) as a domestic necessity—to protect the United States from al-Qaeda. Like the war in Iraq, the surge in Afghanistan is portrayed as taking the fight to the enemy rather than being struck at home. But the surge has more to do with a rising Taliban than a declining al-Qaeda; it is designed to undermine the Taliban's momentum, split it from al-Qaeda, and break it down into more manageable parts to facilitate a political settlement.[146]

Nevertheless, in his addresses to the troops at home and in Afghanistan, Obama equated the Taliban with al-Qaeda. For example, in a December 2009 West Point address, he told his audience that his goal in Afghanistan and Pakistan would be "narrowly defined as disrupting, dismantling, and defeating al Qaeda and its extremist allies."[147] In a surprise visit to Afghanistan four months later, in spring 2010, Obama defended his decision to escalate the fight, telling US troops that their victory is imperative to America's safety. "If this region slides backwards," he said Obama, "if the Taliban retakes this country, al-Qaeda can operate with impunity, then more American lives will be at stake."[148]

In early December 2010 Obama delivered the same message in a surprise visit to US troops in the war-torn country, saying the goal is to disrupt, dismantle, and defeat al-Qaeda and its extremist Taliban allies. He told nearly 4,000 troops gathered in a hangar that they were gaining ground against insurgents and that they are "on the offense" in Afghanistan now, making progress against the Taliban. "We said we were going to break the Taliban's momentum and that's what you're doing, you're going on the offense, tired of playing defense," he said to the crowd, sending a clear signal that he is staying the course in Afghanistan for the foreseeable future.[149]

Under pressure to show progress in a war that a majority of Americans is weary of after nearly a decade, the US president pledged enduring commitment and resolve. "We will never let this country serve as a safe haven for terrorists who would attack the United States of America again," Obama said. "That will never happen." There is increasing evidence that the "December review"—a one-year analysis of Obama's Afghanistan war plan, now seems to be, for the most part, an affirmation of current US strategy. The president's senior aides have already set measured expectations, promising no major policy changes. "I don't think you'll see any immediate adjustments," Doug Lute, Obama's senior adviser on the war effort, told reporters traveling with Obama.[150]

Indeed, the results of a one-year review of Obama's war strategy reflected the same tensions and contradictions that have bedeviled him before. Overall, Obama said, there has been "'significant progress' in the goal of disrupting, dismantling and defeating" al-Qaeda—an objective he set when he announced the surge in Afghanistan, and one that could have been achieved without expanded military and civilian deployment there. Obama also said that "we are on track to achieve our goals" against the Taliban and to "start reducing our forces" in July 2011.[151] But two assessments from the US intelligence community present a gloomy picture of the Afghan war, contradicting Obama and Defense Secretary Robert Gates, who said after visiting the region that he is convinced the administration's strategy is turning around the Afghanistan war.[152]

As I have shown, there are minor operational ties between the Taliban in Afghanistan and some al-Qaeda operatives who provide inspiration, as well as training in how to make roadside bombs. The tactic of suicide bombing is a key point. Compared to the many successful suicide attacks perpetrated by the Pakistani Taliban, the Afghan Taliban have generally demonstrated very poor tradecraft. Nonetheless, there have been signs of increasing sophistication; a reality that can be explained as a function of proximity to al-Qaeda, as well as the adoption of its tactics and ideology.[153] It is worth noting that in his most recent statements, Mullah Omar has clearly said that suicide attacks should be employed sparingly and only after authorization from the highest levels. The Afghan Taliban have also gone out of their way to distinguish themselves from both al-Qaeda and the Pakistani Taliban, although in practice the guidance issued by the leadership is not always followed.

Mullah Omar is more moderate than other Taliban elements, such as the now-defunct Mullah Dadullah of the Quetta Shura, which pioneered suicide attacks in Afghanistan, attacks carried out by the so-called Haqqani network, an independent insurgent organization headquartered in Pakistan and run by Maulvi Jalaluddin Haqqani along with his son Sirajuddin. Dadullah led the more radical wing of the Taliban and reportedly had strong Arab connections. With his death in 2007 the radical wing of the Taliban has been left leaderless. Dadullah's brother accused Taliban leaders of complicity in his brother's death, an accusation widely credited in Afghanistan, despite denials by the Taliban and Pakistan security forces. Nevertheless, Mullah Omar argued bitterly with Dadullah over the latter's extreme behavior.[154]

It is therefore misleading to group together al-Qaeda, a transnational, borderless jihadist group waging a worldwide terrorist campaign, with the Taliban, a local armed, nationalist-Islamist insurgency whose focus has always been the Afghan front. Although the two groups have ties, they are separate and distinct groups with different constituencies and different goals. American authorities have never accused the Afghan Taliban of carrying out strikes or attacks outside Afghanistan. Some Taliban elements, such as the Haqqanis, flirt with al-Qaeda, but the relative consensus that has emerged among scholars of the Taliban is that if the Taliban return to Afghanistan in one form or another, they would most likely try to push al-Qaeda out of their country. Bin Laden's death in Pakistan provides another reason for the Taliban to distance itself from al-Qaeda, though it would be futile to expect Omar and his cohorts to formally disassociate themselves from the Afghan Arabs.

Ridding the Pashtun tribal lands of al-Qaeda and other foreign extremists demands a region-wide political settlement that addresses the legitimate grievances of the tribal communities and nationalist Islamist sentiments, as well as the geo-strategic concerns of Pakistan, Iran, and India. There is also agreement among observers that reform of the political and legal system, integrating the tribal region into the mainstream and lifting the inhabitants out of extreme poverty, is crucial to achieve lasting peace. Unless and until the Western coalition invests in the political economy of the tribal areas and protects civilians, the Taliban will continue to prey on the vulnerabilities of the Pashtun tribesmen and impose their own system of extremism. A negotiated settlement with the Pashtun tribes (which will bring the Taliban into the government) would very likely result in the expulsion of al-Qaeda and other foreign militants from the area.[155]

The case of Iraq is instructive. The challenge is to give the Pashtun tribes a real stake in the political and economic order, and thus to turn them against al-Qaeda. Make no mistake: the Pashtuns harbor no love for al-Qaeda, who brought disaster to the Taliban when they sheltered al-Qaeda in the 1990s. The conventional view is that the two camps are, and have always been, joined at the hip. Yet as we have seen, at the height of al-Qaeda's prowess in Afghanistan in the late 1990s, several senior Taliban leaders, including the foreign minister Mullah Wakil Ahmad Mutawakkil, resented al-Qaeda's presence in the country and lobbied hard to get rid of bin Laden and Zawahiri and expel the foreign fighters. They would have succeeded had Mullah Omar not protected bin Laden.[156] Bin Laden had violated the terms of his stay and brought ruin to the Taliban and was savagely condemned.[157]

According to Douglas Saunders of Canada's *Globe and Mail*, Mullah Omar remains "very opposed" to al-Qaeda, and most allied commanders in Afghanistan Saunders has talked with think it "very unlikely" that al-Qaeda would establish a base there even if the Taliban were to take over. Richard Barrett, a leading specialist on Afghanistan, says of the Taliban, "They don't want Al Qaeda hanging around."[158] In the last several years, after considerable friction with the local population and Taliban fighters, there has been a noticeable decrease in the presence of autonomous groups of Arab fighters. What few Arab fighters remain today are more likely to remain under Afghan command.[159]

The writer and journalist Rahimullah Yusufzai, who for the last three decades has been reporting from inside Afghanistan and Pakistan, and who has interviewed the rank and file of both al-Qaeda and the Taliban—including Mullah Omar, bin Laden, and

Zawahiri—has said that the Taliban would not tolerate al-Qaeda in Afghanistan if and when they return to power. When I pressed Yusufzai as to whether the Taliban would ever, under any circumstances, provide shelter to al-Qaeda in Afghanistan, he replied that he doubted it; Taliban leaders have learned the hard way that al-Qaeda's transnational agenda clashes with their nationalist-Islamist vision. The Taliban have shed blood to expel the US-led occupation of Afghanistan, and once integrated into the government, they would not jeopardize their hard-won gains by allowing al-Qaeda back.[160]

That conclusion was implicitly affirmed by Mullah Mohammed Tayyab Agha, head of the Taliban political bureau, in an interview with *al-Hayat*, a London-based pan-Arab newspaper:

> The solution lies in the Afghan people being left free. This means an end to occupation, leaving Afghanistan, and giving an opportunity to the government that was there before occupation, namely the government of the Islamic emirates, to restore the situation to what it was before, unite the country, strive to bring about stability, and ban drugs! . . . We are prepared to cooperate with the Islamic states and with the states of the world. The world must recognize us before asking us to be committed to anything.[161]
>
> But there are Western and international demands to be met before a withdrawal, mainly disengagement between the Taliban and the al-Qaeda organization, and not allowing al-Qaeda to remain in Afghanistan.[162]

The current marriage of convenience between the Taliban fighters and al-Qaeda operatives will hold as long as the West confuses and conflates them, and wages all-out war against them. Yusufzai cautions against using the current situation in Pakistan and Afghanistan as a yardstick with which to judge the Taliban's behavior after the end of hostilities. He concedes that relations between some elements of the Taliban and al-Qaeda have become warmer because they are both targeted by Western troops; and al-Qaeda has become dependent on the Pakistani Taliban for its survival. But the Taliban in Afghanistan view al-Qaeda as a sword hanging over their necks, as Yusufzai put it. The key is for the West not to confuse the Taliban and the Pashtun with al-Qaeda, but instead try to separate them, just as it did in with the Iraqi Sunni tribesmen in Anbar.[163]

If there is one person who knows the state of relations between the Taliban and al-Qaeda in the past and the present it is Abu al-Walid al-Masri, a legendary figure among the Afghan Arabs and the first foreigner to swear allegiance to Mullah Omar in the 1990s. In an online interview with the *Australian*, Masri—who worked closely with Omar and other Taliban chiefs and was close to bin Laden and his cohorts—said that the differences between al-Qaeda and the Taliban are greater now than they were before the US invasion of Afghanistan in 2001. He is emphatic: the Taliban will no longer welcome al-Qaeda, which stabbed them in the back, in Afghanistan. According to Masri, al-Qaeda's return to Afghanistan would threaten the future Taliban rule because "the majority of the population is against al-Qaeda."[164] In response to the question of why the Taliban do not renounce al-Qaeda as the United States demands, Masri, who is a regular contributor to the Taliban magazine and a longstanding, close supporter and friend of the Taliban leadership, says that this would mean surrender to the "invading Americans" and accepting their conditions for negotiations. "This is something impossible," stated Masri; instead, the Taliban leadership, which trusts no one beyond its borders, including the Pakistani authorities, their current allies, may indirectly dissociate itself from al-Qaeda along similar lines to those of Mullah Mohammed Tayyab Agha, head of the Taliban political bureau.[165]

We must not lose sight of the local context of the Afghan conflict, wherein a power struggle for the soul of Afghanistan is playing out. Although recently President Karzai was harshly criticized in the United States for airing nationalist grievances, his words resonate among ordinary Afghanis. In a private meeting, Karzai reportedly told five American lawmakers that foreign interference in his country's affairs was fueling the insurgency. "He said that the only reason that the Taliban and other insurgent groups are fighting the Afghan government is that they see foreigners having the final say in everything," one lawmaker told the *Wall Street Journal*.[166]

All five lawmakers said that Karzai had told those who gathered at the presidential palace that the Taliban's "revolt" would change to "resistance" should the United States and its allies keep dictating how Afghanistan should be run.[167] In a subsequent interview with the *Washington Post* in November 2010, Karzai, who is pro-American, mildly expressed the sentiments of his people toward the presence of US troops: "The time has come to reduce military operations. The time has come to reduce the presence of, you know, boots in Afghanistan . . . to reduce the intrusiveness into the daily life."[168] Karzai publicly vented his frustration with American military tactics and called for the empowerment of the Afghan people:

> The raiding homes at night. Terrible. Terrible. A serious cause of the Afghan people's disenchantment with NATO and with the Afghan government. Bursting into homes at night, arresting Afghans, this isn't the business of any foreign troops. Afghans have to do that, and one of the important elements of transition that we're working on is to end [these] raids of the Afghan homes and arrest of Afghans by foreign troops in Afghanistan and

civilian casualties. Plus so many other things, the violence and the violation of our laws that these private security firms cause . . .

The raids are a problem always. They were a problem then, they are a problem now. They have to go away. The Afghan people don't like these raids. If there is any raid, it has to be done by the Afghan government within the Afghan laws. This is a continuing disagreement between us.[169]

It would be a mistake to dismiss Karzai's warning as the ramblings of an increasingly isolated, paranoid, and conspiracy-minded partner, as leaked US diplomatic cables portray him. General David Petraeus told the *Washington Post*, on the record, that he read Karzai's remarks with "astonishment and disappointment." Regardless of whether or not American officials view Karzai as a weak "strategic partner," they must not dismiss his warning that the US War on Terror—not only by special-ops forces but also by airstrikes and drones—is radicalizing the population more than it is truly defeating the Taliban and that the Taliban must be diplomatically engaged.[170]

However, despite repeated denials and assertions by top US leaders that the military tide has turned against the Taliban, a subtle and important shift has taken place in American policy. In the past, officials supported only "reintegration" or inclusion of low-level officials and defectors into Afghan society and opposed reconciliation with the Taliban leadership; they now publicly support Karzai's high-level direct peace talks with the dissident movement, notwithstanding the embarrassing acknowledgment by Western officials that a man who presented himself as a senior Taliban leader authorized to negotiate a cease-fire with the Afghan government was an impostor.[171] The *New York Times*, *Washington Post*, Radio Free Europe/Radio Liberty, and other media outlets have widely reported that US-led military forces in Afghanistan have helped to facilitate meetings between the Karzai government and members of the Taliban, in the hopes of fostering political reconciliation. White House spokesman Robert Gibbs said the Obama administration had "long supported" an "Afghan-led reconciliation effort"—a clear indication of the new shift in strategy.[172]

American and NATO officials have confirmed the military's role in the meetings, even though they have been cautious about their progress. Hillary Clinton told a journalist in Brussels that it was too early to tell whether the Afghan reconciliation would work. "We're not yet ready to make any judgments about whether or not any of this will bear fruit on the reconciliation front," she said.[173] The top American commander in Afghanistan, General Petraeus, told reporters that discussions had occurred between senior Taliban leaders and senior Afghan officials.

The new shift in US strategy reflects a stark reality: there is no military solution to the civil strife in Afghanistan. Although US military commanders report limited progress in their campaign against the Taliban, saying that there has been a shift in momentum in favor of the NATO coalition, their conclusion is that the Taliban could not be defeated, only degraded and prevented from taking over the country. America also seeks an end to its costly commitment in Afghanistan, already the longest in US history, a commitment that has eclipsed the Soviet Union's reckless adventure there.[174]

Leaked diplomatic cables covering recent years of US strategy in Afghanistan throw further light on the bleak portrait of the war-torn country, as depicted by American officials. Time and again, US Ambassador Karl W. Eikenberry lamented the difficulty of achieving sustained success against the insurgency and the pervasive corruption at the highest level of the Afghan regime and portrayed President Karzai as erratic, paranoid, and unreliable. Although

President Obama and his military commanders say they have broken the Taliban's momentum, the classified documents show US officials' sense of futility and resignation: "No matter how effective military performance may be, the insurgents will readily fill any vacuum of governance, and without political competence, lasting [counterinsurgency success] . . . will remain one more operation away," Eikenberry concluded in an assessment that echoes concerns expressed over the current coalition offensive in the southern province of Kandahar.[175]

The Taliban have also sustained considerable human losses and appear to be testing the political waters in the form of these talks.[176] Despite the public denials by the Taliban, initial talks with representatives are promising because they seem to be speaking for the Quetta Shura Taliban, the top Afghan Taliban leadership council in Quetta, Pakistan. This therefore represents a dramatic shift in the Taliban's stance. Mullah Omar has, for the first time, supported secret high-level talks with the Karzai government to negotiate an end to the nine-year war, the *Washington Post* said. "They are very, very serious about finding a way out," a source close to the talks told the *Washington Post*.[177] Although it is too early to draw any conclusions given the absence of real progress, both camps appear to have second thoughts about their prolonged deadly embrace in Afghanistan.

If and when that happens, it will signal the end of al-Qaeda Central, which no longer exercises effective operational control over its far-flung followers. One of the major points to emerge out of the hearings of American intelligence chiefs that I have cited is that al-Qaeda's few surviving lieutenants were dispirited and on their own and suffer from low morale and lack operational direction.

There is evidence that al-Qaeda's control of its loosening network of affiliates is limited to the organization's chief of external operations, who often either trains or sanctions freelancers.

The chief of external operations makes these decisions without consulting anyone higher up in the organizational hierarchy. Because of its visibility, this position has always been very vulnerable and its holders are swiftly captured or killed, delivering a significant blow to al-Qaeda: Khalid Sheikh Mohammed Abd al-Hadi al-Iraqi, Abu al-Faraj al-Libi, Hamza Rabia, Abu Layth al-Libi, Abu Sulayman al-Jaziri, Abu Ubayda al-Masri, and Mustafa Abu al-Yazid are the latest operations chiefs to fall prey to a drone attack on September 25, 2010.[178]

The notion of a tightly knit and centralized control presupposes physical links that no longer exist. Although Zawahiri, al-Adl, and others are still at large, they know well the deadly costs of establishing any physical links outside of al-Qaeda's inner "core"—now reduced to fewer than a dozen, according to testimony by disillusioned jihadis returning from the "havens" in the Pakistan frontier zone. Use of a cell phone by any one of them amounts to certain death by a CIA drone. Human carriers are their preferred method of communication. But it has become all but impossible for al-Qaeda to micromanage a global war via human carriers while its leaders are under hot pursuit—as bin Laden's discovery and killing made abundantly clear. Bin Laden relied on only one courier to communicate with the outside world, yet that courier brought about his demise.

As I hope this book has established, there is overwhelming evidence to suggest that the original menace of al-Qaeda is winding down. Most of its seasoned field lieutenants have been either captured or killed, replaced by unskilled and ineffective operators; new recruits are hard to come by. The *Guardian* concluded a series of investigative reports by stating that the 'Core' al-Qaeda was now reduced to "a senior leadership of six to eight men."[179] "Several other Egyptians, a Libyan and a Mauritanian occupy the other top positions. In all, there are perhaps 200 operatives who count."[180] Bin Laden's death will exacerbate a leadership crisis within al-Qaeda, which already lacked a functioning command-and-control structure. There is no one who matches the stature and charisma of bin Laden, a unifying and beloved figure within the organization. Zawahiri, as we've seen, is divisive and prickly, an intellectual giant among the remaining figures in al-Qaeda but not a rallying figure. He is no force-multiplier. Nevertheless, if Zawahiri is passed over for either Abu Yahia al-Libi, a Libyan who serves as al-Qaeda's Afghanistan commander, or al-Adl, another field commander, that would indicate how deep the fault lines truly run.

However, al-Qaeda's crisis is structural and existential and transcends personalities. Its declining operational position and military fortunes must be contextualized within the massive and debilitating crisis of legitimacy and authority discussed previously. It is on this level that the failure of transnational jihad seems most striking.

Now, as we have seen, al-Qaeda consists of a collection of roving bands on the run, concentrated mainly on the Pakistan-Afghan border, its top leaders are deep in hiding.[181] While calling themselves al-Qaeda, local branches are pitted in a fierce local struggle for survival against the near enemy and are unable to coordinate their actions with the parent organization. Remnants of transnational jihad, including al-Qaeda, are in leaderless disarray and face a hostile environment at home and abroad. So profound is al-Qaeda's disarray that one of its field lieutenants, in a message intercepted by US intelligence before the raid on bin Laden's compound, had pleaded with bin Laden to come to the group's rescue and provide some leadership. His plea fell on deaf ears. Bin Laden chose personal safety over organizational survival—but to no avail.[182]

Although besieged and in retreat and lacking its founding father, al-Qaeda—it bears repeating—may nonetheless succeed in carrying out a strike inside the United States or Britain, as it nearly did on two occasions since December 2009. Bottom-up radicals like Shahzad, Abdulmutallab, Zazi, and Abdaly will find a way to infiltrate Western security and try to kill civilians. Top-down attacks hatched by bin Laden's allies, such as the two cargo bombs sent by AQAP, may also get through. Although frightening, this probability makes al-Qaeda more a criminal network than a strategic threat.

And yet many terrorism experts belittle the debilitating crisis of legitimacy faced by al-Qaeda, as well as the substantial erosion of Muslim support for transnational jihadism. They claim that al-Qaeda is on the rise and consider transnational jihadism a success story. Look at what bin Laden has accomplished in the last twenty years, they point out. He has struck at the heart of the greatest power in world history and gotten it bogged down in prolonged and costly wars; he has also established a successful global franchise attracting recruits worldwide; and despite everything that the United States has thrown at al-Qaeda, it has not subdued the organization or put an end to terrorist attacks.

Nonetheless, militants whom I recently re-interviewed—particularly repentant jihadis—know they are at a crossroads. At home and abroad they are blamed for unleashing the wrath of the United States against the umma. Most of their allies have deserted them, and they are censured by clerics and Muslim opinion. Only a miracle will resuscitate transnational jihad. The question is whether the prolonged War on Terror, the breakup of Yemen or Libya, a destabilized Pakistan, a seventh Arab-Israeli war, the destruction of Hamas, or the civil war that will ensue if democratic change does not come to those who demonstrated for it in early 2011, will provide that miracle.

Conclusion: Down to Size

Politically based violence and terrorism is a social plague no more or less destructive than other social ailments. Instead of investing politically based violence and terrorism with civilizational and existential meanings, it is important to understand what created the wave of transnational jihad, a wave that surged in the late 1990s and has recently broken into smaller and weaker ripples. While these ripples might remain dangerous, they will most likely scatter and dissipate.

As I have tried to argue, there is a substantial disconnect between the dominant terrorism narrative based on perception—which portrays al-Qaeda and others who subscribe to its ideology as a strategic, existential threat—and the reality of the threat, which is significantly smaller and primarily tactical. This divide between perception and reality foments unnecessary fear and lubricates a costly national security-industrial complex that includes nearly a million individuals with high security clearances. Furthermore, I argue that the perception many Americans and Westerners have of al-Qaeda has taken hold of the public imagination and is not likely to change anytime soon. Evidence and reality no longer matter in a world built on perception and illusion. Every plot and incident is viewed as an affirmation of al-Qaeda's invincibility and reach: to the American leadership bin Laden and his successors appear to be 100 feet tall.

Time and again, we are told that all plots worldwide have al-Qaeda's signature and fingerprints. Until his death—and even after—the terrorism narrative portrayed bin Laden as a daring captain who guided his men to safety and provided them with operational direction. Before US officials have had time to translate and digest the "treasure trove" of documents seized at his hideout in Abbottabad, they leaked bits and pieces of information designed to show that he was in command and control of al-Qaeda and a "driving force" behind every recent al-Qaeda plot, providing operational direction and advice to his lieutenants worldwide, and not just ideology and inspiration. There was a concerted effort to underscore the significance of eliminating the head of the terrorist organization. Instead of demanding full disclosure and access to evidence and subjecting official leaks to critical scrutiny, commentators and terrorism experts repeated the charges like parrots and refrained from critically challenging the truncated official narrative. Few have wondered whether anyone out there cared about bin Laden's personal journal, and therefore whether—with but one courier by his side—bin Laden could have been a "driving force" behind every plot worldwide for the last five years.

Americans and Westerners are fed a constant diet of catastrophic scenarios and scare tactics. Like the Cold War era, mainstream politicians and analysts neither challenge the dominant terrorism narrative nor educate the Western public about al-Qaeda's self-limiting challenge—more of a security irritant than a strategic threat. The result is that the Western public, particularly Americans, has internalized an exaggerated fear of terrorism, which has become more a state of mind than an actual reality; it shapes their view of the world and themselves.

When asked in a recent poll to rate a list of countries or entities on a 1-to-10 scale based on the threat they pose to the United States,

61 percent of Americans placed al-Qaeda in the 9–10 or "very high" threat level. Nearly two-thirds of Americans consider al-Qaeda and its allies to pose the most serious security threat the United States faces, well above that from a saber-rattling North Korea or a fiery-tongued Iran. Ironically the *Christian Science Monitor*/TIPP poll was conducted between 29 November and 4 December 2010, shortly after North Korea shelled a small South Korean island off its coast, drawing the United States into the Korean Peninsula's heightened tensions and threatening a full-scale war. Nevertheless, al-Qaeda still topped North Korea as a strategic threat.[1]

Bin Laden and Zawahiri shattered Westerners' peace of mind and instilled disproportionate fear into their psyche. On this psychological level al-Qaeda has won the battle, even as they have suffered a shattering military loss. The fear of terrorism is much greater and more powerful than al-Qaeda's actual numbers or capability. All the War on Terror really does is legitimize al-Qaeda's failed ideology and expand the circle of enemies faced by Western and American interests worldwide. There will never be closure to the terrorism narrative as long as a few of bin Laden's men remain alive. In contrast to conventional warfare, it is unlikely that there will be a white flag or a surrender ceremony in the fight against al-Qaeda. In conventional terms, al-Qaeda cannot be defeated because it does not have an army and does not hold territory. Regardless of the death of their emir, bin Laden's remaining followers will carry on the losing fight.

Even Obama, who had been critical of the terrorism narrative before and during his presidential campaign, felt trapped once he assumed his duties as commander in chief. Terrorism experts who advised Obama during the presidential transition and who afterwards fed him alarming reports about al-Qaeda's increasing prowess and reach warned him against any shift of policy. The new strategy linked the Taliban to al-Qaeda and rejected any separation between them. Obama's national security team also impressed on him the need to expand counterterrorism operations worldwide to prevent the unthinkable—the detonation of a nuclear device inside the homeland. In an early fear-riddled report, then CIA Director Michael Hayden informed the new president that clandestine, lethal counterterrorism "'operations were active in more than 60 countries and if al Qaeda planned to detonate a nuclear weapon in an American city or launch an influenza pandemic by use of a biological agent, these covert actions are all you've really got to try to stop them,' Hayden explained."[2]

To drive the point home to the new president, Hayden and Director of National Intelligence Blair warned that one hundred Westerners, including many with US passports or visas, were being trained in Pakistani safe havens to return to their homelands to commit high-profile acts of terrorism: "Al Qaeda is training people in the tribal areas who, if you saw them in a visa line at Dulles, you would not recognize as potential terrorists," Hayden said.[3]

That warning caught Obama's attention. Feeling constrained, the new president bought into the core arguments of the terrorism narrative. In an interview with investigative journalist Bob Woodward, Obama expressed his concern that only one attack by al-Qaeda might reinforce Americans' fears and leave them with a psychological scar:

> What you've seen is a metastasizing of Al Qaeda, where a range of loosely affiliated groups now have the capacity and the ambition to recruit and train for attacks that may not be on the scale of 9/11, but obviously can still be extraordinary . . . One man, one bomb . . . which could still have, obviously an extraordinary traumatizing effect on the homeland.[4]

Moreover, during an Oval Office interview with Woodward, Obama volunteered some extended thoughts on terrorism; these shed light on why the new president bought the doomsday scenarios offered by his national security team. "'I said very early on, as a senator, and continued to believe as a presidential candidate and now as president, that we can absorb a terrorist attack,'" Obama said, to Woodward's surprise. "'We'll do everything that we can to prevent it, but even a 9/11, even the biggest attack ever, that ever took place on our soil, we absorbed it and we are stronger. This is a strong, powerful country that we live in, and our people are incredibly resilient,' the president stressed."[5]

Obama added that his previous thinking has now hardened in light of a greater concern: al-Qaeda's obtaining a nuclear bomb—a game changer in strategic parlance. "'A potential game changer would be a nuclear weapon in the hands of terrorists, blowing up a major American city. Or a weapon of mass destruction in a major American city,'" Obama told Woodward.

> "And so when I go down the list of things I have to worry about all the time, that is the top, because that's one area where you can't afford any mistakes. And so right away, coming in, we said, how are we going to start ramping up and putting that at the center of a lot of our national security discussions? Making sure that occurrence, even if remote, never happens," Obama concluded.[6]

What emerges clearly from Obama's interview with Woodward is the influence of the terrorism narrative on the president's changing views of the nature of the terrorism threat during his time in office. Obama once believed that the United States could withstand and weather any attack by al-Qaeda, including the September

11 suicide bombings, even though they were devastating, deadly, and costly; terrorism was not a strategic or an existential threat. Now, he said, a lone bomber, a lone attack, could psychologically traumatize the nation. President Obama seems to be more concerned about the psychological trauma of the US public than the actual threat by al-Qaeda, a threat which the United States can withstand, as he correctly noted.

This is, in a nutshell, why few politicians, including Obama, challenge the conventional narrative. The fear of terrorism has not only taken hold of the imagination of Americans, but also drives government policy.

The problem with the terrorism narrative is that it cannot be falsified. Any plot anywhere by al-Qaeda or its allies directed at the United States and the West will be deployed as evidence of the durability of the threat. The question is not if al-Qaeda is dangerous—of course it is. Despite its structural weakness, increasing evidence shows it still plots, operationally, to strike inside the United States and other European countries. But most of these plots are dependent on amateurs and freelancers who lack the skills and training and determination of the Afghan pioneer generation. By the time of his death, bin Laden had become overwhelmingly dependent on bottom-up volunteers and recruits, such as the failed underwear bomber, the would-be New York subway bomber, and the foiled Times Square bomber. Instead of explicitly acknowledging al-Qaeda's inherent structural weakness and vulnerability, the terrorism narrative contends that the transnational organization has adapted and shifted tactics to low-level, small attacks, an indirect admission of declining and diminishing ability.

In contrast, al-Qaeda's leadership exercises little operational control over the new phenomenon of bottom-up radicalization, at least beyond ideological incitement. Rather, the US War on Terror, first in Iraq and now in Afghanistan-Pakistan, has triggered a backlash among scores of disillusioned and frustrated young Muslims who live in Western societies, including the United States, as a headline article in the *New York Times* aptly noted after the failed Times Square bombing, "Fighting Terrorism, Creating Terrorists."[7] The presence of Western boots in Muslim lands and the costly wars radicalize important segments of Muslim opinion, particularly the middle class in urban cities, and also militarize a few young men who are ideologically and emotionally susceptible and vulnerable. Despite their apparent tactical success, US counterterrorism measures like the CIA drone attacks further fuel anti-American sentiments and calls for vengeance.

Yet neither the US national security apparatus nor terrorism experts are willing to create a link between the new phenomenon of bottom-up extremism and the US War on Terror, particularly in Afghanistan-Pakistan. While the question of cause and effect is bread and butter for social scientists and historians, it is lost in translation for the terrorism narrative. The latter offers a simpler formula: al-Qaeda's tentacles are spreading poison worldwide and, energized rather than dispirited by the loss of their founding father, its leadership is directing the new terrorist wave.

On its own, al-Qaeda's military losses do not explain its structural crisis and steep decline. Bin Laden's transnational jihad and tactics have been de-legitimized from within the world of Islam— discredited and undermined by prominent religious scholars and clerics and former cohorts who jumped ship. Far from gaining traction, Muslims did not jump on bin Laden and Zawahiri's bandwagon because they view it as aimless and pointless, devoid of a clear roadmap. For millions of Arabs and Muslims who revolted against dismal social conditions and oppression in early 2011, al-Qaeda has nothing concrete to offer them—no socioeconomic blueprint or political vision to the complex challenges and threats facing their societies. Their (on the whole) peaceful and dignified conduct speaks volumes about the disconnect between bin Laden and his small band, on the one hand, and Muslim publics on the other.

Al-Qaeda's social space has shrunk considerably and now faces a hostile environment with fewer recruits and shelter. In Iraq, Yemen, Palestine, Lebanon, Saudi Arabia, the Maghreb, Indonesia, and elsewhere, ordinary Muslims have joined the authorities in chasing al-Qaeda away from their neighborhoods and streets, a development that does not bode well for bin Laden and his men. Al-Qaeda's loss of Muslim public support (which it arguably never had in the first place), coupled with internal fragmentation, spells disaster for its leadership, whose gamble depended on winning Muslim hearts and minds and triggering a clash of cultures between the world of Islam and the Christian West. That crisis has recently been exacerbated by the success of Arab citizens at toppling some of their dictators without resorting to violence and terrorism.

Knowing the debilitating damage that the loss of Muslim public support has exacted on his organization, Zawahiri, now titular head of al-Qaeda, has recently attempted to distance the group from shedding civilian blood. In a largely neglected statement marking the ninth anniversary of the September 11 attacks, Zawahiri urged Muslims to embrace jihad but avoid indiscriminate slaughter: "We disown any operation which a jihadi group carries out in which it doesn't show concern for the safety of the Muslims," he said in a audio message, a message designed to respond to critics and change how Muslims view al-Qaeda.[8]

There is no doubt that al-Qaeda and its allies still actively plot to attack Western interests. If history is a guide to understanding the rise and fall of violent groups, there is often an interval between their loss of public support and their ideological and operational erosion and decay. Although al-Qaeda's low-level violence will persist for the foreseeable future, the rot that has set in is unstoppable. Plots against Western societies will persist as long as the United States is embroiled in wars in Muslim lands, a painful truth that terror pundits and Western officials refuse to acknowledge. The root causes of many recent homegrown terror plots lie in the raging conflicts in Iraq, Afghanistan, Pakistan, Somalia, and elsewhere.

The US War on Terror inflames anti-American sentiment in Muslim countries and creates more terrorists; it has allowed a ragtag guerrilla force to portray themselves as legitimate Muslim warriors and defenders of the umma. In this sense, America's overreaction provides the oxygen that sustains al-Qaeda.

The cultural reverberations of the terrorism narrative, such as the spreading of Islamophobia and intolerance and the undermining of liberal values and constitutional rights, are widely felt in United States and Western societies. The irrational fear of terrorism, coupled with a concerted ideological campaign by the far-right to equate Islamic ideals and precepts with Islamist militancy, has caused a public backlash against Islam and Muslims in the United States and Europe. Opinion polls—alarmingly—show that ever increasingly numbers of Westerners equate Islam and Muslims with violence and extremism. By overblowing the al-Qaeda threat and overlooking distinctions and differences among various religious groups, the terrorism narrative sows the seeds of cultural mistrust and suspicion and has supplied bin Laden and his successors with powerful ammunition to deploy in their ideological battle against Western societies. Time and again, they have used examples of Islamophobia to incite Muslims to carry out attacks against the West.

This book does not seek to offer extensive policy prescriptions—the analysis speaks for itself. However, I would argue that there are a few simple lessons to learn from it. The first is that US policymakers must bring a closure to the War on Terror. Second, there must be a concerted effort to debunk the terrorism narrative and break al-Qaeda's hold on the American imagination. Americans must be told that its ideology and tactics have been de-legitimized from within the world of Islam. There is no better way to gauge the irrelevance and insignificance of al-Qaeda than to heed the millions of peaceful Arabs who rebelled against their oppressive governments and called for freedom and open society.

Al-Qaeda has lost the struggle for Muslim hearts and minds and is hemorrhaging from its loss of Muslim public support, middle leadership, and skilled lieutenants and fighters. While al-Qaeda still actively plots to attack the United States and other Western societies, it no longer possesses the capabilities to carry out spectacular operations along the lines of September 11 or to inflict any significant damage.

In short, Americans and Westerners should be told that the war is over. One hopes that bin Laden's demise will mark the end of al-Qaeda's grip on the American imagination, as well as put a closure to the War on Terror. It is time to close this costly chapter and shift to a containment strategy to deal with the remnants of al-Qaeda and its local partners. Any containment strategy must now involve the empowerment of Muslim societies and the exercise of judicious restraint in the use of force. Western leaders must level with their citizens and make a plea for reflexivity; a plea that there is no absolute security and that their own security is organically linked to the rest of humanity. It must also be a plea about the limits and costs of force in international affairs. Terrorism cannot be eradicated by pushing a button, as in drone attacks, or even military intervention, because that is likely to cause a backlash—and ultimately more, not less, terrorism.

As for how to deal with recent terror plots and homegrown rad-icalization, there is an urgent need to expedite the withdrawal of Western, particularly American, boots from Muslim territories.[9] For Muslims, the presence of tens of thousands of US and NATO troops in their homeland remains a constant and deeply painful and humil-iating reminder of the European colonial legacy, a legacy of domina-tion and subjugation. Contrary to the typical view in the terrorism narrative, neither Iraqis nor Afghanis view the US military presence as benign and disinterested, nor designed to bring them security, peace, and democracy; rather, they see it as a foreign occupation, an intrusive, humiliating violation. Most of the recent bombing plots were a blowback against American military tactics and campaigns in Muslim countries.

US officials now know that their over-reliance on militarism and excessive use of force radicalizes Muslim populations and instigates calls for resistance and vengeance at home and abroad. Since Sep-tember 11, America's wars have created many more anti-American jihadis than al-Qaeda has ever fielded. For example, the US-led in-vasion and occupation of Iraq militarized Muslim opinion, shaped a new generation of jihadis, and generated hundreds of additional terrorist attacks and tens of thousands of civilian casualties, according to the US government's National Intelligence Estimate on "Trends in Global Terrorism: Implications for the United States."[10] Numerous independent studies have confirmed this trend.

Before the US invasion, Iraq never experienced suicide terrorism, and yet after the occupation, the country produced the largest arse-nal of "martyrs" ever seen, demonstrating additional evidence of the possible relationship between foreign occupation and suicide ter-rorism. Other examples can be found in Lebanon, Kashmir, and Sri Lanka, though one can reasonably argue that in the case of Kashmir and Sri Lanka the troops are not "foreign."[11] Now the conflicts in

Afghanistan-Pakistan (and Somalia, to a lesser extent) have replaced the Iraq war as a major source of radicalization, including that of homegrown terrorism. There is also a real danger that the longer the United States wages war on terrorism in Afghanistan-Pakistan, the more durable the threat that will come to haunt American and Western interests in the future. Pakistan's slide into anarchy will be a far greater catastrophe for American interests and regional stability than the current mess in Afghanistan.[12]

Even should the United States withdraw its troops from Iraq and Afghanistan in the next few years, as President Obama has pledged, the US military "footprint" in the greater Middle East would still be substantial enough to rankle opponents in the region. At the very moment Obama announced "the end of our combat mission in Iraq," the Pentagon dug deeper in the Middle East, in order to expand and upgrade military bases and other facilities throughout the Persian Gulf, including Kuwait, Qatar, Bahrain, the United Arab Emirates, Oman, and Saudi Arabia. This formidable, long-term military presence in the countries surrounding Iraq and encircling Iran is, indeed, likely to inflame anti-American sentiment in a region where distrust and suspicion of American objectives runs high.[13]

Neither al-Qaeda factions in Iraq nor al-Qaeda in the Arabian Peninsula in Yemen can survive a direct frontal confrontation with their own societies and governments. They are well aware that such a confrontation would trigger a public backlash against terror methods and ultimately doom them. The clash between militant Islamists and the Egyptian and Algerian authorities in the 1990s was a case in point. In the first half of the 1990s, Western security specialists feared that the Islamist insurgency would triumph in both countries and overthrow the pro-Western regimes there. Ultimately, the militants' destructive methods, coupled with their lack of a political and social vision, turned public opinion against them and brought about their defeat.

Time and again, domestic and transnational jihadis have proven to be their own worst enemies; their indiscriminate violence has alienated ordinary Muslims in Egypt, Algeria, Iraq, Lebanon, Saudi Arabia, Indonesia, and elsewhere. The al-Qaeda branch in Yemen and the remnants in Pakistan seem to be pursuing similar tactics and falling into a similar trap. The United States, together with the international community, can and should assist Yemen and Pakistan in rebuilding their institutions and empowering them to address their complex security threats. But the United States must resist the temptation of directly waging war on terrorism, as it is doing now, and turning the struggle into a confrontation between al-Qaeda and the West. That is precisely what bin Laden wanted America to do— to become militarily embroiled in Muslim lands and transform an internal political struggle into a clash of cultures and civilizations.

While in the short term it would be significant to begin removing Western troops from Muslim lands, that by itself will not be sufficient to resolve the underlying tensions and suspicions between the world of Islam and the Christian West. On both sides there is an urgent need to deactivate the cultural and political minefields that constantly threaten to explode. Both have a common moral responsibility to cut the fuse and stop the small minority within their rank. In particular, the United States should stop viewing the Middle East through the terrorism prism, the Israeli prism, and the black-gold prism—oil.

The democratic revolutions in various Arab countries represent a window of opportunity for the United States to rebuild broken bridges of trust with embattled societies in the region and support their quest for freedom and self-determination. The changes in North Africa and the Middle East represent a moment of great potential because the protesters are focused on jobs and human rights and appear to have little or no anti-Western or Islamist flavor. The United States must seize the moment and chart a new beginning with the people of the Middle East by taking a risk on people's aspirations for open and representative government, for promoting the rule of law and human rights, and for making structural investments in institution-building, including the economy. The United States can help tranform the Middle East. America should not just be on the right side of history. America must realize that Middle Eastern dictators have not only brought ruin to their societies, they have fueled anti-American and anti-Western sentiments there. A widespread belief among Middle Easterners holds that the United States is a partner in their oppression because of its support for their ruling tormentors.

Second, the excessive influence (more like a veto power) that Israel exercises over US mideast policy is a major contributing factor to the widespread Muslim hostility against the United States. The Israeli prism not only hinders the construction of a balanced, rational American foreign policy toward the region, but also poisons the wellsprings of relations between the West and the Muslim world in general. From Iran to Indonesia, America is held responsible for perpetuating the Palestinian predicament and empowering and allowing Israel to occupy Palestinian territory. The Palestine-Israel conflict is the fundamental fault line in the Islamic arena, not just the Arab region, and the source of 70 percent (in my estimation) of tensions and suspicions between Muslims and Americans.

In this sense, the establishment of a viable independent Palestinian state has become linked to US national strategic interests in the Muslim world. One good example of this came during President Obama's visit to Indonesia in November 2010. Responding to President Obama's speech at the University of Indonesia and his strategy of outreach to Muslims, Anis Matta, secretary general of the Prosperous Justice Party, Indonesia's largest Islamist political party, said the president's outreach to Muslims here and elsewhere would be influenced by a single issue. "What will Obama do in resolving the Israeli-Palestinian conflict?" Matta said. "If we don't see any progress, what he says is just a speech."[14]

The ongoing Palestine tragedy has also radicalized large segments of Muslims, undermined liberal voices in the Arab world and beyond, and empowered Islamist forces. In his acceptance speech for the CATO Institute's Milton Friedman Prize for Advancing Liberty, the Iranian dissident Akbar Ganji argued that the "gushing wound of Palestine is the most appropriate site for the worsening infection of fundamentalism."[15] Accordingly, a just solution to the Palestine predicament, and the formation of an independent Palestinian state, next to Israel, is essential to reconstructing the image of the United States in the Muslim world and the democratic transformation of the region.[16] But despite his occasional efforts to do so, President Obama has not succeeded in changing the Israeli lens through which the US foreign policy establishment and, above all, members of Congress view the Middle East.[17]

Obama and his administration have subscribed to the dominant narrative on Israel and, as millions of Arabs revolted against their dictators, his administration vetoed an Arab resolution at the UN Security Council condemning Israeli settlements in the Palestinian territories as an obstacle to peace. The irony is that the resolution— sponsored by at least 130 countries and backed by all 14 other members of the Security Council—is consistent with Obama's official stance on the construction of Jewish settlements. As the first veto exercised by the Obama administration under pressure from Congress and Israel's friends, it risks alienating Arabs and Muslims with whom he had promised to improve relations. This is a recipe for perpetual misunderstanding and conflict because, regardless of what types of governments emerge from the rubble of political authoritarianism in the Arab world, they will have assertive foreign policies that challenge Israel's hegemony and further consumption of Palestinian lands.

Meanwhile, Abbas' softened approach to the settlement issue and scandalous revelations shown in the Palestine Documents collectively demonstrate the huge challenge that Abu Mazen and Fatah face in the upcoming elections. He has lost significant authority and credibility in the eyes of many Palestinians because he has not delivered tangible progress on the peace front, and his regime is seen as corrupt. His close alliance with the US has hurt him and strengthened Hamas' narrative about the futility of making further concessions to the Israelis. The leaked negotiation documents obtained by al-Jazeera known as the "Palestine Papers"—offering wide-ranging concessions to the Israeli side—were the final nail in the Palestinian Authority's coffin. Hamas has gained more popularity at the expense of Abbas' PA and has emerged as a major winner of the social turmoil sweeping the Arab landscape, including Palestinian society.

The recent reconciliation agreement between Hamas and Fatah reflects three processes at work: (1) a weakened Palestinian Authority whose leader, Abu Mazen, gambled on President Obama to help deliver a Palestinian state; (2) failure of American diplomacy to deploy its political and material assets to broker a peace settlement; and (3) the revolution in Egypt which has brought an important shift in the country's foreign policy and approach towards Palestine. Obviously, Abbas has concluded that the Israeli leadership is not interested in a genuine settlement and that the Obama administration won't deliver the Israelis. He has decided to press for a United Nations declaration of statehood in September

2011 and has shifted focus to putting the Palestinian house in order and national unity.

The most effective means for Israel to escape its security dilemma would be to accept a peace settlement along the lines suggested by the international community, including the United States, its long-time ally: a two-state solution—one secure Jewish state and one secure Palestinian state living side by side in peace. The challenge facing the United States is to limit the preponderant influence that Israel exercises over its mideast foreign policy, which will serve US and Israeli interests alike. For example, in a major speech laying out his approach to the Middle East in May 2011, Obama was the first US president to publicly reaffirm that the borders between Israel and Palestine "'should be based on the 1967 lines with mutually agreed swaps." But when addressing the American Israel Public Affairs Committee (AIPAC), the pro-Israeli lobby, the following day, Obama took indirect aim at Netanyahu who flatly rejected Obama's vision, first by repeating what the Israeli prime minister objected to—the phrase pre-1967 borders—and then qualifying his statement by making a critical concession to Israel. "Mutually agreed swaps," he said, meant "that the parties themselves—Israelis and Palestinians—will negotiate a border that is different than the one that existed on June 4, 1967." It is difficult to see how the weak Palestinians can negotiate "mutually agreed swaps" with the superior Israelis who do not accept a return to the boundaries that existed before the war in June 1967.[18]

More importantly, there was no hint in Obama's much-heralded speech of any concrete US action or new initiative to implement the vision of two states, Israeli and Palestinian, living side by side in peace. In other words, Obama has deferred the resolution of Palestine-Israel to his second presidential term, that is, if he wins reelection.

Finally, clouding the vision of American policymakers is the country's addiction to oil and opposition to real, fundamental change in the greater Middle East. For the last sixty years, US foreign policy has, for the most part, sacrificed the rule of law and human rights at the altar of stability and security, narrowly defined. The fear of disruption of the oil flow and increased financial costs has blinded American officials and caused them to support local autocrats as guardians of the status quo. With very few exceptions, the United States has not taken the risk of supporting progressive and democratic voices and has backed oppressive Muslim rulers who frequently violate the human rights of their citizens. Bin Laden and his cohorts have exploited America's support for authoritarian clients to incite young Muslims to join their crusade against the "far enemy." On a deeper level, the lack of an open political space to debate and argue has created a vacuum of legitimate political authority: a vacuum that false prophets like bin Laden and Zawahiri try to fill.

The United States cannot and should not dictate the reformist agenda in the Middle East. However, as millions of Arab voices have, since early 2011, stridently called for real change, American leaders can and should lend support by pursuing a consistent approach toward the promotion of the rule of law and human rights and freedom at home and abroad and supporting the universal aspirations of millions of Arabs. America's equivocation on democratic principles, coupled with torture of terror suspects and illegal practices in US-run prisons after the September. 11 attacks, has undermined its moral authority and emboldened Middle Eastern rulers to tighten their grip on power. The United States must close the gap between rhetoric and reality via democratic promotion of universal rights, and by sending an unequivocal message to friend and foe alike about its commitment to these cherished goals. To do so would further dent the iron wall of authoritarianism and repression in the greater Middle East and ultimately bring about its collapse.

In his May 2011 speech laying out his approach toward the Arab revolutions, Obama sought to realign US foreign policy in the Arab region by saying the United States has a stake not just in the stability of nations, "but in the self-determination of individuals." The policy of the United States will promote political and economic reform across the region, a set of universal rights, and support transitions to democracy; said Obama: "Our support for these principles is not a secondary interest—today I am making it clear that it is a top priority that must be translated into concrete actions, and supported by all of the diplomatic, economic and strategic tools at our disposal."[19] Obama indirectly acknowledged that his administration has not been consistent in its stance toward allies like Bahrain and Yemen that have suppressed dissent, though he mildly reproached them with only a slap on the wrist. If Obama translates rhetoric into concrete policy toward America's friends and foes alike, that would herald a new chapter in Arab-American relations. However, as the recent peaceful revolutions have shown, only Arabs and Muslims—with the support of the international community—can transform their society and embark on a democratic journey. Like their eastern European counterparts in the 1980s and 1990s, the Arabs' democratic journey will be rocky, messy, uneven, and long. There is no assurance of successful democratic transformation, and there will undoubtedly be setbacks. Despite the removal of the Tunisian and Egyptian strongmen, the army still calls the shots in almost every Arab country. The most difficult challenge is to institutionalize the relationship between the army and civilian leadership and put an end to domination by the senior ranks of the military. Like eastern Europe, the Arab transition from political authoritarianism to more open, pluralistic societies will take decades, not just years.

Nevertheless, the democratic virus is spreading and creating a new language—and a new era—of politics in the Arab world: an era in which Arabs and Muslims will not allow a small misguided minority to seize their voice. In this new landscape, al-Qaeda and like-minded factions will lack the oxygen to survive unless, of course, the democratic promise is aborted and legitimate grievances are not met. The risks are real but the rewards are worthwhile. The role of the United States, together with the United Nations and the international community, is critical in keeping pressure on the military in Egypt, Tunisia, and elsewhere, to honor their pledges of guiding the transition to a democratic government.

Only Muslims, with the support of the international community, can undermine al-Qaeda's transnational ideology and disfranchise bin Laden and his cohorts. Since September 11, prominent Muslim clerics and opinion-makers have condemned al-Qaeda's violent tactics and twisted interpretation of religious texts and doctrines, particularly the institution of jihad. Nevertheless, there is a widespread, false belief among Muslims that al-Qaeda is an American invention, more of a myth than a reality, that is not worth serious engagement. In contrast to the terrorism narrative in the West that paints al-Qaeda as a strategic threat, many Muslims dismiss it as irrelevant and even nonexistent. While al-Qaeda has taken hold of the imagination of Westerners, it has not had a major impact on the imagination of Muslims. The two opposing narratives shed light on the degree of misunderstanding and suspicion between the two sides.

Muslims must directly confront al-Qaeda's ideology and formulate a concerted and systematic campaign to educate the youth about its theological pitfalls (many have already begun to do so). A high strategic priority must be directed to the education of the Muslim youth and the prevention of radicalization and militarization. Religiously based radical ideologies deploy dubious theological arguments and lift partial scriptural verses and texts out of context to convince young Muslims that Islam justifies violence against civilians.[20]

Muslim civil societies, governments, and the religious establishment must join forces and develop an effective counter-radicalization strategy, one anchored in an ethical foundation of cultural tolerance. There is an urgent need to reclaim the philosophical and moral foundation of the sacred and downplay the political, a difficult and complex task but also a critical one. Identity politics must not overshadow and trample on universal and humanist principles, a regrettably dominant feature in the authoritarian political order in the region for the last four decades. Phobias about the West are as destructive as Islamophobia, as the September 11 attacks prove.

In the long term, radical ideologies will find shelter in Muslim countries as long as there is a vacuum of legitimate political authority, an increasing gap between those who govern and their citizens. The Arab arena, in particular, has suffered from excessive political repression and dismal social and economic conditions—unemployment among the educated youth is in the double-digits and abject poverty afflicts non-oil-producing Arab states (approximately 40 percent of Arabs live in poverty). That dark climate, coupled with closed political space, makes the Arab area vulnerable to extremist ideologies. For example, between 33 and 50 percent of approximately 120 million young Arabs roughly between the ages of 12 and 25 say they would like to emigrate permanently to another country, according to a 2010 Gallup survey. The Dubai-based poll shows that this desire by the youth to leave is not only about finding better or higher-paying jobs, but also relates to opinions on economic conditions and political governance.[21] It is no wonder that since December 2010 social revolutions have shaken the very foundation of the failed autocratic political and economic order in the Arab world.

Ultimately, the critical variable that is likely to determine the contest/confrontation between al-Qaeda operators and local governments is the degree of legitimacy the latter possess in the eyes of their Muslim populations. Legitimacy requires the establishment of representative and responsive governments and open political systems where grievances can be publicly aired. Without this factor, while pro-Western Muslim regimes are likely to win most of the battles they fight against terrorists simply by force, it is unlikely that they will win the war in any conclusive fashion because there will always be a small, disgruntled constituency that will provide a source of support for terrorists and extremists.

Tyranny, dismal social conditions, authoritarian political systems, and the absence of hope provide the fuel that powers radical, absolutist ideologies in the Muslim world; they are the mother of all ailments that afflict the region, including al-Qaeda, a parasite that feeds on political and social turmoil and repression. It is not enough to simply focus on the violent ideology of al-Qaeda without devoting sufficient attention to the social conditions that give rise to such ideologies. The greatest challenge facing the Arabic-Islamic arena in the years to come is to find a way for a smooth transition from political authoritarianism and one-party, family-based rule, to an open democratic polity where all citizens—men and women—are equal before the law. Democratization, in other words, is now a moral imperative. In this sense, if the Arab revolutions manage to fill the gap of legitimate political authority, they will annihilate al-Qaeda and like-minded local branches. Only then will al-Qaeda, like Osama bin Laden, not only die, but, finally, be allowed to die.

NOTES

Introduction

1. "A New Approach to Safeguarding Americans," remarks by John O. Brennan, Assistant to the President for Homeland Security and Counterterrorism—as prepared for delivery (Center for Strategic and International Studies, Washington, DC), The White House, Office of the Press Secretary, 6 August 2009.

2. Eamon Javers, "Clinton: Al Qaeda More 'Agile,'" Politico, 2 July 2010, http://www.politico.com/news/stories/0210/32633.html (with video clip).

3. Ross Colvin and Caren Bohan, "Obama: al Qaeda Bid to Go Nuclear Is Top Threat," Reuters, 11 April 2010, http://www.reuters.com/article/idUS-TRE63A1YJ20100412.

4. Ibid.

5. Lucy Madison, "Attorney General Eric Holder: Threat of Homegrown Terrorism 'Keeps Me Up at Night,'" ABCNews.com, 23 December 2010.

6. John Mueller, *Atomic Obsession* (New York: Oxford University Press, 2010), pp. 155–236.

7. Scott Wilson and Mary Beth Sheridan, "Obama Leads Summit's Nuclear Security Efforts; 'This Is Truly a Global Issue' Challenge Is in Persuading Others," *Washington Post*, 11 April 2010; Colvin and Bohan, "Obama: al Qaeda Bid."

8. Peter D. Zimmerman and Jeffrey G. Lewis, "The Bomb in the Backyard," *Foreign Policy* (November/December 2006), pp. 32–39. According to Mueller, Zimmerman and Lewis understate the costs wildly: the conspirators would be lucky to buy off three people with such a paltry sum of $10 million. Moreover, the terrorists would be required to expose their ultimate goals to at least some

215

of the corrupted, and at that point (if not earlier) they would become potential extortion victims. They could not afford to abandon unreliable people who know their goals (though they could attempt to kill them), and such people would now enjoy essentially monopoly powers to ever escalate their price. The cost of the operation in bribes alone could easily become ten times the sum suggested by Zimmerman and Lewis. And even at that, Mueller notes, there would be, of course, a considerable risk that those so purchased would, at an exquisitely opportune moment of their own choosing, decide to take the money and run—perhaps to the authorities representing desperate governments with essentially bottomless bankrolls and an overwhelming incentive to expend resources to stop the atomic plot and capture or kill the scheming perpetrators. See Mueller, *Atomic Obsession*, p. 178.

9. Ibid., pp. 155–236.

10. Ibid.

11. On level "A" threat, see Ashton B. Carter and William J. Perry, *Preventive Defense: A New Security Strategy for America* (Washington, DC: Brookings Institution Press, 1999), pp. 11–15; Joseph S. Nye, Jr., "Redefining the National Interest," *Foreign Affairs* 78, no. 4 (July–August 1999).

12. In their forthcoming book, *Terror, Security, and Money* (New York: Oxford University Press, 2011), Mark Stewart and John Mueller calculate that the enhanced costs of the War on Terror—increased costs of domestic security beyond those in place on 10 September 2001 have totaled more than $1 trillion. The costs for overseas ventures like the Afghanistan and Iraq wars, part of the War on Terror, have so far come to at least an additional $2 trillion and may well be twice that.

Joseph Stiglitz and Linda Bilmes estimate that the direct and indirect costs of the Iraq war will top $3 trillion, and they say that their estimates are conservative: at least $600 billion would be needed for the lifetime healthcare costs for injured US soldiers, $400 billion due to loss of workers to the economy, both injured and those serving in the National Guard, $600 billion for interest on money borrowed to finance the war, and $1–$2 trillion is the macro-economic impact of the war. See Linda Bilmes and Joseph Stiglitz, *The Three Trillion Dollar War: The True Cost of the Iraq Conflict* (New York: W. W. Norton and Company, 2008).

Congress has allocated $1.05 trillion to the Iraq and Afghanistan wars. See "Notes and Sources: Cost of War Counter," National Priorities Project, http:// www.nationalpriorities.org/cost_of_war_counter_notes.

As of 2008, the United States has spent more than $300 billion on a new post–September 11 Department of Homeland Security, a second "defense" department. The $300 billion does not include what local and state governments and private businesses have spent on homeland security. In addition, the cumulative increased cost of counterterrorism for the United States since September 11 (the federal, state, local, and private expenditures as well as opportunity costs) has topped $1 trillion. See Mueller, "Terrorphobia: Our False Sense of Insecurity," *American Interest* (May/June 2008), http://www.the-american-interest.com/article.cfm?piece=418.

In addition, "An assessment of increased United States federal homeland security expenditure since 2001 and expected lives saved as a result of such expenditure suggests that the annual cost ranges from $64 million to $600 million (or even more) per life saved, greatly in excess of the regulatory safety goal of $1 million to $10 million per life saved. As such, it clearly and dramatically fails a cost-benefit analysis. In addition, the opportunity cost of these expenditures, amounting to $32 billion per year, is considerable, and it is highly likely that far more lives would have been saved if the money (or even a portion of it) had been invested instead in a wide range of more cost-effective risk mitigation programs." See M. G. Stewart and J. Mueller, "Assessing the Costs and Benefits of United States Homeland Security Spending," Research Report No. 265.04.08, Centre for Infrastructure and Reliability, University of Newcastle, Australia.

Since September 11, the US defense budget for foreign counterterrorism has increased considerably. It is hard to find comprehensive data on foreign aid related to counterterrorism, especially key "front-line" states in the "War on Terror"—Pakistan, Afghanistan, Yemen, Turkey, Jordan, Lebanon, Indonesia, Philippines, and others—a category of security assistance used during the Cold War to provide support to key geopolitical allies. For example, the level of development assistance "nearly tripled from approximately $10 billion in 2000 to $28.5 billion in 2005. In October 2009, President Obama allocated $7.5 billion for Pakistan." See Stephen Kaufman, "Bush's Budget Request Would Continue Increase in Foreign Aid: USAID Administrator Says U.S. Aid Has Nearly Tripled Since 2000," America.gov, 5 February 2007, http://www.america.gov/st/washfile-english/2007/February/20070205173017esnam fuak8.193606e-02.html#ixzz0i9F93xof; Jim Lobe, "U.S. Foreign Aid Budget Takes on Cold War Cast," Inter Press Service (IPS News), 3 February 2004, http://www.ipsnews.net/interna.asp?idnews=22232; "Obama Signs Big Pakistan Aid Bill," BBC News, 15 October 2009, http://news.bbc.co.uk/1/hi/world/americas/8309643.stm.

13. There is a tremendous volume of foreign policy literature on bureaucracies and their natural tendency to grow and multiply over time. Scholars argue that government bureaucracies develop internal pressures for self-aggrandizement and expansion. See William A. Niskanen Jr., *Bureaucracy and Representative Government* (Chicago: Aldine-Atherton, 1971); Hugh Heclo and Aaron B. Wildavsky, *The Private Government of Public Money: Community and Policy Inside British Politics* (London: Macmillan, 1974); Anthony Downs, "A Theory of Bureaucracy," Rand Paper, 1964; Daniel Tarschys, "The Growth of Public Expenditures: Nine Modes of Explanation," *Scandinavian Political Studies* 10 (1975).

14. Dana Priest and William Arkin, "Top-Secret America: A Hidden World, Growing beyond Control," *Washington Post*, 18 July 2010 (part 1). See also "Top-Secret America: National Security Inc," *Washington Post*, 20 July 2010 (part 2); "Top-Secret America: The Secrets Next Door," *Washington Post*, 21 July 2010 (part 3); Kimberly Dozier, "Total U.S. Intelligence Bill Tops $80 Billion," Associated Press, 28 October 2010.

15. Priest and Arkin, "Top-Secret America: A Hidden World."

16. Ibid.

17. Ibid.

18. "Obama: Human, Systemic Failure to Blame in Terror Attempt," CNN.com, 30 December 2009, http://edition.cnn.com/2009/POLITICS/12/29/airline.terror.obama/index.html; "Obama on Intel System: 'This Was a Screw-Up,'" CNN.com, 6 January 2010, http://edition.cnn.com/2010/POLITICS/01/05/obama.terror.meeting/index.html.

19. "Obama on Intel System," CNN.com.

20. Priest and Arkin, "Top-Secret America: National Security Inc."

21. Mark Mazzetti and Scott Shane, "Data Show Bin Laden Plots; C.I.A. Hid Near Raided House," *New York Times*, 5 May 2011.

22. For a strong overview of the privatization of American national security policy, see Peter W. Singer, who provides an excellent overview in his work *Corporate Warriors: The Rise of the Privatized Military Industry* (Ithaca, NY: Cornell Security Studies, 2003).

23. Ibid.

24. Ibid.

25. Rohan Gunaratna and Anders Nielsen, "Al Qaeda in the Tribal Areas of Pakistan and Beyond," *Studies in Conflict & Terrorism* 31, no. 9 (September 2008), pp. 775–807.

26. David E. Singer and Mark Mazzetti, "New Estimate of Strength of Al Qaeda Is Offered," *New York Times*, 30 June 2010.

27. Mazeetti and Shane, "Data Show Bin Laden Plots," Associated Press, 3 May 2011; Mazeetti and Shane, "Phone Call by Kuwaiti Courier Led to bin Laden," Associated Press, 3 May 2011.

28. Jonathan Marcus, "Osama Bin Laden: At al-Qaeda's Helm in Abbottabad," BBC.com, 12 May 2011; Pierre Thomas and Martha Raddatz, "Osama Bin Laden Operational Journal among Evidence from SEAL Raid," ABC NEWS.com, 11 May 2011; Pete Williams, "Al-Qaeda Aspired to Attack U.S. Train on 9/11/11: Records Seized in bin Laden Raid Show Anniversary Plot under Consideration," NBC News.com, 6 May 2011.

29. See the Pew research polls or Shibley Telhami's 2010 poll of Arab opinion available here: http://www.brookings.edu/reports/2010/0805_arab_opinion_poll_telhami.aspx. Also see John Esposito and Dalia Mogahed, *Who Speaks for Islam? What Do A Billion Muslims Really Think?* (New York: Gallup Press, 2008).

30. Ibid.

31. In his press conference after Egyptian President Mubarak was forced to resign, Obama echoed a similar sentiment: "Egyptians have inspired us, and they've done so by putting the lie to the idea that justice is best gained through violence. For Egypt, it was the moral force of non-violence—not terrorism, not mindless killing—but non-violence, moral force that bent the arch of history toward justice once more." Robert Mackey, "Updates on Day 18 of Egypt Protests," *New York Times*, 11 February 2011.

32. Juan R. Cole, *Engaging the Muslim World* (New York: Palgrave Macmillan, 2009); Rashid Khalidi, *Resurrecting Empire: Western Footprints and America's Perilous Path in the Middle East* (Boston: Beacon Press, 2005); Robert Jervis, *American Foreign Policy in a New Era* (New York: Routledge, 2005); Francis Fukuyama, *America at the Crossroads: Democracy, Power, and the Neoconservative Legacy* (New Haven: Yale University Press, 2006); "Iraq/Middle East," Project for the New American Century, http://www.newamericancentury. org/iraqmiddleeast2000-1997.htm.

33. Loretta Napoleoni, *Insurgent Iraq: Al Zarqawi and the New Generation* (New York: Seven Stories Press, 2005); Jean-Charles Brisard, *Zarqawi: The New Face of Al-Qaeda* (Cambridge: Polity Press, 2005).

34. Priest and Arkin, "Top-Secret America: A Hidden World."

35. John Barry and Evan Thomas, "A War Within," *Newsweek*, 12 September 2010.

36. Benjamin Friedman, Jim Harper, and Christopher Preble, eds., *Terrorizing Ourselves: Why U.S. Counterterrorism Policy is Failing and How to Fix It* (Washington, DC: Cato Institute, 2010).

37. Daniel Luban, "The New Anti-Semitism," *Tablet*, 19 August 2010, http:// www.tabletmag.com/news-and-politics/43069/the-new-anti-semitism-2/; Emran Qureshi and Michael Sells, eds., *The New Crusades: Constructing the Muslim Enemy* (New York: Columbia University Press, 2003); Matti Bunzl, *Anti-Semitism and Islamophobia: Hatreds Old and New in Europe* (Chicago: Prickly Paradigm Press, 2007); Peter Gottschalk and Gabriel Greenberg, *Islamophobia: Making Muslims the Enemy* (Lanham, MD: Roman and Littlefield, 2007); Bobby Ghosh, "Does America Have a Muslim Problem," *Time*, 30 August 2010. For a deeper historical account, see Thierry Hentsch, *Imagining the Middle East* (Montreal: Black Rose Books, 1992); Norman Daniel, *Islam and the West: The Making of an Image* (Oxford: Oneworld, 2009).

38. James Shanahan and Erik C. Nisbet (Media & Society Research Group of Cornell University), "Restrictions on Civil Liberties, Views of Islam, & Muslim Americans," 17 December 2004, Institute for Social Policy and Understanding, http://www.ispu.org/reports/articledetailpb-64.html.

39. Luban, "The New Anti-Semitism."

40. Martin Peretz, "The New York Times Laments 'A Sadly Wary Misunderstanding of Muslim-Americans.' But Really Is It 'Sadly Wary' or a 'Misunderstanding' at All?" 4 September 2010, *New Republic*, http://www.tnr.com/

blog/77475/the-new-york-times-laments-sadly-wary-misunderstanding-muslim-americans-really-it-sadly-w; Nicholas D. Kristof, "Is This America?" *New York Times*, 11 September 2010.

41. Martin Peretz, "An Apology," 13 September 2010, *New Republic*, http://www.tnr.com/blog/the-spine/77607/martin-peretz-apology.

42. Laurie Goodstein, "Across Nation, Mosque Projects Meet Opposition," *New York Times*, 7 August 2010; Ron Scherer, "Ground Zero and Beyond: Four Mosque Battles Brew across US," *Christian Science Monitor*, 19 August 2010.

43. "Address by Newt Gingrich, America at Risk: Camus, National Security and Afghanistan," 29 July 2010, American Enterprise Institute for Public Policy Research.

44. Andy Barr, "Newt Gingrich Compares Mosque to Nazis," Politico, 16 August 2010, http://www.politico.com/news/stories/0810/41112.html; Maureen Dowd, "Our Mosque Madness," *New York Times*, 17 August 2010.

45. Richard Kim, "The Center Cannot Hold: Why the Mainstream Media Can't Stop the 'Ground Zero Mosque' Hysteria," *Nation*, 19 August 2010, http://www.thenation.com/blog/154077/center-cannot-hold-why-mainstream-media-cant-stop-ground-zero-mosque-hysteria.

46. "Under Fire, Obama Clarifies Support for Ground Zero Mosque," Fox News, 14 August 2010; Dowd, "Our Mosque Madness."

47. From http://en.wikiquote.org/wiki/James_Madison.

48. Gallup and the Co-Exist Foundation, "Religious Perceptions in America."

49. James Carroll, "How to Spot an Islamophobe," Daily Beast, 30 January 2010, http://thedailybeast.com/blogs-and-stories/2010-01-30/how-to-spot-an-islamaph.

50. Ibid.

51. "National Security Strategy," May 2010, The White House, http://www.whitehouse.gov/sites/default/files/rss_viewer/national_security_strategy.pdf.

52. "A New Approach to Safeguarding Americans," remarks by John O. Brennan.

53. "Remarks by the President at United States Military Academy at West Point Commencement," The White House, Office of the Press Secretary, 22 May 2010, http://www.whitehouse.gov/the-press-office/remarks-president-united-states-military-academy-west-point-commencement.

54. "National Security Strategy," May 2010, The White House.

55. "A New Approach to Safeguarding Americans."

56. In terms of language, Obama's national security advisers have removed terms such as "Islamic radicalism" from a new document outlining national security strategy and will use the new version to emphasize that the United States does not view Muslims through the lens of terrorism. Distancing themselves from the Bush National Security Strategy, which outlined his doctrine of preventive war and which states, "The struggle against militant Islamic radicalism is the great ideological conflict of the early years of the 21st century," Obama's

advisers say that changing terminology is part of a larger effort, one that seeks to change how the United States talks to the Muslim world, as well as what it talks about, from technology transfer to health care, education, and business startups. See Matt Apuzzo, "Not All Terrorism: Obama Tries to Change Subject," Associated Press, 7 April 2010.

57. In a revealing interview, former Vice President Richard Cheney said he was concerned that the Obama national security team is not ready to deal with the new threats facing the United States in the post–September 11 era. He noted that there "are a lot of people who did good work and were honorable civil servants and public servants during the Clinton administration coming back in. One of the things I worry about, though, is they'll assume they can pick up right where they left off. And the fact is the world has changed in major ways since January of '01 when we took over. And that break in service of some eight years, I think, they will find has been a period of time when the threat to the nation has changed in fairly dramatic ways." See "Political Punch: Cheney Assails Obama Decision to Close Gitmo; Expresses Concern That Democrats About to Take Over Don't Realize World Has Changed," ABC News, 13 January 2009, http://blogs.abcnews.com/politicalpunch/2009/01/cheney-assails.html.

In a speech to the American Enterprise Institute, Cheney questioned Obama's decision to close Guantanamo Bay and his approach to national security. He said, "What's more, to completely rule out enhanced interrogation methods in the future is unwise in the extreme. It is recklessness cloaked in righteousness, and would make the American people less safe." According to Cheney, "There is never a good time to compromise when the lives and safety of the American people are in the balance." Criticizing Obama's approach in the fight against terrorism in general, Cheney said that "behind the overwrought reaction to enhanced interrogations is a broader misconception about the threats that still face our country. You can sense the problem in the emergence of euphemisms that strive to put an imaginary distance between the American people and the terrorist enemy. Apparently using the term 'war' where terrorists are concerned is starting to feel a bit dated. So henceforth we're advised by the administration to think of the fight against terrorists as, quote, 'Overseas contingency operations.'" See "Transcript of Former Vice President Dick Cheney's Speech on Interrogation," delivered at the American Enterprise Institute, 21 May 2009, About.com Guide by Justin Quinn, http://usconservatives. about.com/od/capitalpunishment/a/Cheney_AEI_Speech.htm.

58. Noah Feldman, "How Different Is Obama from Bush on Terrorism," *Foreign Policy*, 3 September 2010.

59. *Washington Post*, 14 February 2010; *New York Times*, March 17, 2010; David Cole, "License to Kill," *Nation,* 16 April 2010.

60. Adam Entous, "Special Report: How the White House Learned to Love the Drone," Reuters, 18 May 2010; Feldman, "How Different Is Obama."

61. "U.S. Believes It Can Now Destroy al Qaeda," Reuters, 3 May 2011.

62. Karin Brulliard, "Anger Simmers in Pakistani Army over bin Laden Raid," *Washington Post*, 19 May 2011).

63. Adam Levine, "Bin Laden Raid Was Humiliating to Pakistanis, Gates and Mullen Say," CNN.com, 18 May 2011.

64. Bergen and Tiedemann, "The Year of the Drone"; "Latest Drone Strikes in Northwest Pakistan Kill 15," CNN.com, 16 September 2010. Bergen and Tiedemann reach a similar conclusion in their policy paper that analyzes drone attacks from 2004 to 2010. They found that since Obama entered office, the use of drone attacks has risen considerably. Using US military sources and media reports, they observe that the civilian casualty rate of drone attacks is 32 percent and that the majority of the time these attacks have hit their target. While the accuracy of the drone attacks is convincing, Bergen and Tiedemann call into question their efficacy. First, they have not stopped the rise of terrorist attacks in Afghanistan and Pakistan, and the attacks have not stopped the replacement of new operatives and the launching of new operations. Second, the drone attacks are questionable under international law. Third, the employment of drones is a tactic and not a strategy, and they do not provide a solution to winning the war against the Taliban. Finally, they have been received very negatively by the Pakistani public and serve as a recruitment tool for the Taliban and al-Qaeda. However, the accuracy of these attacks has been greatly underestimated in this study. Pakistani and human rights organization sources calculate the casualty rate to be significantly higher. Thus, the accuracy and the efficacy of drone attacks indicate that the costs of these attacks far outweigh the benefits. Bergen and Tiedemann, "The Year of the Drone."

    In his book, *Dying to Win: The Strategic Logic of Suicide Terrorism* (New York: Random House, 2005), Robert Pape sheds light on the reasons for suicide terrorism and the linkage between drone attacks and the occurrence of suicide terrorism plots against the United States. He examined over 400 terrorist attacks between 1980 and 2003 and concluded that instead of ideological motivations or economic reasons, the logic of suicide terrorism is driven by strategic means—to end foreign occupation of Muslim lands. Individuals who carry out suicide attacks are often used by groups to achieve their strategic objectives, and on the personal level, their actions are supported by their community and motivated by the perceived altruism for their actions.

65. "Analysis: Obama Being Re-evaluated after Gutsy Raid," Associated Press, 6 May 2011.

66. Dozier, "Mullen Says Al-Qaeda Threat from Yemen Is Serious"; "Qaeda Thousand Cuts Threat 'Very Serious,' Says Mullen," Agence France-Presse (AFP), 21 November 2010.

67. "Qaeda Thousand."

Chapter 1

1. Rohan Gunaratna, *Inside Al Qaeda: Global Network of Terror* (New York: Columbia University Press, 2003), p. xxxiii.

2. Ibid., p. xxxv.

3. For example, see Paul Berman, *Terror and Liberalism* (New York: W. W. Norton, 2003).

4. Ahmed al-Khatib, "Second Revisions of Tanzim al-Jihad: Sayyid Fadl, Mufti al-Jihad, Responds to Zawahiri's 'Exoneration': Al-Qa'ida's Second-in-Command is a 'Hypocrite,'" no. 12, 1 December 2008; Muntasir al-Zayyat, *Ayman al-Zawahiri kama araftuhu* [Ayman al-Zawahiri as I knew him] (Cairo, 2002). See Zawahiri's memoirs in which he acknowledges Qutb's influence, *Fursan tahta rayat al-nabi* [Knights under the prophet's banner] (serialized in *al-Sharq al-Awsat,* December 2001).

5. Sayyid Qutb, *Ma'alam fi al-tariq* [*Milestones*] (Cedar Rapids, IA: The Mother Mosque Foundation, n.d.); Qutb, *Limaza a'damunani* [Why they executed me] (n.p and n.d, http://www.tawhed.ws); Ibrahim M. Abu-Rabi, *Intellectual Origins of Islamic Resurgence in the Modern Arab World* (New York: State University of New York Press, 1996).

6. Zawahiri, *Fursan*.

7. Khatib, "Second Revisions," no. 3, 21 November 2008.

8. See also the memoirs of Hani al-Sibai, a former leader of al-Jihad: Kamal Tawil, a series of four lengthy interviews with Egyptian Islamist Hani al-Sibai [in Arabic] *al-Hayat,* 1–4 September 2002; Zayyat, *Ayman al-Zawahiri*; Khatib, "Second Revisions," no. 11, 30 November 2008. See also *al-Hayat,* 24 January 2001.

9. Muntasir al-Zayyat, "al-Gamaa al-Islamiya: ruiya min al-dahil" [in Arabic; "Islamic groups: An inside-out view"] (the book was serialized in *al-Hayat,* 10–14 January 2005); Zayyat, *Ayman al-Zawahiri*.

10. Khatib, "Second Revisions," no. 11, 20 November 2008. See Zawahiri, *Fursan*.

11. This section on bin Laden relies heavily on Steve Coll, *The Bin Ladens: An Arabian Family in the American Century* (London: Penguin Books, 2008); Peter Bergen, *The Osama bin Laden I Know: An Oral History of al-Qaeda's Leader* (New York: Free Press, 2006).

12. See Join the Caravan: http://www.kavkazcenter.com/eng/content/2007/05/28/8351.shtml. See also Defense of the Muslim Lands: http://www.religioscope.com/info/doc/jihad/azzam_defence_1_table.htm.

13. Abdel Bari Atwan, *The Secret History of Al-Qa'ida* (London: Saqi, 2006), p. 74.

14. Khatib, "Second Revisions," no. 8, 27 November 2008.

15. Ibid., no. 12, 1 December 2008.

16. Gunaratna, *Inside Al Qaeda*, p. 3.

17. Azzam's definition of *al-qaeda al-sulba* is a similar to Qutb's vanguard and refers to a tactic: "Every principle needs a vanguard to carry it forward, and while

focusing its way into society, [it] puts up with heavy tasks and enormous sacrifices. There is no ideology, neither earthly nor heavenly, that does not require such a vanguard that gives everything it possesses in order to achieve victory for this ideology. It carries the flag along the sheer, endless and difficult path until it reaches its destination in the reality of life, since Allah has destined it should make it and manifest itself. This vanguard constitutes al-Qaeda al-sulba for the expected society." See Abdullah Azzam, "al-Qaeda al-sulba," *al-Jihad*, no. 41, April 1998, p. 46.

18. Khatib, "Second Revisions," no. 10, 29 November 2008.
19. Jason Burke, *Al Qaeda: The True Story of Radical Islam* (London: I.B. Tauris, 2003), p. 2.
20. Gunaratna, *Inside Al Qaeda*, pp. xxviii, 1–3.
21. Khatib, "Second Revisions," no. 9, 28 November 2008.
22. Lawrence Wright, *The Looming Tower: Al Qaeda and the Road to 9/11* (New York: Alfred A. Knopf, 2006), p. 131.
23 Yaroslav Trofimov, *The Siege of Mecca: The Forgotten Uprising* (London: Penguin Books, 2007), p. 7.
24. Khatib, "Second Revisions," no. 3, 21 November 2001. See ibid., no. 10, 29 November 2008.
25. Wright, *The Looming Tower*, p. 151.
26. Peter L. Bergen, *Holy War, Inc.: Inside the Secret World of Osama bin Laden* (New York: Touchstone, 2001), pp. 81–82.
27. Gunaratna, *Inside Al Qaeda*.
28. Burke, *Al Qaeda*, pp. 2–10.
29. Mohammed Salah, "Al-Hayat in the Egyptian Tura Prison Speaks with the author of 'Rationalizing Jihad in Egypt and the World,'" no. 1 of 6, 9 December 2007.
30. See *The Encyclopedia of Afghan Jihad*, a copy of which was acquired by Associated Press, 2 October 2001. Burke, *Al Qaeda*, pp. 3–4.
31. *Al-Quds al-Arabi*, 24 November 2001. For an English translation, see "Part One of a Series of Reports on bin Laden's Life in Sudan: Islamists Celebrated Arrival of 'Great Islamic Investor,'" *Al-Quds al-Arabi*, 24 November 2001, translated by PBS.
32. Khatib, "Second Revisions," no. 11, 30 November 2001.
33. Ibid, no. 10, 29 November 2008.
34. Salah, "Al-Hayat," no. 4 of 6, 11 December 2007.
35. Burke, *Al Qaeda*, p. 4.
36. Ibid., pp. 142, 154. Lawrence Wright reaches a similar conclusion to Burke's: "The actions [attacks] in Aden, Somalia, Riyadh, and Dhahran may have been inspired by his [bin Laden] words, but it has never been demonstrated that he commanded the terrorists who carried them out. Although Ramzi Yousef had trained in an al-Qaeda camp, bin Laden was not connected to the 1993

World Trade Center bombing. Bin Laden told the London-based Palestinian editor Abdel Bari Atwan that al-Qaeda was responsible for the ambush of American forces in Mogadishu in 1993, the National Guard Training Center bombing in Riyadh in 1995, and the Khobar Towers bombing in 1996 but there is no evidence to substantiate these claims." Wright, *The Looming Tower*, pp. 208–212, 246.

37. *Messages to the World: The Statements of Osama Bin Laden*, edited and introduced by Bruce Lawrence and translated by James Howarth (London and New York: Verso, 2005), pp. 15–16.

38. Wright, *The Looming Tower*, p. 175.

39. Usama bin Muhammad bin Laden, "An Open Letter to King Fahd on the Occasion of the Recent Cabinet Reshuffle," August 1995, Center for Combatting Terrorism Center, West Point, AFGP-2002-000103-HT-NVTC, http://www.ctc.usma.edu/aq/pdf/AFGP-2002-000103-Trans.pdf. *Messages to the World*, p. 23.

40. Salah, "Al-Hayat," nos. 1 and 2 of 6, 7 and 9 December 2007.

41. Ibid., 29 June 2005, 1, 6 July 2005 and 8 December 2004.

42. Ibid., 6 July 2005.

43. Ibid.

44. Ibid., 10 July 2005.

45. Ibid., 8 December 2007; "Interview with Muntasir al-Zayyat," Ahmed al-Khatib, *al-Misri al-Yawm*, 17 November 2007.

46. See Sibai, "Kamil Tawil"; Zayyat, *Ayman al-Zawahiri*; Khatib, "Second Revisions," no. 9, 28 November 2008; Zawahiri, *Fursan*.

47. "Al-Hayat Talks to 'Dr. Fadl' in Tura Prison," *al-Hayat*, 8 December 2007.

48. Salah, "Al-Hayat," 28 December 1998.

49. *The 9/11 Commission Report: Final Report of the National Commission on Terrorist Attacks Upon the United States* (New York: W. W. Norton, 2004), p. 232.

50. Andrew Higgins and Alan Cullison, "Strained Alliance: Al Qaeda's Sour Days in Afghanistan," *Wall Street Journal*, 2 August 2002.

Chapter 2

1. Zayyat, *Ayman al-Zawahiri*; Zawahiri, *Fursan*; Diya Rashwan, "The Renunciation of Violence by Egyptian Jihadi Organizations" in *Leaving Terrorism Behind: Individual and Collective Disengagements*, ed. Tore Bjorgo and John Horgan (London: Routledge, 2009); Y. Feldner, Y. Carmon, and D. Lav, "The Al-Gama'a Al-Islamiyya Cessation of Violence: An Ideological Reversal," *Middle East Research Institute* 309 (21 December 2006) http://www.memrijttm.org/content/en/report.htm?report=1802&param=IDTA;

Fawaz A. Gerges, *The Far Enemy: Why Jihad Went Global* (Cambridge: Cambridge University Press, 2009), ch. 4.

2. E.g., Usama Ibrahim Hafiz and Asim Abd al-Majid, *Hurmat al-ghuluww fi al-din wa-takfir al-Muslimin* (Riyadh: Maktabat al-Ubaykan, 2004), and idem, *Taslit al-adwa ala ma waqa fi al-jihad min al-akhta* (Riyadh: Maktabat al-Ubaykan, 2004).

3. For a comprehensive survey of the ideological and theological views of the movement's founding fathers, see the two volumes collected and edited by Rifat Sayyid Ahmad, *al-Nabi al-musalah* [The militant prophet: The rejectionists], vol. 1 (London: Riad El-Rayyes Books, 1991); Rifat Sayyid Ahmad, ed., *al-Nabi al-musalah* [The militant prophet: The revolutionaries], vol. 2 (London: Riad El-Rayyes Books, 1991).

4. Interviews with Habib in Cairo in September, October, November, and December 1998 and January and February 1999. See my profile of Habib in Fawaz A. Gerges, *Journey of the Jihadist: Inside Muslim Militancy* (Orlando, FL: Harcourt Press, 2007).

5. Interview with Habib, Cairo, February 1999.

6. Ibid.

7. Rashwan, "The Renunciation of Violence."

8. *Messages to the World*, p. 17.

9. Ibid., p. 27.

10. B. Ganor, *Defining Terrorism: Is One Man's Terrorist Another Man's Freedom Fighter?* (Washington, DC: International Policy Institute for Counter-Terrorism, 1999), p. 6.

11. See the critical works of Patrick Porter, *Military Orientalism: Eastern Wars through Western Eyes* (London: Hurst and Company, 2009); Tarak Barkawi, *Globalization and War* (New York: Rowman and Littlefield, 2006), pp. 153–155; Jeremy Black, "Determinisms and Other Issues," *Journal of Military History* 68 (2004), pp. 127–132.

12. Dan Gold, *Hatred's Kingdom: How Saudi Arabia Supports the New Global Terrorism* (Washington, DC: Eagle Publishing, 2003), p. 6.

13. Mahmood Mamdani, "The Politics of Naming: Genocide, Civil War, Insurgency," *London Review of Books* 29, no. 5 (8 March 2007), pp. 5–8.

14. G. M. Steinberg, "Israel's Right to Self-Defense," *Wall Street Journal*, 23 February 2010; Daniel Pipes, "Faisal Shahzad, Jihadi, Explains Terrorism," National Review Online, 25 June 2010.

15. *Messages to the World*, pp. 33, 61.

16. Gerges, *The Far Enemy*, see chs. 3 and 4.

17. Zawahiri, *Fursan* Khatib, "Second Revisions," no. 11, 30 November 2008; Zayyat, "al-Gamaa al-Islamiya." See also Sibai, "Kamil Tawil"; Hani al-Sibai, "Introduction" in Zayyat, *Ayman al-Zawahiri*; Mohammed Salah, *Narratives of the Jihad Years: The Journey of the Arab Afghans* [in Arabic] (Cairo, 2001).

18. Gerges, *The Far Enemy*, ch. 4.
19. Andrew Higgins and Allan Cullison, "Terrorist's Odyssey: Saga of Dr. Zawahiri Illuminates Roots of Al Qaeda Terror," *Wall Street Journal*, 2 July 2002; Shafi'i, "Zawahiri's Secret Papers," part 2, 14 December 2002.
20. Sibai, "Introduction" in Zayyat, *Ayman al-Zawahiri*; Shafi'i, "Zawahiri Expelled Two Jihadi Leaders"; Shafi'i, "Zawahiri's Secret Papers," part 1, 13 December 2002.
21. Sibai, "Introduction" in Zayyat, *Ayman al-Zawahiri*; Higgins and Cullison, "Terrorist's Odyssey"; Salah, *Narratives of the Jihad Years*, ch. 5.
22. Interview with Habib, October 1999; Sibai, "Introduction."
23. Khatib, "Second Revisions," no. 2, 19 November 2008.

Chapter 3

1. *9/11 Commission Report*, ch. 5.
2. Ibid.
3. Ibid.
4. Ibid.
5. Ibid.
6. Ibid.
7. Ibid.
8. Ibid.
9. Salah, "Al-Hayat."
10. Leah Farrall, "Hotline to the Jihad," *Australian*, 7 December 2009.
11. See http://www.aawsat.com/english/news.asp?section=3&id=627. For the entire Arabic text, see *al-Sharq al-Awsat*, December 2004.
12. Ibid., 8 December 2004 and 29 June 2005.
13. Ibid., 9 December 2004 and 1 July 2005.
14. Ibid.
15. Ibid., 29 June 2005 and 1 July 2005.
16. Ibid., 1 July 2005.
17. In particular, the four books released by al-Gamaa al-Islamiya, written in Arabic and widely distributed and disseminated in Egypt and the Arab world (Cairo, 2002), were reviewed and approved by all of the "historical leaders" of al-Gamaa. Their translations of the individual titles are "Initiative of Cessation of Violence," "Shedding Light on the Mistakes Committed in the Jihad", "The Ban on Narrow Positions on Religion and on the Excommunication of Muslims," and "Advice and Clarification to Rectify Concepts of Those Who Assume Responsibility for Society." See also Essam Mohammed Derbala, "Al-Qaeda's Strategy: Mistakes and Dangers" [in Arabic], serialized by *al-Sharq al-Awsat*, 6–9 August 2003; Interview with Karam Zuhdi [in Arabic], *al-Mussawar*, 21 and 28 June 2002; *al-Sharq al-Awsat*, 15–16 July 2003. See discussion in Umar

Ashour, "De-radicalization of Jihad?" at http://www.terrorismanalysts.com/pt/index.php?option=com_rokzine&view=article&id=39&Itemid=54.

18. Derbala, "Al-Qaeda's Strategy," 6–9 August 2003 and 12 January 2004.

19. Ibid.

20. Nagih Abdullah Ibrahim, "Islam and the Challenge of the Twenty-First Century" [in Arabic], al-Sharq al-Awsat, 21 and 24 June 2004; Derbala, "Al-Qaeda's Strategy."

21. Ibrahim, "Islam and the Challenge"; Derbala, "Al-Qaeda's Strategy."

22. Ibid.

23. Derbala, "Al-Qaeda's Strategy."

24. Ibrahim, "Islam and the Challenge."

25. Ibid.

26. Ibid.

27. Ibid., 23, 24, and 27 June 2004.

28. Ibid., 24 June 2004.

29. Ibid., 26 June 2004.

30. "al-Sharq al-Awsat Talks to the Leader of Egyptian Islamic Group Inside a Prison," al-Sharq al-Awsat, 15–16 July 2003. See the series of interviews with Zuhdi in the pro-government newspaper al-Mussawar, 21 and 28 June 2002. Paul Schemm, "Egypt Lets the World Know That the Gamaa Islamiya Is out of the Terrorism Business," Cairo Times, 27 June 2002–3 July 2002.

31. al-Mussawar, 8 August 2003; al-Sharq al-Awsat, 15–16 July 2003.

32. "Chapters from the Charter of Islamic Political Action," compiled by Ahmad, al-Nabi al-musalah, vol. 1, pp. 165–78.

33. See Sibai, "Kamil Tawil," 1–4 September 2002.

34. "Usama Rushdi, Former Media Official and Member of the Shura Council of 'al-Jamaa al-Islamiya': Bin Laden's Speech Is Provocative and Full of Terms Only Muslims Understand," al-Sharq al-Awsat, 25 January 2005.

35. Ibid.

Chapter 4

1. Fou'ad Hussein, "Al-Zarqawi . . . The Second Generation of al-Qa'ida—Seif al-Adl's Testament"; Mohammad A. Shafi, "Seif al-Adl: Al-Qa'ida's Ghost," al-Sharq al-Awsat, 1 June 2005; Associated Press, "Lawmaker: Yemen Holding 104 People Suspected of Terror Ties," 23 September 2020; Tony Karon, "Nine Years After 9/11. Is Al-Qaeda's Threat Overrated?" Time, 11 September 2010; Robert F. Worth, "Is Yemen the Next Afghanistan," New York Times, 6 July 2010.

2. Associated Press, "402 Al Qaeda Suspects Arrested, Pakistan Says," 10 September 2002; Kamran Khan and Dana Priest, "Pakistan Pressures Al Qaeda: Military Operation Results in Alert and Arrests," Washington Post, 6 August 2004.

3. United Press International, "Intelligence Good but Not Actionable on bin Laden," 14 September 2010.

4. See "Transcript of President Bush's Address," September 20, 2001, CNN, http://articles.cnn.com/2001-09-20/us/gen.bush.transcript_1_joint-session-national-anthem-citizens?_s=PM:US.

5. Associated Press, "Al Zarqawi Group Vows Allegiance to Bin Laden," 17 October 2004; Dan Murphy, "In Iraq, a Clear-Cut bin Laden-Zarqawi Alliance," *Christian Science Monitor*, 31 December 2004.

6. Hussein, "Al-Zarqawi"; Shafi, "Seif al-Adl: Al-Qa'ida's Ghost," *al-Sharq al-Awsat*, 1 June 2005.

7. Laura Jordan and Katherine Shrader, "Bin Laden Enlisting Al-Zarqawi for Attacks," Associated Press, 1 April 2005.

8. Hussein, "Al-Zarqawi," parts 6 and 7, 19–20 May 2005; Marwan Shahada, "The al-Zarqawi-al-Maqdisi Dispute . . . ," *al-Hayat*, 5 July 2005; Mahari al-Zaydi, "Abu Muhammad al-Maqdisi: Al-Zarqawi's 'Spiritual Godfather,'" *al-Sharq al-Awsat*, 26 July 2005.

9. Office of the Director of National Intelligence (ODNI) News Release No. 2-05, available at http://www.fas.org/irp/news/2005/10/dni101105.html.

10. Ibid.

11. Zawahiri presents Zarqawi with a series of questions that show the danger inherent in attacking the Shiites: "Is the opening of another front now in addition to the front against the Americans and the government a wise decision? Or, does this conflict with the Shiites lift the burden from the Americans by diverting the mujahedeen to the Shiite, while the Americans continue to control matters from afar? And if the attacks on Shiite leaders were necessary to put a stop to their plans, then why were there attacks on ordinary Shiites? Won't this lead to reinforcing false ideas in their minds, even as it is incumbent on us to preach the call of Islam to them and explain and communicate to guide them to the truth? And can the mujahedeen kill all of the Shiites in Iraq? Has any Islamic state in history ever tried that? And why kill ordinary Shiites considering that they are forgiven because of their ignorance? And what loss will befall us if we did not attack the Shiites? And do the brothers forget that we have more than one hundred prisoners—many of whom are from the leadership who are wanted in their countries—in the custody of the Iranians? And even if we attack the Shiites out of necessity, then why do you announce this matter and make it public, which compels the Iranians to take counter measures? And do the brothers forget that both we and the Iranians need to refrain from harming each other at this time in which the Americans are targeting us?" See ibid.

12. Ibid.

13. ODNI News Release No. 2-05.

14. Ibid.

15. Esposito and Mogahed, *Who Speaks for Islam?*

16. "Results of a New Nationwide Public Opinion Survey of Saudi Arabia," Terror Free Tomorrow: Center for Public Opinion, December 2007, http://www.terrorfreetomorrow.org/upimagestft/TFT%20Saudi%20Arabia%20Survey.pdf.

17. "Results of a New Nationwide Public Opinion Survey of Pakistan before the February 18th Elections," Terror Free Tomorrow: Center for Public Opinion, January 2008, http://www.terrorfreetomorrow.org/upimagestft/TFT%20 Pakistan%20Poll%20Report.pdf.

18. Pew Global Attitudes Project, "Pakistani Public Opinion: Growing Concerns about Extremism, Continuing Discontent with U.S.," Pew Research Center, 13 August 2008, http://pewglobal.org/reports/pdf/265.pdf.

19. Pew Global Attitudes Project, "Global Opinion Trends 2002–2007: A Rising Tide Lifts Mood in Developing World," Pew Research Center, 24 July 2007, http://pewglobal.org/reports/pdf/257.pdf (reprinted).

20. Ibid.

21. Pew Global Attitudes Project, "Support for Suicide Bombings," Key Indicators Database, Pew Research Center, http://pewglobal.org/database/?indicator=19&survey=10&response=Rarely/never%20justified&mode=table.

22. "Public Opinion in Iran and America on Key International Issues," Program on International Public Attitudes (PIPA), December 2006, http://www.worldpublicopinion.org/pipa/pdf/jan07/Iran_Jan07_quaire.pdf.

23. "Results of a New Nationwide Public Opinion Survey of Saudi Arabia."

24. "Results of a New Nationwide Public Opinion Survey of Pakistan before the February 18th Elections."

25. Pew Global Attitudes Project, "Confidence in Osama bin Laden," Key Indicators Database, Pew Research Center, http://pewglobal.org/database/?indicator=20&group=6&response=Confidence.

26. Ian Black and Richard Norton-Taylor, "Al-Qaeda Faces Recruitment Crisis, Anti-terrorism Experts Say," *Guardian*, 11 September 2009; "Terrorism: Al-Qaida under Pressure," *Guardian*, 11 September 2009.

27. Robert Lacey, *Inside the Kingdom: Kings, Clerics, Modernists, Terrorists, and the Struggle for Saudi Arabia* (New York: Viking, 2009); Rachel Bronson, *Thicker Than Oil: America's Uneasy Partnership with Saudi Arabia* (Oxford: Oxford University Press, 2008); "Saudi Arabia Tackles Terrorism," *Economist*, 17 July 2008, http://www.economist.com/specialreports/displaystory.cfm?story_id=11701258; Caryle Murphy, "Saudi Arabia Announces Arrest of 110 Al Qaeda Suspects," *Christian Science Monitor*, 24 March 2010, http://www.csmonitor.com/World/Middle-East/2010/0324/Saudi-Arabia-announces-arrest-of-110-Al-Qaeda-suspects; "Saudi Arabia Arrests 701 Al Qaeda-Linked Militants Plotting 'Oil Attacks,'" Fox News, http://www.foxnews.com/story/0,2933,371267,00.html; "Saudi Arabia Arrests 172 in Anti-terror Sweep," MSNBC, 28 April 2007, http://www.msnbc.msn.com/id/18349238/; Christopher Boucek, "Saudi Arabia's 'Soft' Counterterrorism

Strategy: Prevention, Rehabilitation, and Aftercare," Carnegie Endowment for International Peace, September 2008, http://www.carnegieendowment.org/publications/index.cfm?fa=view&id=22155&prog=zgp&proj=zme; Black and Norton-Taylor, "Al-Qaeda Faces Recruitment Crisis."

28. On 12 February 2008, the Qatari daily *al-Arab* published an interview with an al-Qaeda commander in northern Iraq, Abu Turab al-Jazairi. The interview, at an al-Qaeda hideout in northern Iraq, was conducted according to al-Qaeda's stipulations—including no disclosure of the region where it took place and no communications or recording equipment of any kind brought to the site. See http://www.memri.org/report/en/0/0/0/0/0/0/2593.htm. See also http://www.aliraqi.org/forums/showthread.php?t=84183.

29. "Declassified Key Judgments from 'Trends in Global Terrorism: Implications for the United States,'" ODNI, April 2006, http://www.dni.gov/press_releases/Declassified_NIE_Key_Judgments.pdf.

30. Islamtoday.com, http://islamtoday.com/; Fawaz A. Gerges, "His Mentor Turns on bin Laden," *International Herald Tribune*, 21 September 2007.

31. Gerges, "His Mentor Turns on bin Laden."

32. *Messages to the World*, p. 26.

33. Ibid.

34. Ibid.

35. Ibid.

36. Fawaz A. Gerges, "Osama bin Laden's Growing Anxiety," *Christian Science Monitor*, 26 October 2007.

37. Ibid.

38. "Letter to al-Zarqawi from al-Zawahri," MSNBC, 11 October 2005, http://www.msnbc.msn.com/id/9666242/.

39. "Bin Laden: "Message to the People of Iraq," October 22, 2007, http://www.nefafoundation.org/miscellaneous/nefabinladen1007.pdf; Ahmed Rahim, "Bin Laden Concedes Making Mistakes . . ." *al-Hayat*, 2 December 2007.

40. Ibid.

41. Ibid.

42. BBC News, ABC News, and NHK, "Iraq Poll September 2007," September 2007, http://news.bbc.co.uk/2/shared/bsp/hi/pdfs/10_09_07_iraqpoll.pdf.

43. See "Al-Qaeda Commander in Northern Iraq: We Are in Dire Straits," 11 March 2008, http://www.memri.org/report/en/0/0/0/0/0/0/2593.htm. See also http://www.aliraqi.org/forums/showthread.php?t=84183.

44. "Al-Hayat in the Egyptian Prison Tora Talks to the Author of the Document 'Rationalizing Jihad,'" *al-Hayat*, 13 December 2007.

45. "Tarshid al-Jihad fi Misr wa-l-Alam" [Rationalizing jihad], serialized in *al-Masri al-Yawm*, 18 November 2007–2 December 2008.

46. Ibid.

47. Ibid.
48. Ayman Al-Zawahiri, "Exoneration: A Treatise Exonerating the Community of the Pen and the Sword from the Debilitating Accusation of Fatigue and Weakness," NEFA Foundation, 2 March 2008, http://www.nefafoundation.org/miscellaneous/FeaturedDocs/Zawahiri_Exoneration_ciaosc.pdf. See also Zawahiri's initial reaction in a video to Fadl's statement, "Advice of One Concerned," 5 July 2007; Ian Black, "Violence Won't Work: How Author of 'Jihadists' Bible' Stirred Up a Storm," *Guardian*, 27 July 2007, http://www.guardian.co.uk/world/2007/jul/27/alqaida.egypt.
49. Zawahiri, "Exoneration."
50. Ibid.
51. Khatib, "Second Revisions," nos. 1–13, November and December 2008. See also "Al-Hayat in the Egyptian Prison, Tura, Talks to the Author of the Document 'Rationalizing Jihad . . .,'" *al-Hayat*, 8–13 December 2007.
52. "The Open Meeting with Shaykh Ayman al-Zawahiri," NEFA Foundation, 2 April 2008, http://www.nefafoundation.org/miscellaneous/FeaturedDocs/nefazawahiri0408.pdf; "Selected Questions and Answers from Dr. Ayman al-Zawahiri," NEFA Foundation, 6 May 2008, http://www.nefafoundation.org/miscellaneous/FeaturedDocs/nefazawahiri0508.pdf; "Selected Questions and Answers from Dr. Ayman al-Zawahiri," NEFA Foundation, 30 May 2008, http://www.nefafoundation.org/miscellaneous/FeaturedDocs/nefazawahiri0508-2.pdf.
53. "Zawahiri: The Ninth Anniversary of the September 11 Attacks" [in Arabic], *al-Quds al-Arabi*, 9 September 2010.

Chapter 5

1. Richard Esposito, Matthew Cole, and Brian Ross, "President Obama's Secret: Only 100 al Qaeda Now in Afghanistan," ABC News, 2 December 2009, http://abcnews.go.com/Blotter/president-obamas-secret-100-al-qaeda-now-afghanistan/story?id=9227861; Joshua Partlow, "In Afghanistan, Taliban Surpasses al-Qaeda," 11 November 2009, *Washington Post*, http://www.washingtonpost.com/wp-dyn/content/article/2009/11/10/AR2009111019644.html.
2. Bob Woodward, *Obama's Wars: The Inside Story* (New York: Simon Schuster, 2010), p.71.
3. Joseph Berger, "Pakistani Taliban Behind Times Sq. Plot, Holder Says," *New York Times*, 10 May 2010.
4. Scott Shane and Robert F. Worth, "Earlier Flight May Have Been Dry Run for Plotters," *New York Times*, 1 November 2010.
5. "Al-Qaeda Claimed Responsibility for an Attack on the Headquarters of Intelligence in Southern Yemen" [in Arabic], RayNews.net, 11 July 2010, http://www.raynews.net/index.php?action=showNews&id=3784; "Al-Qa'ida Claims

Responsibility for Yemen Attacks" [in Arabic], Al Jazeera.net, 23 July 2010; "Al-Qaeda Claims Yemen Attack that Killed Six Soldiers," AFP, 12 August 2010; Hammoud Mounassar, "Three Policemen Killed in Yemen 'Qaeda,'" AFP, 17 July 2010; "Gunmen in Yemen Attack Two Southern Yemen Security Offices," BBC, 17 July 2010.

6. "Al-Qaeda Leaders Make Yemen Speech," 22 December 2009, Al Jazeera English, http://english.aljazeera.net/news/middleeast/2009/12/2009122273913988616. html; Scott Shane, Mark Mazzetti, and Robert F. Worth, "Secret Assault on Terrorism Widens on Two Continents," New York Times, 14 August 2010.

7. Ayman al-Zawahiri, "From Kabul to Mogadishu," statement released 22 February 2009, transcript of an Arabic-language audio recording obtained by NEFA investigators and translated into English, http://www.nefafoundation. org/miscellaneous/FeaturedDocs/nefazawahiri0209-2.pdf; Charles Levinson and Margaret Cocker, "Al Qaeda's Deep Tribal Ties Make Yemen a Terror Hub," Wall Street Journal, 22 January 2010, http://online.wsj.com/article/SB 10001424052748704320104575015493304519542.html; Shane, Mazzetti, and Worth, "Secret Assault on Terrorism."

8. "Al-Qaeda Network in Yemen Opens a New Door for the Implementation of Operations" [in Arabic], al-Tagheer.net, 3 September 2010, http://www.al-tagheer.com/news21816.html.

9. "Saudi Al-Qaeda Urges Killing of Christians," Middle East Observatory, 12 August 2010, http://www.meobservatory.com/docpub/Saudi-Al-Qaeda-Urges-Killing-Of-Christians.shtml; "Saudi Al-Qaeda Urges Killing of Christians," RTTNews.com, 11 August 2010.

10. "Al-Qa'ida's Military Commander in Yemen Declares His Intention to Establish a Military" [in Arabic], al-Quds al-Arabi, 13 October 2010; Shuaib M. al-Mosawa, "AQAP Announces Formation of Aden-Abyan Army," Yemen Observer, 14 October 2010, http://www.yobserver.com.

11. Ghaith Abdul-Ahad, "Shabwa: Blood Feuds and Hospitality in al-Qaida's Yemen Outpost," Guardian, 23 August 2010; Shane, Mazzetti, and Worth, "Secret Assault on Terrorism."

12. "Aden Abyan Army: A Chilling Fact or Dark Fiction? Khalid Abd al-Nabi: No Such Thing as Aden-Abyan Army" [in Arabic], al-Maydan.net, 2 October 2010, http://news.al-maydan.net/articles-action-show-id-828.htm.

13. "Al-Qaeda in Yemen Is Waging a Guerrilla War in the Cities of Lauder and Mawadia in Southern Yemen" [in Arabic], YemenNation.net, 19 October 2010, http://www.yemennation.net/news3611.html; "Al-Qaeda in Yemen Is Waging a Guerrilla War in the Cities of Lauder and Mawadia in Southern Yemen" [in Arabic], al-Jazirah.com, 20 October 2010, http://www.al-jazirah. com/20101020/du14d.htm.

14. Khalid al-Hamadi, "Yemen: Abyan Falls between a Rock—al-Qa'ida—and a Hard Place—the Secessionist Movement" [in Arabic], al-Quds al-Arabi, 17 October 2010.

15. Six years after, the Yemeni state has failed to subdue the Houthi rebels who complain of political, social, and religious marginalization. The Saleh government denies Houthis' claims and accuses them of trying to subvert the republic and revive the Imamate—a theocracy based on Zaydi beliefs and practices, a form of Shiite Islam—which was overthrown in the 1960s. Moreover, Yemeni officials have sought to portray the Houthi rebellion as an extension of Shiite Iran's efforts to spread its influence in the heart of Sunni-based Arab states. Clearly, there is no military solution to the Houthi rebellion, and the Saleh regime has acknowledged this fact by exercising military restraint and inviting at least three senior Houthi representatives to participate in a national dialogue involving Yemen's governing coalition and a group of opposition parties. This is a good start to ending the bloodshed and pain in the north.

16. US Department of State, SECRET/NOFORN SANAA 01549, "Brennan-Saleh Meeting September 6, 2009," NSC for APDNSA John Brennan and Denise Moraga, DEPT for NEA/ARP AMA MACDONALD, Wikileaks. See also Scott Shane, "Yemen Helps U.S. Fight Al Qaeda, on Its Own," *New York Times*, 3 December 2010.

17. Steven C. Caton, "Yemen: Not on the Verge of Collapse," *Foreign Policy*, 11 August 2010.

18. A prime example of this came in August 2010, when the newspaper *Hadith al-Madina* reported that the Saudi crown prince, Sultan Bin Abdulaziz, was threatening to stop money that "flows from Saudi Arabia to Yemeni tribes for security." According to the newspaper, the reason was "that Saudi Arabia may be inclined to redirect the money to the Houthis," because they were the stronger faction and because they did not provide shelter to al-Qaeda. Mohammad Bin Sallam, "Government and Houthi Delegations Return to Sana'a," Yemen-Times.com, 2 September 2010, http://www.yementimes.com/DEFAULT-DET.ASPX?SUB_ID=34694.

19. "Obama Blames al-Qaeda for Christmas Day Jet 'Bomb,'" BBC News, 2 January 2010, http://news.bbc.co.uk/1/hi/8437496.stm/; Mohamed Sudam, "Yemen President Tackles Boosting Security with U.S.," Reuters, 2 January 2010, http://www.reuters.com/article/idUSTRE60116K20100102; Roger Runningen, "Obama Counterterror Aide Confers with Yemen's Saleh on Fighting Al-Qaeda," *Bloomberg*, 20 September 2010, http://www.bloomberg.com/news/2010-09-20/obama-counterterror-aide-confers-with-yemens-saleh-on-fighting-al-qaeda.html.

20. US Department of State, SECRET/NOFORN SANAA 000004, "General Petraeus' Meeting with Saleh on Security Assistance, AQAP Strikes," Wikileaks; Shane, "Yemen Helps U.S."

21. Ben Wedeman, "Is Yemen Crying 'al Qaeda'?," CNN, 8 November 2010; Phil Stuart, "The United States Has the Resources and Allies Needed to Combat al Qaeda," Reuters, 9 November 2010.

22. Kimberly Dozier, "Mullen Says Al-Qaeda Threat from Yemen Is Serious," Associated Press, 21 November 2010.

23. Greg Miller and Peter Finn, "CIA Sees Increased Threat from al-Qaeda in Yemen," *Washington Post*, 24 August 2010. See also Adam Entous and Siobhan Gorman, "U.S. Weighs Expanded Strikes in Yemen," *Wall Street Journal*, 25 August 2010; Shane, Mazzetti, and Worth, "Secret Assault on Terrorism Widens on Two Marib Provinces, East of Yemen's Capital Continents."

24. Shane, Mazzetti, and Worth, "Secret Assault on Terrorism Widens"; Miller and Finn, "CIA Sees Increased Threat."

25. US Department of State, SECRET/NOFORN SANAA 000004, "General Petraeus' Meeting with Saleh on Security Assistance, AQAP Strikes," Wikileaks.

26. Shane, Mazzetti, and Worth, "Secret Assault on Terrorism Widens." See also Ghaith Abdul-Ahad, "Shabwa: Blood Feuds and Hospitality."

27. Reuters, AP, "The Deputy Governor of Maarib Killed in an Air Raid by Mistake" [in Arabic], al-Riyadh.com, 26 May 2010, http://www.alriyadh.com/2010/05/26/article529112.html.

28. US Department of State, SECRET/NOFORN SANAA 01549, "Brennan-Saleh Meeting September 6, 2009," NSC for APDNSA John Brennan and Denise Moraga, DEPT for NEA/ARP AMA MACDONALD, Wikileaks. See also Shane, "Yemen Helps U.S.," *New York Times*, http://www.nytimes.com/2010/11/29/world/29cables.html?pagewanted=2.

29. *al-Hayat*, 30 September 2010; see also Mohammed Jamjoom, "Yemen: U.S. has Carried Out Airstrikes in Yemen," 30 September 2010.

30. Miller and Finn, "CIA Sees Increased Threat."

31. Entous and Gorman, "U.S. Weighs Expanded Strikes in Yemen."

32. Julian E. Barnes and Adam Entous, "Yemen Covert Role Pushed: Failed Bomb Heightens Talk of Putting Elite U.S. Squads in CIA Hands," 1 November 2010.

33. Ibid.

34. Ibid.

35. US Department of State, SECRET/NOFORN SANAA 01549, "Brennan-Saleh Meeting September 6, 2009," NSC for APDNSA John Brennan and Denise Moraga, DEPT for NEA/ARP AMA MACDONALD, Wikileaks.

36. Entous and Gorman, "U.S. Weighs Expanded Strikes in Yemen."

37. Shane, Mazzetti, and Worth, "Secret Assault on Terrorism."

38. Ibid.

39. Ibid.

40. "Analysis: Yemen gives wounded al Qaeda a chance to regroup," *Reuters*, May, 27, 2011.

41. Anwar al-Awlaki, "Message to the American People" [speech in Arabic and English], 25 April 2010, Global Islamic Media Front.

42. "Yemeni Scholars Threaten to Declare Jihad against Any Foreign Military Intervention," NabaNews.Net, 14 January 2010, http://www.nabanews.

net/2009/23437.html; Scott Peterson, "In Yemen, 158 Clerics Vow Jihad if US Military Intervention Broadens," *Christian Science Monitor*, 14 January 2010.

43. Khalid Abdullah, "Unmanned Drone Attacks Fuel Mistrust of the Government and America" [in Arabic], *al-Quds al-Arabi*, 28 October 2010.

44. Mark Mazzetti, "Drone Strike in Yemen Was Aimed at Awlaki," *New York Times*, 6 May 2011.

45. Philip Johnston, "Anwar al Awlaki: The New Osama bin Laden?" *Daily Telegraph*, 17 September 2010.

46. Cited in Ravi Somaiya, "Tracking the News on Air Cargo Explosives," *New York Times*, 30 October 2010.

47. Ghaith Abdul-Ahad, "Blood Feuds and Hospitality."

48. Mohammed Jamjoom, "Official: Yemen Plans to Prosecute al-Awlaki," CNN, 2 November 2010.

49. Mohammed Ghobari, "Yemen al Qaeda Warned Tribe against Helping Government," Reuters, 3 November 2010.

50. "Yemen in al Qaeda Manhunt as Preacher Appears in Tape," Reuters, 24 October 2010; "Yemen Hunts al-Qa'ida in Shabwa," Al Jazeera.net, 24 October 2010.

51. "Surrender of 15 al-Qaeda Fighters in Southern Yemen" [in Arabic], *al-Quds al-Arabi*, 26 October 2010; "Local al-Qaeda Leader Surrenders to the Authorities" [in Arabic], *al-Quds al-Arabi*, 28 October 2010.

52. "Fourteen al-Qaeda Operators in Yemen Surrender" [in Arabic], al-Jazeera.net, 1 November 2010.

53. *Al-Quds al-Arabi* [in Arabic], 8 November 2010.

54. Khalid Hamadi, "Sana Complains That Her Allies Do Not Share Intelligence Information" [in Arabic], *al-Quds al-Arabi*, 2 November 2010.

55. Ahmed Al-Haj, "Yemeni Leader Says He'll Leave, Warns of al-Qaida," Associated Press, 21 May 2011.

56. *Washington Post*, 18 March 2010.

57. Ibid.

58. Ibid.

59. Office of the Coordinator for Counterterrorism, "Chapter 1. Strategic Assessments," *Country Reports on Terrorism 2009*, US Department of State, 5 August 2010, http://www.state.gov/s/ct/rls/crt/2009/140882.htm.

60. Greg Miller and Jerry Markon, "Radicalization of Times Square Suspect Was Gradual, Investigators Say," *Washington Post*, 7 May 2010; "Times Square Suspect Was Upset Over Drone Attacks, Source Says," FOXNews.com, 5 May 2010.

61. "The Radicalization of Dr. Al-Balawi," *My Direct Democracy*, 13 January 2010, http://mydd.com/users/mainstreet/posts/the-radicalization-of-dr-al-balawi. Also available at Juan Cole's *Informed Comment Blog*, http://www.juancole.com.

62. "Profile: Major Nidal Malik Hasan," BBC News, 12 November 2009, http://news.bbc.co.uk/1/hi/8345944.stm; Bill Roggio, "US Army Major behind Fort Hood Murders Expressed Sympathy for Islamic Terrorists," *The Long War Journal*,

5 November 2009, http://www.longwarjournal.org/archives/2009/11/muslim_
army_major_be.php#ixzz0kjGxnsWI.

63. Jeremy Markon, Pamela Constable, and Shaiq Hussein, "Va. Suspects in Pakistan Say Mission Was Jihad Not Terrorism," *Washington Post*, 5 January 2010, http://www.washingtonpost.com/wp-dyn/content/article/2010/01/04/AR2010010400800.html.

64. Mark Mazzetti, Sabrina Tavernise, and Jack Healy, "Suspect Is Said to Admit to Role in Plot," *New York Times*, 5 May 2010.

65. Scott Shane, "Fighting Terrorism, Creating Terrorists," *New York Times*, 4 July 2010; Tom Hays, "Guilty Plea in Failed N.Y. Car Bombing," Associated Press, 22 June 2010.

66. Larry Neumeister and Tom Hays, "Faisal Shahzad, Times Square Car Bomber, Details His Chilling Plot," Associated Press, 22 June 2010.

67. Shane, "Fighting Terrorism."

68. Neumeister and Hays, "Faisal Shahzad."

69. Basil Ktaz, "Defiant Times Square Bomber Gets Life in Prison," Reuters, 5 October 2010; Deborah Feyerick, "Times Square Bomb Plotter Sentenced to Life in Prison," CNN, 5 October 2010.

70. A. G. Sulzberger and William K. Rashbaum, "Guilty Plea Made in Plot to Bomb New York Subway," *New York Times*, 22 February 2010.

71. Ibid.

72. Pierre Thomas, "NYC Subway Plot; Dangerous New Phase in Threat by Al Qaeda," ABC, 23 February 2010.

73. Eric Schmitt and Eric Lipton, "Officials Point to Suspect's Claim of al Qaeda Ties in Yemen," *New York Times*, 26 December 2009, http://www.nytimes.com/2009/12/27/us/27terror.html?_r=1.

74. Michael Velardo, "Nidal Malik Hasan: His Own Patient?" *Detroit Substance Abuse Examiner*, 6 November 2009, http://www.examiner.com/x-8358-Detroit-Substance-Abuse-Examiner~y2009m11d6-Nidal-Malik-Hasan-His-own-patient.

75. Spencer S. Hsu, "Suspect in D.C. Metro Bomb Plot Sought to Fight U.S. Troops Overseas, Records Say," *Washington Post*, 28 October 2010.

76. David Morgan, "Man Arrested in DC Plot Trained for Afghanistan," Reuters, 28 October 2008; "FBI Learned of Subway Terror Suspect in January," Associated Press, 28 October 2010.

77. Evan Perez, "Trip Plan Sparked FBI's Terror Sting," *Wall Street Journal*, 29 October 2010.

78. Ibid.

79. According to the *Wall Street Journal*, the stings have become a staple of the Justice Department's efforts to ensnare terrorists since September 11. Some cases receive a rocky reception from skeptical juries. But in recent years, juries have handed down lengthy sentences against defendants in sting cases.

Some sting cases have drawn criticism from defense lawyers for seeming to entrap defendants. For example, in 2006, the FBI arrested seven members of a religious group in Miami's Liberty City neighborhood and charged them with plotting to attack the Sears Tower in Chicago and federal buildings. Defense lawyers said an informant overreached and two juries balked at the government's case, which ended in mistrials. It took a third trial before five of the defendants were convicted on terrorism-related offenses.

The fear of terrorism was causing law enforcement to try to prevent attacks at all costs, "even at the expense of ensnaring possibly innocent people," said Albert Levin, a Miami defense lawyer who represented suspects in the Miami case.

Earlier in October 2010, a Jordanian man was sentenced to 24 years in a case in which an FBI informant posed as a terrorist operative. The suspect attempted to detonate what he thought was a truck bomb near a Dallas skyscraper. See Ibid.

80. Hsu, "Suspect in D.C. Metro Bomb."

81. Jonathan Githens-Mazer, "'Radicalisation via YouTube'? It's Not So Simple: There Are Real Lessons to Take from the Roshonara Choudhry Case—But We're in Danger of Missing Them," 4 November 2010; Michael Seamark, "This Gross Insult," *Daily Mail*, 4 November 2010.

82. Gordon Rayner, Andy Bloxham, and Laura Roberts, "Stockholm Bomber Was Thrown out of Luton Mosque for Trying to Recruit Extremists," *Telegraph*, 13 December 2010.

83. Julian Borger and Richard Norton-Taylor, "Sweden Suicide Bomber's British Connections under Investigation," *Guardian*, 12 December 2010.

84. Eric Schmitt and Scott Shane, "Christmas Bombing Try Is Hailed by bin Laden," *New York Times*, 24 January 2010, http://www.nytimes.com/2010/01/25/world/25binladen.html.

85. Pam Benson, "Homegrown Terrorist Threat to Be Part of National Security Strategy," CNN, 26 May 2010.

86. US Department of State, Office of the Coordinator for Counterterrorism, "Chapter 1: Strategic Assessments," *Country Reports on Terrorism 2009*.

87. Peter Bergen and Bruce Hoffman, "Assessing the Terrorist Threat: A Report by the Bipartisan Policy Center's National Security Preparedness Group," *Bipartisan Policy Center*, 10 September 2010, pp. 14–17, http://bipartisanpolicy.org/sites/default/files/NSPG%20Final%20Threat%20Assessment.pdf.

88. Ibid., p. 14.

89. Ibid., p. 31.

90. Ibid., pp. 31–32.

91. Ibid., p. 31.

92. According to an authoritative study by the Triangle Center on Terrorism and Homeland Security, 48 of 120 cases involving terrorist plots came from tips from the Muslim-American community. The study also points out that

not only did tips from Muslim Americans provide information that helped authorities thwart terrorist plots, but also that "Muslim Americans have been so concerned about extremists in their midst that they have turned in people who turned out to be undercover informants." Charles Kurzman, "Muslim-American Terrorism Since 9/11: An Accounting," 2 February 2011, Triangle Center on Terrorism and Homeland Security, Duke/UNC/RTI, http://sanford.duke.edu/centers/tcths/about/documents/Kurzman_Muslim-American_Terrorism_Since_911_An_Accounting.pdf, p. 6.

93. Bob Drogin and April Choi, "Teen Held in Alleged Portland Plot," *Los Angeles Times*, 28 November 2010.

94. Ibid.

95. Ibid.

96. Hal Bernton, "Was FBI Grooming Portland Suspect for Terror?" *Seattle Times*, 30 November 2010.

97. Marisol Bello, "Experts Predict More Terror Plots in the U.S.," Associated Press, 29 November 2010.

98. Bernton, "Was FBI Grooming Portland Suspect for Terror?"

99. Eric Schmitt and Charlie Savage, "In U.S. Sting Operations, Questions of Entrapment," *New York Times*, 29 November 2010, http://www.nytimes.com/2010/11/30/us/politics/30fbi.html.

100. Bob Drogin and April Choi, "Mixed Portrait of Oregon Terrorism Suspect," *Los Angeles Times*, 29 November 2010.

101. Drogin and Choi, "Teen Held in Alleged Portland Plot"; Drogin and Choi, "Mixed Portrait"; Bernton, "Was FBI Grooming Portland Suspect for Terror?"; Schmitt and Savage, "In U.S. Sting Operations, Questions of Entrapment."

102. Tim Fought, "Ore. Terror Suspect Pleads Not Guilty," Associated Press, 29 November 2010.

103. Similarly, less than three weeks after the arrest of Mohamud, FBI agents detained a Baltimore man—described as a 21-year-old American who converted to Islam—on suspicion of plotting to bomb a military recruiting station in Catonsville, Maryland. According to court records, the suspect, identified as Antonio Martinez and also known as Muhammad Hussein, made public postings on his Facebook page discussing how the "rein of oppression is about 2 cease" and calling for violence to stop the oppression of Muslims. He communicated through the social networking site with an FBI informant, saying he wanted to go to Pakistan or Afghanistan and join the ranks of the "mujahideen." Once again, Martinez's case shows how the wars in Pakistan and Afghanistan are triggering blowback and radicalizing homegrown Muslim men. In discussion with the FBI's confidential source, Martinez said if the military continued to kill Muslims, they would need to expand their operation by killing U.S. Army personnel where they live, records show. Justin Fenton, "Arrest Made in Plot to Blow up Baltimore-area Military Recruiting Center," *Baltimore*

Sun, 8 December 2010; "Authorities in Maryland Arrest Man in Alleged Bomb Plot," CNN.com, 8 December 2010; Michael Langan, "'Facebook Sting' Nets US Muslim in Car Bomb Case," AFP, 8 December 2010.

104. Stephan Pauly and Michael Slackman, "Device at Namibian Airport Was a Security Test," *New York Times,* 19 November 2010; "Germany Reconsiders Terror Risk," BBC, 17 November 2010; "In Germany, Evidence Emerges of Attack Plans," CNN, 17 November 2010.

105. "Muslims in Europe: A Report on 11 EU Cities," *Open Society Institute,* December 2009, http://www.soros.org/initiatives/home/articles_publications/publications/muslims-europe-20091215; Pew Global Attitudes Project, "Muslims in Europe: Economic Worries Top Concerns About Religious and Cultural Identity," Pew Research Center, July 2006, http://pewglobal.org/reports/display.php?ReportID=254; Gallup Center for Muslim Studies, "Muslims in Berlin, London, and Paris," *Gallup,* 2007, http://www.gallup.com/consulting/worldpoll/26410/gallup-center-muslim-studies.aspx. See also Scott Atran, *Talking to the Enemy: Faith, Brotherhood, and the (Un)Making of Terrorists* (New York: HarperCollins, 2010); "Islamist Threat to Germany Is Growing Say Police," Reuters, 5 September 2010; Kathy Gannon; "Pakistan: Dozens of Europeans in Terror Training," Associated Press, 3 October 2010; Peter Finn and Greg Miller, "E.U. Cites Nationals Training in Terror," *Washington Post,* 30 September 2010.

106. Shahzad, "Terrorists Appear to Be Planning a Big Attack."

107. Stephen Fidler, "Down but Dangerous: How al-Qaeda Has Been Pushed on to the Defensive," *Financial Times,* 9 June 2008, http://us.ft.com/ftgateway/superpage.ft?news_id=fto060920081527543985.

108. Stephen Fidler, "Down but Dangerous."

109. See the fatwa by the influential shaykh, Muhammad Tahir-ul-Qadri, "Fatwa on Terrorism and Suicide Bombings," 2 March 2010, *minhaj-ul-quran International,* http://www.fatwaonterrorism.com/?page_id=24; Carla Power, "Can a Fatwa Against Terrorism Stop Extremists?" *Time Magazine,* 12 March 2010, http://www.time.com/time/world/article/0,8599,1969662,00.html.

110. Speaking to American troops in Afghanistan in March 2010 President Obama said that "al-Qa'ida was still using the region to plan terrorist strikes against the U.S. and Its allies," *Washington Post,* 29 March 2010; "Al Qaeda Vows to 'Bleed Enemy to Death,'" AFP, 21 November 2010.

111. "Al Qaeda Vows to 'Bleed Enemy to Death.'"

112. Dan De Luce, "Bin Laden 'Hiding in Afghan-Pakistani Border Area,'" AFP, 9 November 2010.

113. Bruce Hoffman, "The Myth of Grass-Roots Terrorism," *Foreign Affairs* (July/August 2008).

114. Woodward, *Obama's Wars,* pp. 88–89.

115. Riedel, *The Search for Al Qaeda.*

116. Woodward, *Obama's Wars*.

117. Ibid., p. 105.

118. Ibid., p. 162.

119. Ibid., p. 167.

120. Ibid., p. 170.

121. Ibid., pp. 185–186, 202.

122. Ahmed Rashid, "Jihadi Suicide Bombers: The New Wave," *New York Review of Books* 55, no. 10, 12 June 2008.

123. John Mueller, "How Dangerous Are the Taliban?" *Foreign Affairs*, 15 April 2009, http://www.foreignaffairs.com/articles/64932/john-mueller/how-dangerous-are-the-taliban; Ahmed Rashid, "A Deal with the Taliban?" *New York Review of Books*, 25 February 2010, http://www.nybooks.com/articles/archives/2010/feb/25/a-deal-with-the-taliban/; Greg Bruno, "Interview: The al-Qaeda-Taliban Nexus," *Council on Foreign Relations*, 25 November 2009, http://www.cfr.org/publication/20838/alqaedataliban_nexus.html; Carlotta Gall and Sabrina Tavernise, "Pakistani Taliban Are Said to Expand Alliances," 6 May 2010. For a detailed study of the TTP, see Hassan Abbas, "A Profile of Tehrik-i-Taliban Pakistan," January 2008, *CTC Sentinel* 1, no. 2, http://www.ctc.usma.edu/sentinel/CTCSentinel-Vol1Iss2.pdf.

124. "Afghan Suicide Bombings," *Jane's Terrorism and Security Monitor*, 8 May 2009; "Suicide Attacks in Afghanistan (2001–2007)," Jabul: UNAMA, 9 September 2007; Jermie Lanche, *Suicide Terrorism in Pakistan: An Assessment, IPCS Special Report* 84, New Delhi, Institute of Peace and Conflict Studies, September 2009; AG's personal communication with security analyst Claudio Franco, 2009.

125. "Pakistan Security Report 2009," Pakistan Institute for Peace Studies, January 2010, http://san-pips.com/download.php?f=29.pdf.

126. Dexter Filkins, "'09 Deadliest Year for Afghans, U.N. Says," *New York Times*, 13 January 2010, http://www.nytimes.com/2010/01/14/world/asia/14kabul.html; Jane Perlez, "U.S. Urges Action in Pakistan after Failed Bombing," *New York Times*, 8 May 2010; "Pakistan Security Report 2009"; "Afghanistan Annual Report on Protection of Civilians in Armed Conflict, 2009," United Nations Assistance Mission in Afghanistan, January 2010, http://unama.unmissions.org/Portals/UNAMA/human%20rights/Protection%20of%20Civilian%202009%20report%20English.pdf/.

127. It was the military campaigns by the army beginning in 2003 that destroyed what was left of the traditional structures; most of the destruction, however, was as a result of the traditional leadership being ousted by the Taliban. Patrick Seale, "Pakistan's Cruel Stalemate," 5 April 2010, Agence Global, http://www.middle-east-online.com/english/opinion/?id=38246; Jane Perlez and Pir Zubair Shah, "Pakistan Regains Control of Remote Area, for Now," *New York Times*, 8 March 2009, http://www.nytimes.com/2009/03/09/

world/asia/09bajaur.html; "Asia Report Number 178: Pakistan: Countering Militancy in FATA," *International Crisis Group*, 21 October 2009, http://www.crisisgroup.org/en/regions/asia/south-asia/pakistan/178-pakistan-countering-militancy-in-fata.aspx.

128. Perlez, "U.S. Urges Action in Pakistan After Failed Bombing."

129. "Pakistan Public Opinion Turning against Taliban," MSNBC, 11 June 2009, http://www.msnbc.msn.com/id/31267869/; Husain Haqqani, "How Pakistan Is Countering the Taliban," *Wall Street Journal*, 30 April 2009, http://online.wsj.com/article/SB124096805456666593.html; "Pakistani Public Opinion on the Swat Conflict, Afghanistan, and the US," *Program on International Policy Attitudes (PIPA)*, 1 July 2009, http://www.worldpublicopinion.org/pipa/pdf/jul09/WPO_Pakistan_Jul09_rpt.pdf; Ibid. Few traditional leaders were left in South Waziristan and Swat was ruled mainly by wealthy landlords. See Jane Perlez and Pir Zubair Shah, "Taliban Exploit Class Rifts in Pakistan," *New York Times*, 16 April 2009, http://www.nytimes.com/2009/04/17/world/asia/17pstan.html.

130. "Pakistan, Its Journalists and the Stories the West Forgets," a panel discussion at Brunei Gallery, SOAS (School of Oriental and African Studies), London, 13 October 2010.

131. Perlez, "U.S. Urges Action in Pakistan After Failed Bombing."

132. Hassan Abbas, "Defining the Punjabi Taliban," April 2009, *CTC Sentinel* 2, no. 4, http://www.ctc.usma.edu/sentinel/CTCSentinel-Vol2Iss4.pdf.

133. It is the long term that many Pakistanis worry about, in particular because unless the severe socioeconomic problems are addressed, the militancy will grow. For the time being, LeT is not affiliated with some of the anti-state groups, though a breakaway faction has done so.

134. Sources within the Pakistani military, April 2010.

135. "Pakistan, Its Journalists."

136. Ismail Khan and Jane Perlez, "Pakistan Halts NATO Supplies to Afghanistan After Attack," *New York Times*, 30 September 2010; "Nato Strike 'Kills Pakistan Troops," *Press Association*, 30 September 2010.

137. Karin Brulliard, "Angers simmers in Pakistani army over bin Laden raid," *Washington Post*, 19 May 2011.

138. Declan Walsh, "Osama bin Laden 'revenge' attack kills scores in Pakistan," *Guardian*, 13 May 2011.

139. David E. Sanger and Eric Schmitt, "As Rift Deepens Between U.S. and Pakistan, Kerry Offers Carrots and Sticks," *New York Times*, 14 May 2011.

140. Ibid.

141. Miller and Markon, "Radicalization of Times Square."

142. Jane Perlez, "Rebuffing U.S., Pakistan Balks at Crackdown," *New York Times*, 15 December 2009, http://www.nytimes.com/2009/12/15/world/asia/15haqqani.html?_r=1.

143. Antonio Giustozzi, *Koran, Kalashnikov, and Laptop: The Neo-Taliban Insurgency in Afghanistan* (New York: Columbia University Press, 2008).

144. This figure only includes full-time fighters inside Afghanistan; it excludes part-timers and facilitators, as well as those that rotate out of the battlefield for rest and recovery.

145. It is worth mentioning that, historically, al-Qaeda fighters seldom do battle; instead, they are tasked with an inspirational role and then training.

146. In his war cabinet meetings, the question was not whether to send more troops but how many. Obama's second major military escalation of the conflict this year, the largest single US deployment since the 2003 invasion of Iraq. There are also 50,000 NATO troops stationed in the country. Notably, there will be as many troops in Afghanistan as in Iraq at the height of the war between 2003 and 2008.

147. Office of the Press Secretary, "Remarks by the President in Address to the Nation on the Way Forward in Afghanistan and Pakistan," 1 December 2009, White House, http://www.whitehouse.gov/the-press-office/remarks-president-address-nation-way-forward-afghanistan-and-pakistan.

148. *Washington Post*, 29 March 2010.

149. Caren Bohan, "Obama Visits Afghanistan, Says U.S. Making Progress," Reuters, 3 December 2010; Carol E. Lee, "Barack Obama, in Afghanistan, Tells Troops They're 'On the Offense,'" Politico, 3 December 2010, http://www.politico.com/news/stories/1210/45923.html#ixzz17GOeDCMj.

150. Ben Feller, "Analysis: Obama's Trip Signals Afghan War Plan Set," Associated Press, 4 December 2010.

151. Karen DeYoung, "Obama Says U.S. Is 'on Track' to Achieve Goals in Afghanistan," *Washington Post*, 16 December 2010.

152. Ken Dilanian and David Cloud, "U.S. Intelligence Reports Cast Doubt on War Progress in Afghanistan," *Los Angeles Times*, 15 December 2010.

153. "The Taliban in Afghanistan: An Assessment," *STRATFOR*, 29 September 2009, http://www.stratfor.com/analysis/20090918_taliban_afghanistan_assessment.

154. "Taliban Issues Code of Conduct," *Al Jazeera English*, 28 July 2009, http://english.aljazeera.net/news/asia/2009/07/20097278348124813.html.

155. After his landslide election, the incoming Obama administration insisted that the war has no military solution and explored a more regional strategy to the Afghan war—including possible talks with Iran; it also looked favorably on the nascent dialogue between the pro-US Kabul government and "reconcilable" elements of the Taliban. Now that seems to have changed. Adm. Mike Mullen, chairman of the Joint Chiefs of Staff, called President Hamid Karzai's meetings with representatives of one of three insurgent groups, Gulbuddin Hekmatyar's Islamic Party, "premature." A US military officer recently threatened Ahmed Wali Karzai, the president's brother, notoriously corrupt, who also maintains links to the Taliban, with death if he is caught talking to the Taliban. See Robert Dreyfuss, "Karzai Quandary," *Nation*, 10 April 2010.

156. See the revealing memoirs by Abu al-Walid al-Masri, "The Story of the Afghan Arabs: From the Entry to Afghanistan to the Final Exodus with the Taliban," penned by a senior member of al-Qaeda Shura Council who is considered a leading ideologue in the organization and who witnessed and participated in the most important decisions. The memoirs were serialized in *al-Sharq al-Awsat*, December 2004. For an English translation, see 29 June and 1, 6, and 10 July 2005.

157. Ibid., 6 July 2005.

158. John Mueller, "The 'Safe Haven' Myth," *Nation*, 28 October 2009; Stephen M. Walt, "The 'Safe Haven' Myth," Stephen Walt's blog on *Foreign Policy.com*, 18 August 2009, http://walt.foreignpolicy.com/posts/2009/08/18/the_safe_haven_myth.

159. AG's personal communication with ISAF officials and security analysts in Kabul, 2009–10.

160. "Pakistan, Its Journalists."

161. "Interview with Mullah Mohammed Tayyab Agha" [in Arabic], *al-Hayat*, 4 December 2009.

162. Ibid.

163. "Pakistan, Its Journalists."

164. Leah Farrall, "Hotline to the Jihad," *Australian*, 7 December 2009.

165. Ibid.

166. *Wall Street Journal*, 4 April 2010.

167. Ibid. Karzai is playing his nationalist and peace cards mainly to restore his own personal credibility, and to decrease the pressure from the international community over corruption and the need for other reforms.

168. "Excerpts from Afghan President Hamid Karzai's Interview with the *Washington Post*," *Washington Post*, 14 November 2010.

169. Ibid.

170. Joshua Partlow and Karen DeYoung, "Petraeus Warns Afghans about Karzai's Criticism of U.S. War Strategy," *Washington Post*, 15 November 2010; Fred Kaplan, "Crazy Like a Fox: What Exactly Is Hamid Karzai Trying to Accomplish with His Latest Comments?" *Slate*, 18 November 2010; Karen DeYoung, "Cables Show U.S. Officials' Sense of Futility in Afghanistan," *Washington Post*, 3 December 2010.

171. Dexter Filkins and Carlotta Gall, "Taliban Leader in Secret Talks Was an Impostor," *New York Times*, 22 November 2010.

172. "Mullah Omar Backs Taliban Talks with Karzai: Report," AFP, 6 October 2010.

173. Karen DeYoung and Craig Whitelock, "U.S.-led Forces Reconciliation Talks between Afghan Government, Taliban," *Washington Post*, 14 October 2010.

174. Ernesto Londono and Perry Bacon Jr., "Obama Tells Troops in Afghanistan: Success Is within Reach," 3 December 2010.

175. "War Logs: Iraq and Afghan War Logs Explorer," Wikileaks, http:// 213.251.145.96/iraq/diarydig/. See also DeYoung, "Cables Show U.S. Officials' Sense of Futility in Afghanistan."

176. Carlotta Gall, Thom Shanker, David E. Sanger, and Eric Schmitt, "Afghan Official Confirms Moves Toward Taliban Talks," *New York Times*, 14 October 2010; Robert Dreyfuss, "United States Supports Taliban Peace Talks," *Nation*, 14 October 2010.

177. Karen DeYoung, Peter Finn, and Craig Whitlock, "Taliban in High-Level Talks with Karzai Government, Sources Say," 6 October 2010.

178. "How al-Qaeda 'Chief' Was Caught," BBC, 4 March 2003, http://news.bbc. co.uk/1/hi/world/south_asia/2818245.stm; Dafna Linzer, "CIA Held Al-Qaeda Suspect Secretly," *Washington Post*, 28 April 2007, http://www.washingtonpost.com/wp-dyn/content/article/2007/04/27/AR2007042700729. html; Robert Windrem, "Who Is Abu Farraj al-Libbi?" MSNBC, 4 May 2005, http://www.msnbc.msn.com/id/7734991/; "Evidence Suggests U.S. Missile Used in Strike," MSNBC, 5 December 2005, http://www.msnbc.msn.com/ id/10303175/; "U.S. Officials: CIA Kills Top al Qaeda Terrorist in Pakistan," CNN, 1 February 2008, http://edition.cnn.com/2008/US/01/31/alqaeda.death/index.html; "US Airstrike Kills 11 Pakistani Soldiers in 'Cowardly and Unprovoked Attack,'" *Times*, 12 June 2008, http://www.timesonline. co.uk/tol/news/world/asia/article4111277.ece; Carlotta Gall and Douglas Jehl, "U.S. Raid Killed Qaeda Leaders, Pakistanis Say," *New York Times*, 19 January 2006, http://www.nytimes.com/2006/01/19/international/ asia/19pakistan.html?_r=1; Frank Gardner, "Death of Mustafa Abu al-Yazid 'Setback' for al-Qaeda," 1 June 2008, http://www.bbc.co.uk/news/10206180.

179. Black and Norton-Taylor, "Al-Qaida Faces Recruitment Crisis."

180. Ibid.

181. *Washington Post*, 18 March 2010.

182. Ibid.

Conclusion

1. Howard LaFranchi, "Al Qaeda? North Korea? Who Americans See as Greatest Security Threat," *Christian Science Monitor*, 8 December 2010.

2. Woodward, *Obama's Wars*, pp. 51–52.

3. Ibid., p. 52.

4. Ibid., p. 123.

5. Ibid., p. 363.

6. Ibid.

7. Scott Shane, "Fighting Terrorism, Creating Terrorists," *New York Times*, 4 July 2010.

8. "Zawahiri: The Ninth Anniversary."

9. In a new book, *Cutting the Fuse: The Explosion of Global Suicide Terrorism and How to Stop it*, which builds on and tests the arguments of their previous work, *Dying to Win: The Logic of Suicide Terrorism*, Robert Pape and James Feldman argue that since 2004, the number of suicide attacks—whether within a country or transnational—has grown with shocking speed. Through a close analysis of suicide attacks by al-Qaeda and other terrorist groups in Iraq, Afghanistan, Pakistan, Lebanon, Israel, Chechnya, and Sri Lanka, the authors provide powerful new evidence that, contrary to popular and dangerously mistaken belief, only a tiny minority of these attacks are motivated solely by religion. Instead, the root cause is foreign military occupation, which triggers secular-nationalist and religious people alike to carry out suicide attacks. Terrorism, it is argued, is a response to foreign military occupation. One can extend the argument to read "foreign military and political intervention." The response, therefore, has to be found in the political realm. Unless political grievances are addressed, counterterrorism policies are unlikely to succeed. See Robert A. Pape and James K. Feldman, *Cutting the Fuse: The Explosion of Global Suicide Terrorism and How to Stop It* (Chicago: University of Chicago Press, 2010).

To counteract the skyrocketing of anti-American suicide terrorism, Pape and Feldman call for the implementation of two strategies.

(1.) "Given the close association between foreign occupation and suicide terrorism, the goal of thwarting the rise of the next wave of suicide terrorism will likely require a major shift in military strategy by those target states with a military presence in foreign areas. This strategy is 'offshore' balancing, which seeks to achieve foreign policy interests in key regions of the world by relying on military alliances and offshore air, naval, and rapidly deployable ground forces rather than heavy onshore combat power." See ibid., p. 8.

(2.) "This strategy of empowering a key local community to better provide for its security independently of the United States, the central government in the country, and the terrorists led to a decline of Iraqi suicide terrorism by over a third in the next year. Most important, the strategy of 'local empowerment' works by recognizing that suicide terrorism is driven by a strategic logic that seeks to remove foreign threats to local culture. A foreign state can remove a local population's primary reason for supporting suicide terrorist campaigns—safeguarding the local way of life—by providing the political, economic, and military wherewithal for the local community to detect and destroy terrorists, tasks that often require deep local knowledge to achieve success." See ibid., p. 9.

10. http://motherjones.com/politics/2007/03/iraq-101-iraq-effect-war-iraq-and-its-impact-war-terrorism-pg-1.

11. Mohammed M. Hafez, *Suicide Bombers in Iraq: The Strategy and Ideology of Martyrdom* (Washington, DC: United States Institute of Peace Press, 2007); http://www.amconmag.com/article/2005/jul/18/00017/, Jeffrey Rudolph, "Can You Pass The Terrorism Quiz," Countercurrents.org, 8 August 2010.

12. Ahmed Rashid, *Descent into Chaos: The United States and the Failure of Nation Building in Pakistan, Afghanistan, and Central Asia* (New York: Viking, 2008).

13. Nick Turse, "The Pentagon Digs in Deeper in the Middle East," TomDispatch.com, 17 November 2010.

14. http://www.nytimes.com/2010/11/11/world/asia/11indo.html?_r=1&emc=eta1.

15. Akbar Ganji, "Dreaming of a Free Iran," *Boston Review*, 26 May 2010. http://bostonreview.net/BR35.3/ganji.php.

16. Ibid.

17. For the latest episode in the continuing saga of America's weak-kneed approach toward Israel, see Rami G. Khouri, "Washington Bends for Israel Once Again," *Daily Star* (Beirut), 27 November 2010.

18. Helene Cooper, "Obama Challenges Israel to Make Hard Choices Needed for Peace," *New York Times*, 22 May 2011; Steven Lee Myers, "Divisions Clear as Netanyahu and Obama Discuss Peace," *New York Times*, 20 May 2011.

19. *San Francisco Examiner*, http://www.sfexaminer.com/blogs/beltway-confidential/2011/05/full-text-obamas-middle-east-speech#ixzz1NDGPRayx.

20. A report published by the Institute for Social Policy and Understanding suggests that the best way to prevent radicalization and terrorism is to educate young Muslims in mainstream Islamic teachings so that they will be able to recognize and place such radical narratives, dubious theology, or ignorant preaching in their proper contexts, and thus reject them. While most Western policymakers attempt to extract Islam and secularize Muslim communities and societies, the report's findings advocate a dramatically different path. More authentic teaching of Islam (from credible sources) is likely to be far more effective in combating extremism and terrorism; therefore, "more Islam" (not less) is likely to be successful. To access the report, see Azeem Ibrahim, "Tackling Muslim Radicalization: Lessons from Scotland," June 2010, http://www.ispu.org/files/PDFs/ISPU%20-%20Radicalization%20Report.pdf.

The above ideas are primarily geared toward preventive efforts to reach Muslim youths before they are radicalized. Another effort that seems to be gaining traction addresses radicalization after the individual becomes violent. De-radicalization is a process of working to combat extremism in groups or individuals that have already perpetrated violence. This de-radicalization effort has been undertaken in the Gulf and other Middle Eastern countries with mixed results. There are three dimensions to the de-radicalization program:

(a.) Behavioral: require the abandonment of violence

(b.) Ideological: de-legitimize the use of violence

(c.) Organizational: make structural changes within an organization's leaderships

The common misconception underestimates the central role that organizational factors play in the appeal of terrorist networks. A better understanding of such causes reveals that the challenge is actually manageable: the key is not to profile and target the most despairing or deranged individual but to understand and undermine the organizational and institutional appeal of terrorists' motivations and networks.

21. See the third Silatech-Gallup survey (www.Silatech.com). Rami G. Khouri, "A Guide to the Young Arab World," Agence Global, 24 November 2010.

INDEX